CYCLING TOURING IN SPAIN

ABOUT THE AUTHOR

Harry Dowdell has been a lifelong cyclist. His first cycle tour, with friends was while still at school, was around the North York Moors staying in youth hostels at Wheeldale and Whitby.

After a lengthy break, when the bike was used only for commuting, he restarted cycle touring round south-west Ireland then France.

Harry's cycle touring in Spain started in Andalucía, and subsequent visits have taken in most of the country including two of the Caminos de Santiago. During these tours he has made notes, drawn sketch maps and collected GPS data. This information is the basis for the maps, profiles and text that appear in this book.

Harry continues to cycle regularly in Spain, North Yorkshire and wherever the fancy takes him. He lives in Nidderdale with Liz and pays the bills working as a fitness instructor at the local leisure centre.

CYCLING TOURING IN SPAIN

by
Harry Dowdell

2 POLICE SQUARE, MILNTHORPE, CUMBRIA LA7 7PY
www.cicerone.co.uk

© Harry Dowdell 2003
First edition 2003
Reprinted 2006 and 2013 (with updates)
ISBN-10: 1 85284 381 0
ISBN-13: 978 1 85284 381 6

Printed by KHL Printing, Singapore.
A catalogue record for this book is available from the British Library.
All photographs, maps and route profiles by the author except where stated
Maps and profiles have been produced from data generated with a GPS.
Temperature and rainfall data is based on information supplied by the Met Office.

ACKNOWLEDGEMENTS

Special thanks are due to two people who have supported me in writing this book: firstly Liz who reintroduced me to cycle touring before our first tentative tours of Andalucía and then allowed me out to do the others; secondly Ivor who joined me on the other tours and was an ever-present sounding board. Sadly Ivor is no longer with us and is greatly missed.

A number of readers have kindly forwarded me changes which are always welcome. So many thanks to Gail, Cameron, Caroline, Martin, Andy, Itsik, Molly and all the others whose names I have lost.

Thanks also go to the Spanish Tourist Office in London who provided most of the accommodation information and also identified options that broadened the scope of this book.

ADVICE TO READERS

While every effort is made by our authors to ensure the accuracy of guidebooks as they go to print, changes can occur during the lifetime of an edition. If we know of any, there will be an Updates tab on this book's page on the Cicerone website (www.cicerone.co.uk), so please check before planning your trip. We also advise that you check information about such things as transport, accommodation and shops locally. Even rights of way can be altered over time. We are always grateful for information about any discrepancies between a guidebook and the facts on the ground, sent by email to info@cicerone.co.uk or by post to Cicerone, 2 Police Square, Milnthorpe LA7 7PY, United Kingdom.

Front cover: Puertos de Aliva and the Ermita Señora de las Nieves (Route 8)

CONTENTS

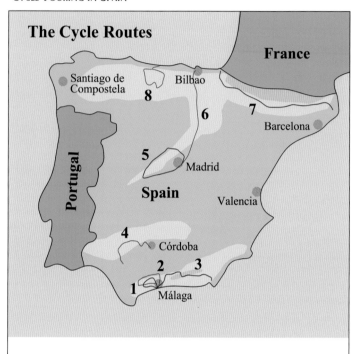

The Cycle Routes

1 Serranía de Ronda

2 Sierra de Grazalema & Torcal

3 Las Alpujarras & Sierra Nevada

4 Sierra Morena

5 Sierras de Gredos & Guadarrama

6 Madrid to Bilbao

7 Los Pireneos

8 Picos de Europa

Legend

Dual carriageway	
Road	
Unpaved road	
Rough unpaved road	
Route	
Optional route	
Railway	
Contour	*500m*
Mountain pass	)(*1,235 m*
Mountain summit	▲ *3,425 m*
Town, Airport	

3500m
3000m
2500m
2000m
1500m
1000m
750m
500m
250m

Alberche valley and Sierra de Gredos from Sierra de la Paramera

INTRODUCTION

Spain, with Portugal, occupies that mountainous square of southwest Europe known as the Iberian Peninsula. It is a country of variety and contrasts for which many claims are made, but one thing is certain: Spain offers some of the best cycling available in Europe.

Forget the non-stop coastal resorts built for packaged pleasure. The cyclist's Spain is not that of the costas, those narrow coastal strips trapped between mountains and sea where millions head for their summer holidays, but of the country where Spaniards actually live, work and play. A world of villages, small towns and vibrant cities, wooded hills and snow-capped mountains, wide valleys and narrow gorges, immense plains, Moorish palaces, Roman ruins and Gothic cathedrals, cave paintings and the works of Picasso, El Greco and Dali, sunshine and warmth, orange and olive groves, small shops and family hotels, a place of history and constant reinvention where Europe and Africa meet; a country that, in short, rewards its visitors.

ROADS

Spain is almost as large as France, considerably bigger than Germany, and more than twice the size of the United Kingdom. Spain would take third place in a league table of the American states, behind Texas but ahead of California.

The population density is higher than that of the Scandinavian countries, but one-third that of the United Kingdom and Germany and one-sixth that of the Netherlands.

As a result Spanish roads are far quieter than those of most other European countries. A spate of recent and ongoing road building means that much of the heavy traffic keeps to the newer, more convenient roads, leaving cyclists to share the old ones with local traffic. Not that 'heavy traffic' in rural areas is a particular problem; on mountain roads no more than five cars per hour can be expected.

Road surfaces are generally very good. The vast majority of new and upgraded roads include a metre-wide lined strip suitable for cycling where traffic is heavy, but otherwise the main carriageways are fine. Regional dual carriageways have a wide hard shoulder for cycling and many have cycle lanes with a specially prepared surface.

The general standard of driving is very good. Motorists do tend to bide their time and wait for a safe place to pass, though a suitable spot can take an embarrassingly long time to materialise. Only mopeds and scooters tend to be a noisy annoyance. Police clampdowns have certainly improved the behaviour of moped and scooter riders and have encouraged the wearing of crash helmets. Having said that,

3642 people were killed on Spanish roads in 1999. A quarter of those deaths occurred during the peak holiday months of July and August when most Spaniards take holidays in the country areas. Annual cyclist fatalities ranged from 78 to 122 per year during the 1990s.

Spain is hilly. If it were levelled off it would leave an immense plateau some 600m high, the altitude of its capital Madrid. The highest mountain in peninsular Spain is Mulhacén (3482m) in the Sierra Nevada, and the Sierra de Gredos to the west of Madrid climbs to over 2500m. The mountain passes can also be very high: in the Sierra Nevada the Veleta road reaches 3200m, while in the Sierra de Guadarrama the Puerto de Navacerrada is at 1860m. The roads are generally well graded (particularly the new ones), using distance not gradient to gain height gradually, so do not expect to have to push very often except where climbs are long. Expect roads in the mountains to climb 50 or 60m/km. There are none of the very steep gradients found in England's Pennines or North York Moors.

With long relentless climbs come long descents, and those lasting 15 or 20km are quite common. Often hard persistent pedalling uphill is amply rewarded with panoramic vistas at the col and scenic revelations during the freewheeling descents. By contrast once away from the mountains the plains can be very flat, and even when undulating allow good, fast travelling.

CLIMATE

Spain can be divided into three main climatic regions: Atlantic Ocean; Mediterranean Sea; the mountains and the plains. See Appendix 1 for temperature and rainfall figures.

The north and north-west are influenced by the proximity of the Atlantic Ocean, particularly in autumn and winter with low-pressure systems sweeping in. Summers are cooler, cloudier and wetter than the rest of the country; rainfall decreases further east. The north-west is known as Green Spain for a good reason; look at the figures for Finisterre and Santander to understand why.

Central Spain has low rainfall, but winter snow can linger on the mountains. Spring is the wettest season, and by midsummer the country has turned from green to brown and feels dry and parched. Summers are hot (and longer the further south you go) and winters can be bitingly cold, particularly in the north. Average midday temperatures for the summer months in Seville reach over 35°C and in Madrid over 30°C. However, while Seville basks in mild winter temperatures Madrid suffers from the bitter cold.

The south and east coasts are influenced by the Mediterranean climate, with lots of sunshine all year round, hot summers and mild winters. The driest area is Almería. It is wetter further north, and also west towards Gibraltar. Barcelona has a wetter autumn than winter.

Cerro Pelado, Sierra de Guadarrama (Route 5)

Deva valley from Invernales de Igüedri (Route 8)

Average temperatures hide the substantial day-to-day variations that can occur. In addition to the air temperature the effect of the heat from the sun should be taken into account. When the average daily maximum exceeds 25°C the heat can become overpowering and cycling uncomfortable. But remember that compared to walking or running cycling creates its own cooling breeze. The cooling effect kicks in above 12km/hr but does not remove the need for protection against sunburn. Only on stopping does the importance of shade become clear. Cycling in the mountains can be cooler; expect a drop of 1°C for every 100m gain in altitude.

When planning a trip think carefully about the best time of year. Depending on how much heat you like consider Andalucía and the south in autumn, winter and spring, Madrid and the centre in spring and autumn, and the north in summer. By chasing the sun it is possible to enjoy pleasant warm cycling all year round. Appendix 1 will help you decide when to go, and every part of Spain has a window of suitability. However, if things do get a little too hot try the following tactics.

- Keep out of the sun whenever possible.
- Wear light clothing that allows the movement of air over the body.
- Acclimatise to the heat in advance: try some rides when it is hot at home. If this proves to be insufficient preparation try

overdressing slightly to help train the body's cooling mechanisms. A body acclimatised to the heat will start sweating at a lower temperature and sweat in greater volume. See 'Eating and drinking en route', below, for information on how to keep hydrated. Heat stroke and exposure are dealt with in 'Coping with extreme weather'.

You can always avoid the worst of the heat by taking a siesta. Siestas developed in rural Spain when workers conformed to the rhythms of nature: work would start early when it was cool, and as temperatures rose workers would stop to take a hearty meal and a couple of hours' rest. Work would be finished off in the late afternoon and early evening when temperatures had dropped and the heat was out of the sun. Although this habit has become less popular in big cities, in rural areas and small towns shops still tend to close for much of the afternoon. There is a noticeable quietening down between 2 and 5pm, so find a shady spot and have a kip.

Spain is one hour ahead of Greenwich Mean Time in winter and two hours ahead in summer. The transition from day to night is surprisingly quick. Even with good-quality lights night-time cycling is not fun, and as the sun sets the warmth also disappears. Try to finish cycling before sunset or at worst within 30min of it. Appendix 2 gives sunrise and sunset times across Spain. Please note that the times are based on a flat horizon and so may vary locally depending on whether you are in a valley or on top of a hill.

HOLIDAYS AND PUBLIC HOLIDAYS

The Spanish take their summer holidays in July and particularly August. It's a good time to visit Spanish cities, which are quieter than usual, with many businesses shutting up shop, although temperatures will be at their highest. Conversely the countryside becomes busier. Booking accommodation in advance during this period is highly recommended.

There are 10 National Holidays in Spain (see below). Public holidays falling on a weekend are not moved. When they fall midweek extra days are often taken to bridge the gap; such holidays are known as *puentes*. Public Holidays and particularly *puentes* see an exodus to the country. Accommodation fills up, making booking in advance advisable.

In addition every Provincial Government and most cities have their own holidays, and these are detailed in each cycle tour.

A SHORT HISTORY

One of the great joys of touring in Spain is discovering and enjoying the architecture, art and cuisine that have resulted from a number of influences that have flowed across the Iberian Peninsula during its turbulent history. The earliest Iberian people were Palaeolithic cave-dwelling invaders from France to the north who left behind them the cave paintings found in the western Pyrenees and around the Bay of Biscay. It is believed that these hunter-gatherers stayed largely in the north of the peninsula.

In the south, Neolithic people from north Africa settled in Alméria between 4000 and 3000BC. They were farmers, living in villages, and by 1000BC these Iberians had spread out to become the dominant inhabitants of the peninsula to which they gave their name. Celts and Germanic peoples from France joined the Iberians to form the Celtiberians in north, west and central Spain.

Public holidays in Spain

1 January	New Year's Day
6 January	Epiphany or Reyes Magos
variable date	Good Friday
1 May	May Day
15 August	Assumption of the Virgin
12 October	National Day
1 November	All Saints
6 December	Día de la Constitución
8 December	Immaculate Conception
25 December	Christmas Day

Alhama de Granada, the old town built high on top of a cliff (Route 3)

The Phoenicians arrived by sea around 1100BC and founded Cádiz and Málaga. These coastal-dwelling people traded widely, particularly in metals, and were joined by Greeks who also established coastal trading colonies.

Around 250BC the Carthaginians came from Sicily to conquer parts of Spain, and founded Barcelona and Cartagena. This heralded the arrival of the Romans, who by 206BC had driven the Carthaginians out. Spain was very important economically and culturally to the Romans, who colonised the country over the next two centuries.

Three centuries later, as the Roman Empire crumbled from within, the barbarian tribes swept in from the north. They were followed by the Visigoths, allies of Rome, and by AD573 they had taken over.

However, in AD711 an army of Berbers invaded from north Africa, and by 718 the Moors had overrun Spain except for parts of the north-west. 'Moor' is a term applied to any Berber or Arab settler, while 'Mozarabs' were Jews and Christians who kept their faith under the Moors. Initially ruled from Baghdad, the Moors soon established Córdoba as their centre, but this unified rule only lasted until 1031 when the country split into a number of independent kingdoms.

Just as the Moors were at their territorial greatest the Catholic Reconquest started from the north-west. It moved south in fits and starts, no doubt aided by antagonism between the independent

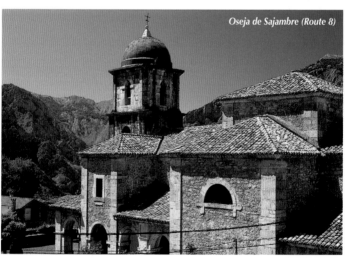

Oseja de Sajambre (Route 8)

Moorish states. Brief periods of unity under the Almoravids and then the Almohads stalled the Reconquest. It was completed when Los Reyes Católicos, Fernando and Isabella, captured Granada in 1492. In the same year Isabella sent Christopher Columbus to search for a westward route to the Indies, only to come across the Americas. It was Los Reyes Católicos who started the Inquisition and ordered the expulsion of nearly all the Spanish Jews.

In 1516 the Hapsburgs came to the throne through the marriage of Carlos V. When elected Emperor of the Holy Roman Empire he also acquired Flanders, Holland and the Americas. Felipe II centralised the Spanish Empire from the newly built palace of El Escorial near Madrid. It was his support of Mary Queen of Scots that led to the Armada in 1588. The War of Spanish Succession was caused when the Bourbon Felipe V came to the throne in 1700 in competition with Charles of Austria who was supported by the British. Spain lost its European territories and the British took possession of Gibraltar in 1714. Nearly a century later, under the influence of France, the Spanish Fleet was destroyed at the Battle of Trafalgar in 1805. This defeat created a power vacuum and Napoleon installed his brother Joseph as king; his reign ended shortly afterwards with the Peninsular War.

The remainder of the 19th and early 20th centuries saw a mixture of monarchy, dictatorship and republican governance. The Second Republic was declared in 1931 and in 1936 the Popular Front won power. Strikes and peasant uprisings led to turmoil, and in July of that year Franco and his garrison in Morocco rebelled. The bloody and bitter Civil War that subsequently took place lasted until 1939.

Franco's fascist Falangist government ruled until his death in 1975 when he was succeeded by King Juan Carlos. Reforms were hesitant, but democracy was restored in the elections of June 1977, and cemented when Juan Carlos refused to support the attempted coup lead by Colonel Antonio Tejero in 1981. EU membership came in 1986 and adoption of the Euro in 1999.

GETTING THERE

Getting to Spain with a bike is surprisingly simple. There are many long-established scheduled and charter airlines flying to Spain from all over the world. Since the mid-1990s various no-frills budget airlines have emerged in Europe, led by the likes of EasyJet and Ryanair, later joined by bmibaby and Jet2. These carriers concentrate on short-haul routes and continue to expand throughout Europe and beyond. As well as bringing more competition to the market they are more flexible than charter airlines and offer one-way tickets at no extra cost, making airport-to-airport routes feasible. From the USA

Noviales (Route 6)

the options are more limited, and for many scheduled airlines will often be the only way.

Air travel is the quickest and can be the cheapest and most flexible way of getting to and from Spain. Flying direct is best in that bikes are more likely to arrive – and to arrive intact. Most airlines will carry a bike, but most have a policy of levying an additional fee, require advance booking and the signing of a waiver, and insist that it is packed in a bike bag or a box. Check at the time of booking what the conditions are as well as what is acceptable in terms of the bag or box. Often a telephone booking is required. A number of airlines will not guarantee that you will travel on the same flight as your bike. In addition a number of airports add their own requirements for the carriage of bikes. The situation is fluid so it is worth checking with the airports concerned or have a look at the various forums on cycling websites such as www.ctc.org.uk or

www.bikeradar.com. If you have any doubts print off a copy of the airline's instructions and also email the airport for their rules. Storage of bags or boxes in Spain can be a problem as only Madrid and Barcelona airports have left-luggage (*consigna*) facilities. Car hire depots and hotels used for first/last night stays are often helpful.

All bikes need to be prepared for a journey by air. Allow plenty of time for this at both ends. Packing is particular to each type of bike bag or box, but the following guidance should help particularly those using a bag. Remove the wheels and place in their pockets. Remove the pedals and re-insert them on the inside of the cranks; position the cranks so that one pedal is inside the frame triangle and the other protrudes below the chainring. This will protect the chainring teeth. Turn the handlebars through 90° to reduce width and lower them. Rotating the handlebars will give protection to brake levers and gear changers. Lower the seat. If possible remove the rear derailleur and tape it inside the rear pannier rack. Some carriers expect you to deflate the tyres. Secure pumps and other accessories. Packing tape can be very useful.

If camping, there are a number of items which must not be carried on an aircraft, all of which can be easily obtained in Spain. Complete lists are available from the airline. Aiport staff will check to see if you are carrying something forbidden. The list includes compressed gases (such as used in camping stoves), flammable liquids and solids (such as methylated spirits and solid fuel) and friction matches (but not safety matches). If taking a decent knife or any sharp or pointed objects put them in your hold luggage as they are likely to be confiscated during baggage checks and will not be allowed into the cabin. Bar locks too are best placed in hold luggage as airport staff can take exception to them as hand luggage. Take all valuables – expensive items and those that cannot be replaced – into the cabin as hand luggage. Tools must travel as hold luggage.

See Appendix 4 for further details on travelling to Spain by air.

GETTING AROUND

This book has been written on the premise that entry into Spain will be via one of the main airports. A number of the routes start or finish some distance from any airport, and for these routes railway stations have been used instead. To get there from the airport one of the following options can be used; these are described in more detail within each tour.

Railways

Bicycles are accepted on regional and long distance trains if there is either sufficient space in the carriage or a specific area for them. At the time of writing there is no easy way to find out which train services will take bikes so it is a case of calling RNFE direct. Cercanías, urban and suburban trains will take bikes with few restrictions and these are detailed on the RENFE website. High speed intercity trains (AVE) do not carry bikes.

RENFE is the state-owned railway (tel: 0034 90 22 40 20 2 [Spain] or at www.renfe.com). FEVE runs trains from Bilbao along the northern coast to Ferrol and allows bikes on all its trains although sometimes with limits as to numbers (tel: 0034 94 42 50 61 5 www.feve.es).

Another agent that can organise tickets and give advice is Rail Europe, tel: 08448 484 064 (UK) or 1 800 361 RAIL (Canada) or 1 888 622 8600 (US) or www.raileurope.com.

Inter-city coaches

Coaches will usually take bikes but may insist they are bagged or boxed. There is often a limit to the number per bus. A fee is usually charged. Be early for your connection and be prepared to do all your own loading. For many

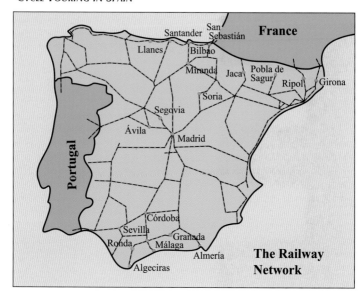

The Railway Network

of the smaller companies the reservation will have to be made in person and ensure that it is clear that you are taking a bike. The coach network is extensive and often connects directly with airport terminals, ports and city centres. Moviela (www.moviela.es) run an industry-wide information and booking service. Companies with known policies are:

Alsa (www.alsa.es) permit booking of tickets and reservations online. To access the bike booking facility passengers must be booked one at a time. Should the facility not appear then it is not available or the bus is full up. There is a limit of four bikes per bus.

Socibus (www.socibus.es) allow bikes subject to available space.

Avanza (www.avanzabus.com) allow bikes subject to available space.

Car hire

One-way car hire is probably the most convenient method of linking airports to tour starts and finishes. Expect to find all the major car hire companies at all the airports, but not necessarily at all the start and finish points, so check before making a reservation.

Making reservations in advance of travel often saves money. However, prices can vary by as much as 50%, so compare prices from several companies before booking. Check what is included in the prepaid price and what is charged locally. Look for mileage limits, insurance and the levels of

20

Invernales de Igüedri on the approach to the Puertos de Aliva (Route 8)

The miners' track traversing the Sierra de la Corta (Route 8)

any excess, Collision Damage Waiver (CDW), bail bond, theft waiver, airport levies, taxes and cost of extra drivers. Confirm age limits of drivers – sometimes they have to be over 25 – and cleanness and type of driving licence. Always check what is being signed for, and always check the condition of the car for dents, scratches and missing items. Any faults must be reported to the car hire company and recorded before setting off. Expect the fuel tank to be full at collection and hand it back full on return or pay heavily for the fuel used. Some operators include a full tank and expect it back empty.

A medium-size five-door hatchback such as a Ford Focus or Renault Megane with the rear seat folded down will easily take two bikes with the wheels removed. If the hire company can provide a bike carrier or roof bars then a smaller car could be used, or more people carried per car. See Appendix 6 for details of car hire companies operating widely in Spain.

PASSPORTS, VISAS, HEALTH CARE AND INSURANCE

A full passport valid for the period of stay is required for entry into Spain. For citizens of EU states that issue National ID cards (as well as Switzerland, Andorra, Monaco and Liechtenstein) the card will suffice. For stays of over 90 days a residence permit is required. For stays of up to a year a temporary permit will suffice; longer stays require a permanent permit. Applications can be made at the Aliens Office of the province in which the residence is to be or at the relevant provincial police station.

Citizens of EU states, Norway, Switzerland and Iceland do not require visas. Holders of passports issued by Canada, Australia, Japan and the USA do not require visas for stays of up to 90 days. For longer stays check with the nearest consulate. Other citizens should check visa requirements.

For emergency services ring 112: this is an EU-wide number that accesses emergency services with the operator speaking your language. The national number for the police is 091. Visitors from EU states receive free medical care from the Spanish Health Service. A European Health Insurance Card is required before travelling. Make applications in the UK at www.ehic.org.uk, tel: 0845 606 2030, or via a form from the post office. If you have a medical condition consider carrying a letter from your doctor, giving details and translated into Spanish. Pharmacies can be a great help if you fall ill and can usually find someone who can speak English fluently. They will also have up-to-date knowledge of local doctors.

Although health care may be free for some there can be considerable incidental expenses, and it is always advisable to get adequate holiday insurance. Prices vary considerably and buying it from your travel agent is rarely the cheapest way; try your bank or insurance broker. Depending on

23

Campo de Zafarraya, a fertile plain surrounded by limestone hills (Route 3)

how often you travel annual insurance can be very good value. Family cover is often available to those who share the same address and substantial discounts if you opt out of luggage and possessions cover providing these are covered under household policy; it is far easier to claim on household than travel insurance. Check the cover and exclusions before signing up.

MOBILE PHONES

There is excellent mobile phone coverage of the whole of Spain, including the Balearic Islands and the Canaries, using the GSM standard (GSM900 and 1800, 3G 2100). It is advisable to check the roaming abilities of your phone with your service provider. Some prepay phones will not permit talk but will allow text messaging. Most service providers have reciprocal arrangements with Spanish-based providers that can significantly reduce call charges. This will usually entail a small service charge covering the period of use and will have to be set up in advance.

Use of your mobile phone in Spain replicates use at home. To call a land line the number starts with the area code; all area codes start with 9. All Spanish mobile numbers start with 6. For international numbers ring 00 or + followed by the country code, area code then telephone number.

MONEY AND BANKS

Spain is an excellent good-value destination, with very reasonable costs of living and accommodation. Expect to get by comfortably on around 50 Euros/£40/US$60 (if sharing rooms) to 65 Euros/£50/US$80 per person per day. Add more for wild partying and upmarket quality hotels!

The road between Ansó and Hecho climbs through the Sierra de Vedao (Route 7)

Ochagavía and the Río Anduña (Route 7)

The currency of Spain is the Euro, which fully replaced the peseta on 28 February 2002 (there were 166.386 pesetas to the Euro). One Euro = 100 cents; coins come in 1, 2, 5, 10, 20, 50 cents and 1 and 2 Euros; notes come in 5, 10, 20, 50, 100, 200 and 500 Euro denominations. Euros are also used in Austria, Belgium, Cyprus, Finland, France, Germany, Greece, Ireland, Italy, Luxembourg, Malta, the Netherlands, Portugal, Slovakia and Slovenia. The exchange rate against sterling, the dollar and other currencies is variable.

Banking hours are typically 09:00 to 14:00 on weekdays and 09:00 to 13:00 on Saturdays. All towns and many of the larger villages have banks and most have cash point machines/autotellers that allow cash withdrawals by Visa, MasterCard and many debit cards. Your own bank will be able to advise which ones will work. Interest on cash withdrawals on a credit card is usually charged immediately. Banks and larger hotels will change sterling and dollars for Euros.

Credit cards are widely accepted in most (but not all) shops, hotels and restaurants, so take some ready cash. Getting Euros from a bank or travel agent in the UK or USA – or post office in the UK – should be straightforward; some offer a cash back service if you return with unspent currency. Do expect to provide evidence of identity as part of the transaction; a passport or driving licence will often suffice.

Hotels

There are thousands of good-value places to stay in Spain. Many are family run with a bar on the ground floor and good home cooking in the restaurant. Prices compare very favourably with elsewhere in continental Europe, and extremely favourably in terms of price and quality with accommodation in the UK. Without exception all have provided secure locations for bicycles when asked. At the bottom end you can usually find bed, breakfast and three-course evening meal with drinks totalling a mere 25 Euros per person. The evening meals can be a real experience, sometimes with a bottle of wine thrown in and virtually as much food as you can eat. Breakfast is usually coffee and toast or bread and jam. Try and avoid croissants, as they have little substance; *churros*, on the other hand – deep-fried 'ropes' of dough – are excellent and will keep you going for ages. *Churros* are traditionally eaten with a hot chocolate drink. Small cakes, *magdalenas*, often make an appearance on Sunday mornings.

Hotels are tightly regulated and must display prices of rooms and meals at reception and in bedrooms. Always check whether meals are available. Complaints' books must be kept and are inspected by the authorities.

Although most hotels have central heating there is a reluctance to switch it on except in extreme circumstances. This can be a problem during a cold snap, and in the mountains the nights can turn chilly. Often there is only one blanket on the bed with others stored away in wardrobes or available for the asking, so make sure you have enough before turning in for the night.

In many hotels marble and polished stone is used in rooms and corridors. While very attractive and easy to clean footsteps can echo and voices boom and, allied with street noise, hotels can be noisy. Take some earplugs if you are a light sleeper.

One of the most welcome recent developments has been the growth of rural accommodation, ranging from bed and breakfast to substantial stylish hotels. The buildings vary from timber-framed medieval town houses to *fincas* (country house/small farm) and *estancias* (large farm/ranch) and stylish modern properties. There is less than national consistency about names or standards expect to see them variously named such as 'Casas Rurales', 'Alojamientos Rurales' and 'Posadas'. The latter in particular (found in Cantabria, and known as Casas Rurales/ Alojamientos Rurales elsewhere) have high standards and offer excellent value. Details can be found at national and provincial tourist offices.

The official classification of hotel-type accommodation can be confusing and there is considerable overlap between classes. Outside each establishment you will find a blue plaque with white lettering identifying the type. The ones likely to be encountered, starting with the most expensive, are in the table.

Details of hotels and guide prices are given at the end of each cycle route description. It is always a good idea to book ahead to make sure you are not left stranded at the end of a hard day. Local telephone directories are a good source of hotel, hostals and pensions often not listed elsewhere. For those able to plan with certainty booking hotel rooms online through a consolidator such as www.laterooms. com may reduce costs.

H *Hoteles*: hotel graded one to five stars. Restaurant, bar etc and everything you would expect of a hotel. Includes the state-run chain of 'Paradores'

HR *Hoteles Residencia*: as *hoteles* except no dining-room facilities, with the possible exception of breakfast

HS *Hostales*: good-value family-owned and run hotels usually with home cooking. Graded one to three stars. Most common in rural areas

HsR *Hostal Residencia*: as *hostales* except no meals, with the possible exception of breakfast

P *Pensiónes*: family-run guest houses. Common in rural areas

CH *Casa de Huéspedes*: similar to *pensiónes*. Not that common

F *Fonda*: rooms, often above a bar, can be excellent value, coupled with good home cooking. Becoming rare

The little-visited forested gorge of the Alto Tajo

Camping

There are some 1200 campsites dotted across the country offering another good-value accommodation option. Many are well equipped with their own bar/restaurant or even swimming pool, though grassy pitches may be hard to come by. However, camsites can be too far apart to make camping-only tours feasible, and some may close down out of season. Wild camping is illegal around built-up areas and forbidden by many landowners, so check before pitching. The difference in price between Hostales and campsites may not be that great, and for a little more money a decent night's sleep in a bed and your own en suite shower at the end of a day in the saddle may be preferable.

Youth hostels

These are often run by the regional Youth and Sports Departments (*Direcciones Generales de la Juventud y el Deporte*) and can be very cheap. They tend to be concentrated in cities and tourist areas.

ABOUT THE BIKE

There are no hard-and-fast rules about which type of bike is best to tour on, unless you are following one of the Caminos de Santiago, in which case a mountain bike is recommended. Otherwise, they are best avoided. They are heavy, and the fat, knobbly tyres make for far harder work than road tyres. The routes described in this book are mostly on

road, with some forest and mountain road sections. Consider using either a dedicated touring bike or a hybrid. A hybrid is a cross between a touring and a mountain bike. It has an upright sitting position, which is great for views but poor for aerodynamics. The routes in this book were ridden on a hybrid apart from those in the Serranía de Ronda and the Sierra de Grazalema. Except where noted in the text, either of the bikes will prove more than adequate.

Gears

Having the right gears is important for getting up those hills in a state to appreciate the challenge and enjoy the view. The right gears allow you to balance height gain and forward movement. The laws of mechanics have it that it takes the same amount of work to transport a bike and rider to the top of a given pass irrespective of gear ratio or forward speed. The length of the road is also irrelevant if there is no resistance from the road surface, wind or mechanical conversion. However, each human has a maximum sustainable work output and optimum pedalling rate or cadence. This is why we have gears.

A simple comparative measure of gears is to calculate how far each full rotation of the pedals moves the bike forward. This is known as 'development', and the development range indicates how suitable a bike is for terrain types and gradients. To calculate the development range, find out

Gearing ratios

Lower limit of development = pi x diameter of wheel x teeth on smallest chainwheel/teeth on largest sprocket

Upper limit of development = pi x diameter of wheel x teeth on largest chainwheel/teeth on smallest sprocket

For my bike

lower limit = 3.14 x 0.7m x 28/34 = 1.8m;

upper limit = 3.14 x 0.7m x 48/14 = 7.5m

(The chainwheel being the front set of cogs and the sprocket set the rear set of cogs.)

The development range is 1.8–7.5m. The upper limit is fine and is only used on the flat and downhill. The lower limit is important in the mountains. Spanish roads are mostly well graded and so most people, including occasional cyclists, can get away with a lower development of around 2.5m. If contemplating mountain and forest tracks think about a lower limit of around 1.8m as the tracks may be steeper and poor surfaces require lower gears. If the terrain is undulating or hilly a lower limit of 3.8m should suffice.

the diameter of your wheel in metres and the number of teeth on the largest and smallest cogs on the chainwheels and on the sprocket set.

Having got the gearing right it is important to use the gears properly. On a bike with 21 gears (three on the front chainwheel x seven on the rear sprocket) only 15 of those ratios should be used. Each chainwheel should only be used to access five of the seven rear sprockets otherwise the chain is flexing too much, resulting in excess wear and adding resistance to the system. The largest chainwheel is used with the five smallest sprockets, the middle chainwheel avoiding the largest and smallest, and the small chainwheel the five largest sprockets.

The same principle applies more so to those with 24 and 27 gears.

Maintenance

Your bike should be well maintained and physically sound. A well-maintained and correctly set-up bike is subject to less resistance and wear. A full service should be carried out prior to going. Cycle shops in rural Spain, although excellent, can be sparse.

Weight

Weight is important for several reasons. A loaded touring bike with rider would typically weigh around 100kg. Every extra kg increases the work required to get up a hill by 1%; conversely, a reduction of 1kg reduces the effort

31

Aisa (Route 7)

by 1%. In stop–start cycling the effort required to get moving depends on the mass of the body to be moved: the lower the mass the lower the effort. The rolling resistance of the tyres is dependent on the amount of tyre in contact with the road at any given time. This is dependent on the load divided by the tyre pressure; the smaller the load the smaller the rolling resistance. Therefore tyres should always be kept to the correct pressure. This is printed on the sidewall of the tyre.

Lights – front and back

Although most cycling will be done during the day you may get caught out in the dark, and a number of the Vías Verdes have very dark tunnels with all-terrain floors. Make sure your lights work and replace existing batteries. Buying replacements in Spain will not be a problem. Position the lights so that when the bike is loaded they can be seen by passing traffic. (UK cyclists

note that traffic will pass on your left.) At night cyclists must wear a reflective jacket that is visible at 150m.

Pannier rack and panniers

There is no need to carry more on your back than the clothes you wear. A loaded backpack can reduce cooling through perspiration, be uncomfortable, and raises the centre of gravity so decreasing stability. Put everything possible in the panniers. For most cycling a couple of rear panniers should suffice; if camping a handlebar bag can provide the extra space required. More kit can be strapped to the top of the pannier rack. If you need more volume think again. Lightweight aluminium racks are fairly cheap and sound. Front panniers tend to be smaller and while giving extra space (and weight) have the advantage of increasing stability by counterbalancing the rear ones. Take at least one elastic bungy cord for fastening things down. Some panniers claim to be waterproof, but line them with bin bags and have a couple of carrier bags to put dirty clothes in. Manufacturers to consider include Ortleib, Carradice and Vaude.

Water bottles

Most bikes have two sets of lugs for fitting water-bottle carriers. Use them both; cycling in warm weather is thirsty work. Plastic bottles can taint the water so fill them with water when new and allow to stand; empty, and repeat until the water tastes acceptable. Top up the bottles at the start of every day and at every opportunity. On long rides through empty country a large bottle of readily available still mineral water can be attached to the rack with a bungy cord.

Flavoured drinks in particular can encourage the growth of mould inside water bottles. Keeping them clean inside and out reduces the chances of contracting gastric disorders.

Tyres and wheels

Make sure they are in good condition at the start, and if in doubt replace them before going. Tyre type and choice is importance for comfort and ease of cycling. Fatter tyres contain more air and give a more comfortable ride, but their higher rolling resistance is more tiring. If travelling light, ie. two full panniers, then a good compromise is to use a 25mm tyre on the front wheel and a 28mm one on the back. If the load is heavier, such as when camping, then consider 28mm front and 32mm rear. This is assuming that the wheels are compatible. Correct tyre pressure will reduce the number of punctures caused by bumps on rough roads. Tyre tread depends on which type of cycling you intend to do – the more off-road riding is planned the deeper the tread should be.

WHAT TO TAKE

Air travellers are typically given a luggage allowance of 20kg (of which 5kg can be taken into the cabin). If the bike is charged for separately it will have its own additional allowance. 20kg should be more than enough. Unless you are camping, if your bike and baggage comes close to or exceeds 20kg in total, then you should seriously reconsider what you are taking as heavy loads can become an unwieldy and tiresome burden.

Bike

Any bike fitting the criteria described earlier will suffice.

Pump

You will certainly need one if going by air. A pump with a pressure gauge is recommended.

Helmet

The wearing of cycle helmets in Spain is compulsory. They must be CE marked and made to international standards such as EN1078. There are exceptions in cases of extreme heat, prolonged climbs or on medical grounds.

Lock

A good U-bolt or cable lock removes worries over security. The weight is worth it.

Tools and spares

A well-maintained sound bike should give very little trouble on a tour. However, do expect to adjust brakes and derailleurs and to repair punctures. The odd spoke may also give way. Tools can easily be shared within a group. If going by air remember to take the tools required to dissemble and assemble your bike before and after the flight.

- Puncture repair kit
- Spare inner tube (one for every two in the party)
- Tyre levers (10cm-long plastics ones are sufficient)
- Spanner to undo the wheel (multi-head is better than adjust-able as it is less likely to damage the nut) – quick-release wheels are even better
- Adjustments: flat blade and Phillips screwdrivers, Allen-keys for all Allen-bolts on bike (typi-cally 4, 5, 6 and 7mm), chain riveter/extractor, oil (3 in 1 or similar in non-aerosol container)
- Spoke replacement: see above for the tools to remove wheel from bike and tyre from wheel. Replace the broken spoke but don't tighten too much; set the wheel back in the upturned bike. Use the bike frame and brake blocks as a jig to measure any buckle. Tighten and loosen the replacement spoke using a small adjustable spanner or a spoke-nipple tool until any buckle has gone. Normally adjusting only the replacement spoke will sort out any problem. The objective is to make your bike sufficiently roadworthy to continue. Small buckles can be sorted out later by someone who has had a bit more practice.
- Spares: very few spares are required. Take a spare inner tube to swap for a punctured one; the repaired one then becomes the spare. Some spokes (taped to the pannier rack); a broken spoke can easily buckle a wheel. A replacement may not make the wheel perfectly true but will be tolerable. Spare nuts and bolts just in case pannier racks or mud-guard lose their means of fixing. A small roll of tape and a length of stiff wire, no use yet – but maybe someday.

Cycling clothes

Wind resistance is reduced with tighter-fitting clothing. As the weather will be perfect clothing can be kept to a minimum.

- Helmet
- Sunglasses: to reduce glare and keep insects and dust out of eyes
- T-shirt or cycling top: avoid mesh tops which do not provide

sufficient protection from the sun, and avoid dark colours that absorb the heat

- Cycling shorts: proper cycling shorts are recommended as the insert is seam free and provides additional padding. Seams in shorts can be very uncomfortable after a few hours.
- Cycling gloves: to protect hands in case of a fall, and to reduce vibrations leading to sore hands and wrists
- Shoes: trainers are fine. Cleated shoes and matching pedals are recommended, but look for cleats that are countersunk into the sole. These shoes are multi functional.
- Suntan lotion: even if it leads to nothing more complex, simple sunburn can be very painful
- Spare T-shirt: to swap for the riding one when stopped for any length of time
- Warm windproof gear: to avoid getting a chill when stopped. At mountain passes it is worth putting such gear on otherwise the descent can be painfully cold. If the weather isn't perfect then lots of additional thin layers built from a thermal top base are best at keeping out the cold. Running bottoms and thermal gloves are welcome additions.

Cycling in rain can be cold and unpleasant, and once cold it is hard to get warm again. Take the following gear with you:

- Reasonably lightweight but fully waterproof top: essential. If cycling at night then make sure it has reflective features to comply with the lighting regulations. On its own it will be fine for showers.
- Fibre-pile fleece jacket: to wear under your waterproof top in heavy or driving rain to keep out the cold. The fibre pile is also good for retaining warmth when wet and it dries quickly
- Fibre-pile hat: to wear under your helmet
- Gloves: waterproof well-insulated gloves are available but can be bulky
- Trousers: it's a choice of close-knit cycling trousers which retain the warmth, uncomfortable waterproof trousers, or just accepting the cold and wet.

Non-cycling clothes

Take what you are prepared to carry, but try and be presentable; the standard of dress in most bars and restaurants is fairly high. The smart casual look is usually acceptable.

Sundries

- Camera and mobile phone: chargers need to work with the local supply. Mains voltage is 220V 50Hz; plugs are of the round two-pin variety
- Earplugs: hotels can be noisy
- Eating implements: daytime eating will often involve a picnic so take a tin and bottle opener,

and knife (usually a Swiss Army knife). Remember to put knives and the like in your hold luggage
- First aid kit: take a small first aid kit. These are readily available from pharmacists, bike and outdoor shops
- Wash kit: soap, towel (can be kept small if staying in hotels), toothbrush etc

CAMPING

If camping the load will increase in terms of volume and weight. Tent, foam sleeping mat, sleeping bag, stove and cooking utensils can easily add 5 to 7kg, not to mention any long-term food items. Front panniers may now be essential. Tents can be broken into their component parts and shared amongst the group.

Tents

Most of the main manufacturers make suitable tents for cyclists: generally two-person, easy to erect and fairly lightweight, ranging from 1kg to just under 4kg. If travelling solo a backpacking/mountain marathon type is both smaller and lighter (1kg or less). Cycling tents tend to have a porch or extension for storage purposes. Manufacturers to consider include Hilleberg, Saunders, Terra Nova, Vango and Vaude.

Stoves

Methylated spirits-fuelled stoves such as those made by Trangia are well proven, pack neatly and come with a matching pan set, which avoids

the separate cooking pans required with a gas burner. Fuel – methylated spirits or gas canisters – will have to be located on arrival. Even so the weight will be 1kg+ excluding cutlery and cleaning materials. If concerned about weight it is possible to get away with a Swiss Army knife and spoon along with a small pan and lightweight mountain stove.

Sleeping gear

A spring or autumn trip means a two- or three-season sleeping bag, but don't forget that most of Spain is above 600m so while daytime temperatures may rise to 25°C in summer, nights (and early mornings) are very cool. If in doubt take a silk liner which is both light to carry and warm to sleep in. A good night's sleep is essential to recovery, so it may be wise to take a Therm-a-rest which, though slightly heavier, is infinitely more comfortable than a basic foam sleeping mat.

EATING AND DRINKING EN ROUTE

Eating

A good breakfast starts the day well, but cycling requires regular intakes of fuel and replenishment will soon be needed. Readily available and convenient foods are fruit, bread, cakes, biscuits and chocolate.

- Bananas (*plátanos*), oranges (*naranjas*) and apples (*manzanas*) are widely available all year round. Other fruits tend to be seasonal.

Sotres and the Collado de Pandébano with their lush hay meadows (Route 8)

- Bread is the carbohydrate staple of Spain: even the smallest village will have a *panadería*, which you can expect to be open mornings (including Sunday) and evenings (rarely Sunday). Getting fresh bread should not be a problem, but many *panaderías* lack any external sign advertising their presence. Most bread uses refined flour, so if you want wholemeal or wholewheat ask for *pan integral*. Cheese and tuna make good fillings. Tuna packed in vegetable or olive oil can remove the need to use butter or margarine, which can be troublesome to carry.

- Small cakes are cheap to buy and make excellent cycling food, but avoid the highly packaged confections that look better than they taste. *Magdalenas*, small cup cakes often flavoured with lemon, can be bought by the dozen and are highly recommended. Avoid the wholemeal variety which tends to be drier and less instantly gratifying. Also recommended are *valencianas*, similar but finger shaped.

In many villages the shops are small and specialised: a bread shop only sells bread, the fruit shop only fruit and vegetables, and the grocer only packaged goods. Purchasing the day's food is a good way of practising the language, especially numbers.

Drinking

Correct hydration is important for good health. Water is essential to biological function. Dehydration, loss of water, thickens the blood and reduces its oxygen-carrying capacity, so reducing performance. Sweating is the main way the body cools itself during hard work. Should sweating be insufficient the body will subconsciously reduce the work level to prevent the body's core temperature from rising to dangerous levels. Conversely too much water, hyperhydration, dilutes the blood salt concentrations and can be life-threatening.

Even without exercise, in warm climates the body would normally lose 2.5kg a day through urination, skin evaporation and breathing. The water is replaced by drinking and metabolising food. Cycling on a hot day can generate one to two litres of sweat per hour going uphill. The body can absorb about 0.8 litres an hour, so the body is bound to endure some water loss during the day. At the very onset of dehydration the body reacts by shutting down urination and initiates a thirst reaction. The thirst reaction and the body's mechanisms for coping with dehydration may diminish with age.

Drinking to maintain correct hydration should be considered a whole-day process. Drink freely to satisfy your thirst. Drinking in anticipation of sweat loss or to match rates of sweating can lead to hyperhydration and is best avoided. Coffee and tea are diuretics but one

The Vía Verde out of Andoain soon crosses the viaduct and continues between steep hills (Route 7)

Embalse de El Pintado in the Parque Natural Sierra Norte (Route 4)

or two cups should have no effect on hydration status. Water is good for hydration and readily available. Many find a flavoured drink more palatable. Fruit juices diluted to between 30 and 50g of sugars per litre, with an optional small pinch of salt, are about the right strength for quenching that thirst. The sugars are a good source of energy. The quantity of sugars in a carton of fruit juice should be listed on the label. Making the drinks stronger reduces their absorption by the stomach, so keep them dilute. On the road keep your drinks bottles topped up. Drinking at meal times is recommended and generally plain water will be fine. An easy test of hydration is that urine should be clear and pale straw coloured. This test is most reliable just after getting up. Alcoholic drinks are diuretics and

should in theory be avoided – but hey, you're on holiday…!

COPING WITH EXTREME WEATHER

Long days of exposed cycling in the mountains in wind and rain can, in extreme circumstances, lead to a severe chilling of the body resulting in exposure. Similarly long days in hot weather in the full glare of the sun can lead to excessive fluid loss, heat exhaustion or a breakdown in the body's heat control mechanism, and heatstroke. Although heatstroke, heat exhaustion and exposure are most unlikely to occur it is worth being aware of their symptoms, prevention and treatment; if not dealt with properly all can be life threatening. The box below is not intended to alarm, but to highlight the appropriate precautions that can be taken to prevent problems.

Heatstroke (hyperpyrexia)

Heatstroke occurs when the body's heat production becomes greater than its heat loss and the body's temperature rises. A body temperature above 40°C can become life threatening.

Physical effort produces heat which is lost through radiation and convection from the body's surface. When these mechanisms are insufficient the body starts to sweat and so loses heat through evaporation. Hot still air, hard physical work and heat absorbed from the sun bring on sweating and so body cooling. The inability to sweat properly may be due to lack of acclimatisation, existing illness, or wearing heat-retaining or waterproof clothes. Some common drugs used to treat motion sickness and diarrhoea, and antihistamines, can also suppress sweating.

Symptoms include:

Tiredness, feeling of weakness, dizziness, headache, possible vomiting and nausea, muscle cramps, loss of coordination, reduction in sweat production, hot skin, fast strong pulse, thirst, drying out and collapse.

Prevention:

- Acclimatise for the likely high temperatures, or progressively build up distance once in Spain
- Avoid cycling if you are running a temperature
- Keep correctly hydrated to replace lost fluids
- Wear light clothes that allow heat and moisture transfer, block the sun and reflect its radiation
- Rest and keep in the shade wherever possible
- Avoid drinking alcohol

Treatment:

- Increase cooling by constantly wetting clothing or immersing patient in water, but be careful not to cause excessive cooling and hypothermia
- Lie the patient down, with the feet raised (to maintain blood flow to the brain)
- Seek medical help as effects can be delayed

Heat exhaustion

Rather than a failure of the heat control mechanisms this is caused by excessive fluid loss (usually through sweating) so thickening the blood.

Symptoms include:

Fatigue, weakness, excessive sweating followed by slow pulse, cold clammy skin, disorientation and possible collapse.

Prevention: same procedures as for heatstroke

Treatment: the objective is to get the blood back to its normal viscosity while keeping the brain fed with oxygen.
* Lie the patient flat with the head slightly down (to maintain blood flow to the brain)
* Get the patient to drink small quantities of sweetened water

Exposure (hypothermia)

Exposure occurs when the body surface is severely chilled, leading to a fall in the core body temperature; this can be fatal.

Either wind and rain alone can chill the body. When they combine they can cause severe heat loss, far more so than low external temperatures.

Symptoms include:

palour and shivering, disinterest and listlessness, distorted vision, slurred speech, irrational behaviour and collapse.

Prevention:
* Wear windproof and waterproof clothing with heat-retaining properties
* Eat at regular intervals throughout the day

Treatment: this primarily involves stopping further heat loss, and if possible providing some heat.
* Get out of the wind and rain
* Get into warm dry clothing and lie down, remembering to insulate the patient from the ground. Use a sleeping bag if available
* If possible share body warmth
* If conscious take warm drinks and easily digestible foods such as sugar
* Avoid tea, coffee or alcohol
* Avoid increasing blood flow to the skin by rubbing or massaging
* Seek medical help as effects can be delayed

HOW TO USE THIS GUIDE

This guide details eight self-contained multi-day cycling routes. Each route is composed of a number of stages; each stage can be done in a day by cyclists of moderate fitness. However, accommodation possibilities along the whole of each route have been given to allow the reader to tailor the ride to his/her own preferences and abilities.

The eight routes described have been designed for maximum enjoyment. The cycling is excellent, passing through the most beautiful parts of the country and visiting many historic and interesting towns and cities. The routes are distributed throughout Spain so each one is distinct in character, geography and topography.

Newcomers to cycle touring or cycling in Spain may wish to consider Routes 1 and 2 which are relatively short but offer an excellent introduction to the country. Routes 4 and 6 pass through some of the less visited parts of Spain without encountering too much hard going. The other routes are more physically challenging, but not excessively so.

These routes are not part of any official network or itinerary, although these do exist. The Camino de Santiago is widely known and well documented for those travelling on foot, horseback or bicycle. The less well-known Ruta de la Plata from Sevilla to Astorga, where it joins the Camino de Frances, is another well-documented cyclable pilgrim route.

The distances of the stages are accurate, as is the amount of climb on the routes described. The cycling times are those recorded by the author and are a measure of the actual amount of time spent cycling and do

not include rest breaks, view stops and the like. Riders should use them as a comparative measure when planning a day's ride.

Many stages have alternatives that provide either easier or harder options to the main route. A number of optional loop routes are described that allow further exploration of some of the more interesting parts of Spain.

The maps are principally to locate and help describe the routes. The maps recommended in the text should be used for navigation purposes and to supply more information about the area.

The accommodation listed is not exhaustive, but finding somewhere to sleep is generally not a problem. However, when heading for towns with a single hotel, reserving a room in advance by telephone is strongly recommended. This is even more important on public holidays, Friday and Saturday nights throughout the year, and during the peak Spanish holiday months of July and August.

If this guide has done its job readers are now ready to head off on their bikes to discover something of Spain. However, some may wish to have like-minded company, a degree of support or to experience the lie of the land before doing their own thing. Appendix 7 lists some companies that organise cycle tours in Spain along with some questions as to the degree of support required.

Alhama de Granada overlooks the gorge of the Río Alhama, with several water mills (Route 3)

ROUTE 1
SERRANÍA DE RONDA

ROUTE SUMMARY

From	To	km	Type	Cycling time
Airport	Yunquera	59	Fairly hilly	4hr 55min
Yunquera	Ronda	36	Hilly through mountains	3hr 20min
Ronda	Teba	67	Hilly, plateau and valley	5hr 10min
Teba	Álora	44	River valley but not flat	2hr 50min
Álora	Airport	40	River valley	2hr 15min

The objective of this tour is to visit Ronda – popular with tourists and an excellent base for exploring, set amongst the limestone hills – via a number of *pueblos blancos* (white villages). By contrast the return takes in the spectacular El Chorro Gorge and follows the Río Guadalhorce back to Málaga.

Yunquera

ROUTES 1 AND 2: CLIMATE DETAILS

	Jan	Feb	Mar	Apr	May	Jun	Jul	Aug	Sep	Oct	Nov	Dec
Málaga												
av min temp °C	8	9	11	13	15	19	21	22	20	16	12	9
av max temp °C	16	17	18	20	23	27	29	30	27	23	20	17
rainfall mm	61	51	62	46	26	5	1	3	29	64	64	62
sunrise	08:28	08:18	07:47	08:02	07:23	07:00	07:01	07:22	07:48	08:12	07:41	08:12
sunset	18:10	18:40	19:11	20:38	21:05	21:38	21:39	21:22	20:46	20:00	18:21	18:02
Best time	G	G	VG	VG	VG	–	–	–	–	VG	VG	G

(G = good time to go; VG = best time to go)

Public holidays
Andalucía: 28 February
Province of Málaga: 9 August and 8 September
Province of Cádiz: Carnival Monday (Monday before Shrove Tuesday) and 7 October

The route can be divided into five stages and is a good introduction to cycling touring in Spain, and is covered by the Instituto Geográfico Nacional 1:200 000 Mapa Provincial of Málaga. (A small part of the route lies in Cádiz, but the Málaga map is sufficient.) The Michelin 1:200 000 map no 124, Zoom Costa del Sol, is recommended, and the *Rough Guide to Andalucía* describes the area well.

Málaga tends to be slightly wetter and warmer than Almería (to the east) but drier and slightly warmer than Cádiz (to the west). Inland temperatures are not moderated by the sea and are often higher outside winter, but the temperature drops approximately 1°C for every 100m of climb and the mountains are generally a bit wetter than the coast. The highest point of the ride is the Puerto de Ventas (1190m); Ronda is about 730m above sea level. The table (left) gives climate details for Málaga, and will enable you to work out the best time for your trip.

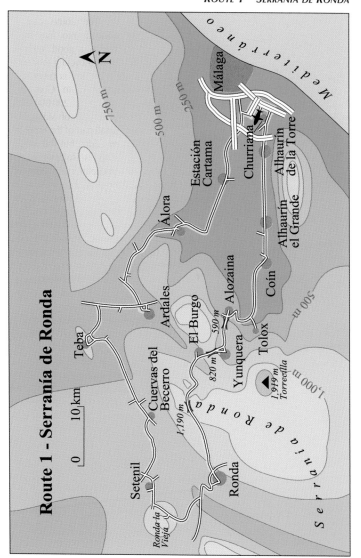

Route 1 - Serranía de Ronda

STAGE 1
Málaga airport to Yunquera

Málaga's modern airport, situated 8km south-west of the town, provides a convenient entry point into Spain.

Distance	59km (36.6 miles)
Type	Fairly hilly
Climb	835m (2740ft)
Cycling time	4hr 55min

Leave the airport terminals as described in Appendix 5, keeping right as the road splits in anticipation of the MA-21, and join it following signs for Torremolinos and Marbella. Keep on this busy dual carriageway for 1.5km before turning right, and head due west along the A-404 skirting to the south of the centre of **Churriana**. Follow the road signs for **Alhaurín de la Torre**, then **Alhaurín el Grande**, and then **Coín**; the route passes through these three small towns on roads numbered alternatively A3-66 and A-404. The road climbs up and away from the coast and is at first busy, but gradually quietens and becomes more suburban, then rural. After Alhaurín de la Torre the road is even less busy; enjoy the more relaxed cycling with pleasant views to the north. All three towns have shops, bars and restaurants. **Coín** has experienced less recent development and has retained character, and is a good place for a break. There is also a good bike shop on the right as the town is entered.

Leave Coín, following road signs to **Ronda**. The next 20km to **Alozaina** is rural and peaceful, with olive and almond trees as far as the eye can see, and occasional

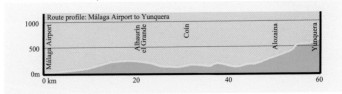

Route profile: Málaga Airport to Yunquera

orange groves and characteristic eucalyptus trees lining river banks and valley bottoms. Ignore the left turn to the spa town of **Tolox**. Once across the not-so-large Río Grande the road climbs more steeply, with superb views. ▶

Alozaina is located just beyond the turn for Yunquera and is worth a detour. Built on a spur, with a viewpoint at the far end, it provides an opportunity to review the route so far. Returning to the Yunquera road the route now twists and turns up through rocky pinewoods on a relentless climb, the toughest cycling of the day. The road levels somewhat after the Puerto de Jorox (590m) – the village of the same name can be seen below – before climbing again towards **Yunquera**. The village is bypassed by the main road, so turn left at the cemetery and follow the narrow streets to find the Hostal Asencio.

Yunquera is a typical Andalucían *pueblo blanco*, its white church set on a rise surrounded by white houses on the edge of a precipice. For the cyclist, thirsty, hungry and drained after a hard day in the heat, it is a welcome stop, particularly in the early evening, when the farmers

Oranges (*naranjas*) are often on sale by the roadside. These will have been been ripened naturally on the tree, and are simply delicious. *Zumo de naranja* is the freshly squeezed juice of ripe oranges and is exquisite, although its bottled form is a poor substitute. Most bars possess a squeezing machine, a welcome sight for the passing cyclist.

Sierra Prieta viewed from the Sierra de las Nieves

Staying on in Yunquera

Although charming, the village will not detain you for long. Cycling excursions are limited to the mountain tracks in the Parque Natural de la Sierra de las Nieves: take the road towards El Burgo and turn left after the first steep rise.

return from the fields on their ponies, saddlebags laden with black and green olives – a pleasant contrast to the harsh country experienced earlier.

STAGE 2
Yunquera to Ronda

Today's stage is through sparsely populated mountains so stock up with bread and other groceries in Yunquera, or at El Burgo in 12km.

Distance	36km (22.3 miles)
Type	Hilly through mountains
Climb	820m (2690ft)
Cycling time	3hr 20min

The road climbs sharply from the *pueblo* before getting the chance to warm up. It continues up through impressively terraced olive groves to the Puerto de las Abejas (Pass of the Bees) at 820m. The road now descends via gentle curves through enormous cultivated fields before a short climb to **El Burgo**, set back from the road and built around a domed hill. This is the last chance to top up with water: the next few hours are through dry limestone mountains with no roadside springs. El Burgo has two places to stay, including the Posada del Canónigo.

The route ahead is through the Serranía de Ronda proper. Having crossed the Río del Burgo at El Burgo, the road continues to climb along its northern bank. It soon reaches the treeline and runs through pine forest on a well-graded and hence very bendy road, the hardest going in Route 1. There is plenty of time to take in the views and to note the kilometre posts that mark progress. The Mirador del Guarda Forestal, located high up the hill, provides views over the upper reaches of the Río

Route profile: Yunquera to Ronda

del Burgo as well as due south to Torrecilla (1919m), the highest peak in the Sierra de las Nieves. The pine trees provide welcome shade.

The stretch to the Puerto del Viento (Pass of the Wind, 1190m) is the most scenic of the day. The road continues its ascent from the mirador, leaving the pine woodland and entering rocky limestone country. It is very dry with little vegetation except in early spring. Having crossed a small plateau the road drops steeply through a craggy defile into the upper valley of the Río Guadalteba before climbing again. There are views to the right of the Sierra de los Merinos, and the pass is clearly visible straight ahead. From the Puerto del Viento

Countryside south El Burgo

View east from the Mirador del Guarda Forestal

the road sweeps downward to **Ronda** over high plains with the odd limestone outcrop covered in scrubby oaks. On the approach to Ronda the road passes under a very impressive aqueduct; unfortunately modern demands have punctured its lines with one hole each for the road, railway and power line.

After two days in the saddle cycling through largely empty country bustling **Ronda** comes as something of a shock. As a major tourist destination in its own right it

Ronda comprises two distinct halves, the older La Ciudad (the city) and the newer El Mercadillo (the merchants' quarter) separated by El Tajo (cleft or gorge) through which runs the Río Guadalevín. These are joined by the spectacular Puente Nuevo (new bridge) and the restrained Puente Viejo (old bridge). In the early evening the town comes to life and the cafés fill up as families gather for the *paseo*, a time for catching up with friends and watching the world go by whilst drinking coffee and eating cake.

has more than a dozen hotels and many more places to eat. Most visitors are day trippers who return to the coast in the late afternoon.

Staying on in Ronda

Try the Turismo just off the Plaza de España (tel: 952 871272) for up-to-date information on accommodation, details of the sites and a map of the town.

Alameda del Tajo: formal gardens on the edge of El Tajo with views over the mountains.

Baños Arabes: refurbished Moorish baths.

Casa del Rey Moro: a stepped passage cut through the rock leads down to the river – take a torch – and Moorish gardens overlook El Tajo.

Palacio de Mandragón: Moorish palace with formal gardens and patios and a small museum.

Plaza de Toros: the bullring, where the modern rules of bullfighting (for the whole of Spain) were laid down. Not to everyone's taste.

Around Ronda

Cueva de la Pileta: escorted tour of caves (fee-paying) with Palaeolithic rock paintings, illuminated by gas lamps.

Cycling: there are too many combinations of roads, tracks and villages to the south and west of Ronda to describe here. Any route, long or short, will reward exploration.

Walking: the Serranía de Ronda provides opportunities for excellent walks among the hills and cork forests. The limestone hills are a good place for alpine plants – many unique to the area – that flower very early in the year. Birds of prey predominate; eagles and vultures may be seen gliding on thermals as they scour the valley sides seeking out carrion. Ask at the Turismo.

STAGE 3
Ronda to Teba

Although this is the longest day in terms of distance, the hills are moderate and there is plenty of cycling on lofty plains with extensive panoramas. Stock up with food for the day before leaving Ronda.

Distance	67km (41.6 miles)
Type	Hilly, plateau and valley
Climb	795m (2608ft)
Cycling time	5hr 10min

Leave Ronda heading north, following the 'Salida Ciudad' signs, turning left to join the A-374 signed to Seville. After an extended downhill cross the Río Guadiaro and after another 600m turn right onto the MA-7402 towards **Setenil**. The road climbs out of the valley through oak-woods where pigs feed on falling acorns. After the woods end the road keeps to the high ground.

After 11km on this road a turn-off left leads to the abandoned hilltop Roman town of **Ronda la Vieja**, which has a new visitor centre. Although there is plenty of fallen stonework the main attraction is the amphitheatre, still with bench seats and backdrop. A modern steel plat-form provides a stage.

Back on the route the MA-4800 takes us, with a right turn at the T-junction, to **Setenil** (or Setenil de las Bodegas), a winemaking centre until phylloxera destroyed the vines. It is a very pretty whitewashed vil-lage with many of the houses built into the cliffs in order to keep the wine cool. The village is unique in this part of the world in that it was not built in a defensive hilltop or precipice-edge location.

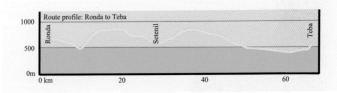

The good cycling continues on to **Teba** on quiet and largely empty roads with only the town of **Cuevas del Becerro** to detain us. Pass to the west then south of the town, first ignoring the left turn to Olvera and then the right turn to Ronda. Beyond Setenil the cycling is mostly through oak *dehesa*. ▶

Two kilometres from Setenil turn right at the roundabout and gradually climb to the Estación de Setenil. The descent is pleasant, firstly through rocky *dehesa*, then huge fields rimmed with limestone cliffs. At **Cuevas del Becerro** turn left on the A367 for 20km of pleasant downhill cycling along the valley of the Río Guadalteba on a high-quality road. Ignore all junctions to right and left.

Teba sits below its castle, on the saddle of a ridge of rocky hills to the north of the main road. Take the signed turn left, followed by a steep uphill pull into the village.

Dehesa is forested pasture, found extensively in southern Spain and Portugal and across north Africa from Morocco to Ethiopia. It supports grazing farm stock as well as rabbits and other animals that provide carrion for raptors and live food for lynx. Unfortunately the lynx is under serious threat and will not be found here, but you may see griffon and Egyptian vultures.

Setenil

55

Staying on in Teba

The castle is the only real tourist attraction in the village. For an excursion consider either the Laguna Dulce or the Laguna de la Fuente de Piedra some 10 and 15km respectively to the north-east: both host flocks of migratory flamingos. A non-cycling option is to take the train from the station to the north of Teba to Granada for a day trip to the Alhambra.

STAGE 4
Teba to Álora

An easy and relaxed day of cycling.

Distance	44km (27.3 miles)
Type	Undulating river valley
Climb	98m (322ft)
Cycling time	2hr 50min

Leave Teba by retracing yesterday's route back to the main road (A367) and turn left for 5km. At the Campillos to Ardales road (A357) turn right and soon cross the western fork of the Embalse del Guadalteba-Guadalhorce, climbing before a good descent to **Ardales**. The reservoirs are part of a large network of dams that control the waters of the Río Guadalhorce, the river we follow down to the sea.

After crossing the Río Turón take the right turn towards Ardales, turning right again at the T-junction to cycle away from the town. Pass under the road just exited. This is the road to the Garganta del Chorro (literally the 'throat of el Chorro'). The road climbs (ignoring the left turn to the reservoir), then soon sweeps downhill

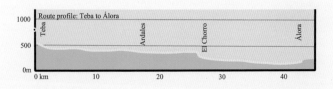

Route profile: Teba to Álora

Garganta del Chorro with the Caminito del Rey and railway bridge

(ignoring the right turn to Bobastro) through the spectacular sheer-sided dry gorge of the Desfiladero de los
Gaitanes. As the gorge widens the Garganta del Chorro
appears on our left. The freewheeling downhill is one of
the highlights of this trip. Look out for the picture-book
hermitage up on the left and later for the railway line
from Málaga that threads its way along the cliffs before
spanning the gorge. The Garganta del Chorro has been
cut by the Río Guadalhorce and provides some of the
best rock climbing in southern Spain.

The ride down to **Álora** is pleasant, but has more
uphill sections than expected.

Bustling **Álora** comes as something of a surprise. The only accommodation is the Hostal Durán, just off the main square. Some rooms have
balconies that overlook the town's Moorish castle.

Staying on in Álora

Apart from the castle there is little to see; Álora is best considered a convenient staging point. There are frequent trains to Málaga, one of the more
historic towns on the coast, with a Roman theatre, Moorish castles, parks
and seafood restaurants.

STAGE 5
Álora to Málaga airport

Distance	40km (24.8 miles)
Type	River valley
Climb	15m (49ft)
Cycling time	2hr 15min

From the Hostal Durán head east, taking the maze of side
streets that lead downhill to the main road skirting the

town centre. Join it by turning right and continue downhill, passing the railway station. Cross the Río Guadalhorce and turn right at the T-junction. After 1km keep left at the confusing junction (forking right leads back across the river); the route is down the east bank. The superior Málaga to Ardales road on the west bank takes most of the traffic. The road is pleasant but busier than the mountain roads, and the landscape becomes more urban as the coast is approached. Pass to the west of the centre of Pizarra, through **Estación Cártama** and the centre of Campanillas.

After crossing the Río Campanillas pass under two motorways, keeping to this road. Approximately 6km from the centre of Campanillas turn right at the roundabout signed 'Pol. Ind. Guadalhorce'. The road passes through a developing business and commercial district, then climbs over a railway line becoming a dual carriageway. The road swings left then passes under a railway bridge. Continue straight ahead at all the roundabouts. Approaching the MA-21 fork right immediately after the roundabout signed to Torremolinos and the airport, taking great care on this busy road. After a couple of kilometres again bear left onto the airport spur road. Go straight ahead at the roundabout and head for Salidas (Departures) by following the signs.

The easiest day's cycling of the tour, going gently down the river valley on good-quality, reasonably quiet roads. If catching an afternoon or evening flight this short stage is a relaxed way to end the tour. For a morning flight consider the Churriana and Málaga options detailed below.

CHURRIANA AND MÁLAGA OPTIONS

For early flights Churriana is just the closest place to stay that retains its Spanish feel. There are a couple of places to stay. Follow the route detailed above but turn right at the roundabout in **Estación Cártama** towards Cártama. Cross the river and at the next roundabout turn left to Churriana on the MA-9002. The road changes to the A-7052 then

Ronda

to the A-404 before arriving in **Churriana**. To get to the airport from Churriana follow the signs firstly for Málaga and then the airport. Join the MA-21. After 1.5km bear right onto the airport slip road. Take care having crossed the dual carriageway as traffic joins from your right. Go straight ahead at the roundabout and head for Salidas (Departures).

The other option is to continue straight on at Campanillas into **Málaga**, which is certainly worth a visit. It has some 65 hotels and many more bars and restaurants. The route to the airport is a not-too-pleasant 8km ride, very well signposted from the centre of town.

Time to spare at Málaga airport

One option is to head for the coast. From the Churriana dirrection, get onto the airport slip road and turn right, following the signs to San Julián. Head west through the village, turning left after the Restaurante El Kiosko, through the fields and under the motorway. Enter the coastal strip town and keep heading west. Soon the coast is reached, close to the mouth of the Río Guadalhorce, but beware: the sand is far from golden. From the Málaga direction go as far as the roundabout on the airport link road and double back as if returning to Málaga. San Julián is signed from the flyover.

ACCOMMODATION ON OR CLOSE TO ROUTE 1

Please note that this is not an exhaustive list. Hotel guide prices are in Euros, based on a double room with an en suite bathroom at high season. Rooms without en suite are typically 20% cheaper, as are single rooms. Please note that hotels are constantly opening, closing or being refurbished; it is always advisable to book ahead. Prices (where known) are indicated as follows: (1) up to 50 Euros; (2) 50–75 Euros; (3) 75–100 Euros; (4) over 100 Euros.

Alhaurín de la Torre

(3) Cortijo Chico, Poligono Ind. Nave 57, Bajo (tel: 952 41 02 03)

(1) Pensión El Patio, Álamos, 45 (tel: 952 41 21 60)

Camping Malaga Monte Parc, Arroyo Hondo, s/n (tel: 951 29 60 28)

Alhaurín el Grande

(3) El Mirador, C. A-404, km 8 (tel: 952 49 07 89)

(2) Finca La Mota, Ctra. De Mijas (tel: 952 49 09 01)

(2) La Palmera, Pl. de la Palmera, s/n (tel: 952 49 11 00)

(2) Kadampa, Fuente del Perro, s/n (tel: 952 59 56 83)

Coín

(2) Hostal Coín, Dr, Palomo (tel: 952 45 32 72)

(2) Hostal Santa Fe, Ctra. Monda, km 3 (tel: 952 45 29 16)

Tolox

(3) Cerro de Hijar, Cerro de Hijar s/n (tel: 952 11 21 11)

(2) Del Balneario, Extramuros, s/n (tel: 952 48 70 91)

(1) Las Flores, Avda. Balneario, 13 (tel: 952 48 70 01)

Alozaina

(2) Posada del Río, Málaga, 4 (tel: 952 33 31 21)

Yunquera

(1) Asencio, Mesones, 1 (tel: 952 48 27 16)

Camping Pinsapo Azul, Avda. Sierra de las Nieves, s/n (tel: 952 48 26 48)

El Burgo

(2) La Casa Grande del Burgo, Mesones, 1 (tel: 952 16 02 32)

Hotel Sierra de los Nieves, C/ Real Comandante Benítez, 26 (tel: 952 16 01 17)

Ronda

(4) Polo, Mariano Soubirón, 8 (tel: 952 87 24 47)

(4) San Francisco, María Cabrera, 18–20 (tel: 952 87 32 99)

(3) El Tajo, Cruz Verde, 7 (tel: 952 87 40 40)

(3) El Espejo, Ctra. Del Cuco, s/n (tel: 952 16 60 40)

(2) Marcías, Pedro Romero, 3 (tel: 952 87 42 38)

(2) Virgin de los Reyes, Lorenzo Borrego, 13 (tel: 952 87 11 40)
(2) Royal, Virgin de la Paz, 42 (tel: 952 87 11 41)
(1) Andalucía, Avda. Martinez, 19 (tel: 952 87 54 50)
(1) Berlanga, Genal, 16 (tel: 952 87 56 26)
(1) Arunda II, José Marío Castello Madrid, 10 (tel: 952 78 25 19)
(1) Morales, Sevilla, 51 (tel: 952 87 15 38)
(1) Colon, Pozo, 1 (tel: 952 87 00 80)
(1) Arunda I, Tabares, 2 (tel: 952 19 01 02)
Camping El Sur, Ctra. Algeciras, km 1.5 (tel: 952 87 59 39)
Camping El Abogao, Ctra. Campillos km 5 (tel: 952 87 58 44)

Setenil
(2) El Almendral, Ctra. Setenil-Puerto De Monte (tel: 956 13 40 29)
(2) Villa de Setenil, Calle Callejón, 10 (tel: 956 13 42 61)

Teba
(3) Molino de las Pilas, Ctra. Vieja de Ronda, km 2 (tel: 952 74 86 22)
(3) Posada Los Olivos, Avda. Flores, 1 (tel: 951 19 16 28)
(3) Cortijo El Puntal, Lugar Zona El Puntal, s/n (tel: 952 30 61 45) houses for rent

Ardales
(2) La Posada del Conde, Bariada Conde de Guadalhorce, 16–18 (tel: 952 11 24 11)
(1) Pensión El Cruce, Ctra. Ardales-Campillos 2 (tel: 952 45 90 12)
Camping Parque Ardales, Bariada de los Embalses, s/n (tel: 952 11 24 01)

El Chorro
Estación de El Chorro (tel: 952 49 50 04)
Camping El Chorro, Paraje Natural de El Chorro (tel: 952 49 52 44)

Álora
(1) Durán, La Parra, 9 (tel: 952 49 66 42)
(2) Pensión Don Pera, Veracruz, 39 (tel: 952 49 96 75)
(1) Valle de Sol, Carambuco, 27 (tel: 952 49 73 47)

Estación Cártama
(1) Moya, Avda. Andalucía, 84 (tel: 952 42 02 69)

Churriana
(2) Los Rosales, Avenida Ricardo Gross, 8 (tel: 952 62 25 26)
Casa Ramos, Calamón, 7 (tel: 952 621 297)

Málaga
With some 65 hotels and pensiónes accommodation should not be a problem. The Turismo in Pasaje de Chinitas near to the cathedral should be able to help (tel: 951 30 89 11, fax: 951 30 89 12, email otmalaga@andalucia.org).

ROUTE 2
SIERRA DE GRAZALEMA AND TORCAL

ROUTE SUMMARY

From	To	km	Type	Cycling time
Álora/Airport	Carratraca	18/58	Fairly hilly	1hr 15min/3hr 25min
Carratraca	Ronda	54	Hilly through mountains	3hr 40min
Ronda	El Bosque	61	Hilly through mountains	4hr 10min
El Bosque	Zahara	32	Hilly through mountains	2hr 40min
Zahara	Teba	76	High plateau and hills	4hr 40min
Teba	Antequera	43	High plateau	2hr 30min
Antequera	Airport	66	Hilly then river valley	4hr 40min

This route visits some of the same ground as Route 1 and is a good introduction to Spain for the keener touring cyclist. However, the routes only share 30km of road and the towns of Ronda and Teba.

The route includes two stages in the splendid Parque Natural de la Sierra de Grazalema west of Ronda. There are more white mountain villages, more hills to climb and more ancient remains to visit. The two large towns passed through are Ronda and Antequera, both of which cater well for travellers. Other stops are in small, quiet towns, each offering something unique to the curious.

This route is covered by the Instituto Geográfico Nacional 1:200 000 Mapas Provinciales of Málaga and of Cádiz. The Michelin 1:200 000 map no 124 Zoom Costa del Sol, is recommended but it does not extend much beyond west of the route, and the *Rough Guide to Andalucía* describes the area well.

See the introduction to Route 1 for information on the climate of the area and for the best time to plan your trip. The western part of Route 2 is affected by the Atlantic weather systems meeting high ground, and can be wet. The highest point of the ride is the Puerto de la Palomas at 1183m; Ronda is at about 730m, and many of the villages visited are fairly high.

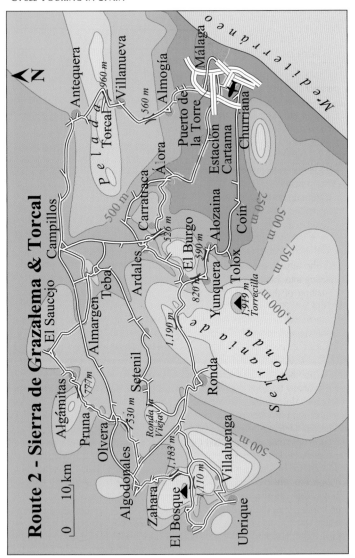

Route 2 - Sierra de Grazalema & Torcal

STAGE 1
Álora or Málaga airport to Carratraca

Distance	18/58km (29.1/36 miles)
Type	Fairly hilly
Climb	510/730m (1673/2395ft)
Cycling time	1hr 15min/3hr 25min

Although the cycling by the Río Guadalhorce is pleasant, and the surroundings rural by the time Álora is reached, the section up the valley can be cut out using one of the frequent trains between Málaga and Álora. The route can be cycled in its entirety and this option is described.

TRAIN OPTION

Leave the airport terminals as described in Appendix 5, moving into the left-hand lane as the road divides in anticipation of the MA-21. This left-hand lane passes over the MA-21 before swinging right and joining it in the direction of Málaga. Keep straight ahead on this road into **Málaga** and eventually pick up and follow the signs to the RENFE railway station. The local trains (*Cercanías*) for Álora leave every 30min and take around the same time to get there. The general rule is up to 3 bikes per carriage at any time of the day.

Leave **Álora** railway station and immediately join the main road by turning right. This road skirts around the outside of the old town via a stiff uphill climb, passing the tourist office and the Red Cross on the way. At

The Spanish coast and its hinterland have experienced a great deal of development with the result that the roads can be very busy. Development also extends along wide low-lying valleys that run into the mountains.

The Spanish version of the RENFE website allows one bike per carriage on the airport to Málaga line but the English version does not. The Spanish version has no time limits on the Álora line whereas the English one allows bikes after 09:00. Go local.

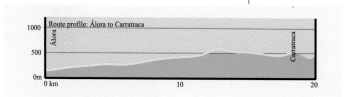

Carratraca has sufficient shops to top up with food for the day.

the traffic lights go straight ahead and follow this road all the way to **Carratraca**. ◀ The road continues climbing with varying gradients but never levels out until a few kilometres before the town where it drops gently. Beyond Álora the countryside quickly becomes rural; the hillsides have been extensively reforested. **Carratraca** is built on a steep hillside above the road. It has been famous for its sulphurous water since the times of the Greeks, and the *balneario* has been refurbished and is now open from mid-June to mid-October. However, the fumes can be experienced all year round! The only accommodation is a Fonda opposite the *balneario*. Over Easter passion plays are performed in the town's bullring, which is carved out of solid rock.

NON-TRAIN OPTION

This option extends the stage to 58km with a height climb of 730m and should take 3hr 25min of cycling time. It is the reverse of the Álora to Málaga airport route described in Route 1. Leave the airport terminals as described in Appendix 5, moving into the left-hand lane as the road divides in anticipation of the MA-21. This left-hand lane passes over the MA-21 before swinging right and joining it in the direction of Málaga. Keep on this road for 1.5km towards **Málaga**. Fork right up the slip road to go over the MA-21 on the flyover. Keep to this road heading in a north-west direction, going straight ahead at the roundabout and under the railway bridge. After 2.6km on this road bear right, crossing over a railway, and at the roundabout at the end turn left. The general instruction is to keep going straight ahead to **Álora** passing through Campanillas, Sta. Rosalía, Estación **Cártama** and Pizarra. When you have travelled 6.4km from Pizarra take the left turn signposted to **Álora**. At the railway station join the main route described above.

STAGE 2
Carratraca to Ronda

Distance	54km (33.5 miles)
Type	Hilly through mountains
Climb	960m (3150ft)
Cycling time	3hr 40min

Leave the town and rejoin the road from Álora. The road climbs before turning right towards **Ardales** at the T-junction with the new road. Once over the pass the road descends into the collection of linked valleys that contain the reservoirs that trap the Río Guadalhorce. Halfway down the hill turn right onto what was the old road; this then swings under the new road. Continue before turning left at the roundabout into **Ardales**, easily identified by its ruined Moorish castle on a rocky outcrop overlooking the town.

Keep straight ahead uphill into the centre of the town, going straight on at the roundabout. The route out of town is signed to **El Burgo**, and is on the left or south-west side of the wide main street with the orange-tree-lined *rambla* (a long, broad pedestrian area). The road climbs out of town before levelling and going up the east side of the Río Turón valley, with good views west to the hills, of which Ortegícar is the highest. Keep going straight ahead to **El Burgo**, ignoring the left turn to Casarabonela. The valley is rich with olive groves,

67

which are widespread around here. The road continues upward with a steep climb through pine forest before coming out high above the river with wide vistas. The road skirts to the north of **El Burgo**, avoiding the low round hill on which it is built. At the A366 turn right towards **Ronda**.

The route from here to Ronda, and all the information relating thereto, is the same as that described for Route 1 (Stage 2: Yunquera to Ronda).

STAGE 3
Ronda to El Bosque

A quiet day's cycling through rugged mountains on benign hills, with superb views and stretches through sun-dappled woodland. Stock up with food for the day before leaving Ronda.

Distance	61km (37.8 miles)
Type	Hilly through mountains
Climb	450m (1476ft)
Cycling time	4hr 10min

Leave Ronda heading north, following the 'Salida Ciudad' signs, turning left to join the A-374 signed to Seville. After an extended downhill cross the Río Guadiaro. Soon after the road climbs and enters a lush country of pasture and woodland. Keep to this road, turning left onto the A372 16km from Ronda and then left again 1.5km later. From here to Algodonales the route is in the Parque Natural de la Sierra de Grazalema. The road continues to climb

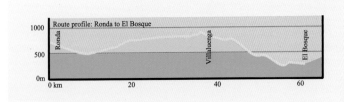

Route profile: Ronda to El Bosque

and soon enters the cork oak forest that is so typical of the area. ▶

Having entered the Province of Cádiz the road contours along the valley side with Grazalema visible opposite. At the T-junction 28km from Ronda turn left signposted to **Ubrique**. The cork forests have been left behind and the country is pasture surrounded by high limestone ridges. The road climbs gently again, funnelled into a narrowing valley before dropping into the rocky valley of Villaluenga del Rosario (870m), reportedly the highest village in the province. Here the valley is at its narrowest, closed in by steep stark limestone mountains and with fertile flat fields filling its floor.

The road continues down the valley floor before swinging right through the Puerto de Manga where the vista opens up. Below the mirador and just round the bend is a picnic site, from which a track leads via a very rough Roman road to Ubrique. The route, however, contours along the valley side below Benaocaz before swinging left and dropping down though a very rocky limestone hillside to the Ubrique road. At the A373 turn right heading north to **El Bosque**. The road climbs, drops, climbs then drops again towards El Bosque. After 8.5km along this road turn right to take the old road which leads downhill into the town centre. Most hotels are located on the Avenida Disputacíon, to the left off the main square.

The cork oaks are easy to spot as the bark is peeled off every 11 or so years, leaving behind a bright orange trunk that darkens to brown as the bark regrows. The use of plastic corks in wine bottles is threatening the economic viability of the industry and this established ecosystem.

Staying on in the Parque Natural de la Sierra de Grazalema

There are limited man-made distractions in the park; it's a superb place for nature lovers. The high limestone mountains have karst topography, and are home to a wide variety of fauna and flora including the Spanish or Pinsapo fir, uniquely stranded here after the last Ice Age. The area has the highest rainfall on the Iberian Peninsula as its mountains are the first to be encountered by Atlantic weather systems. There are many outdoor activities, and the park has information offices at El Bosque in the Avenida Disputacíon, and at Grazalema in the Calle Las Piedras.

STAGE 4
El Bosque to Zahara

Distance	32km (19.8 miles)
Type	Hilly through mountains
Climb	1024m (3360ft)
Cycling time	2hr 40min

Although this is a relatively short stage in cycling terms it is quality, not quantity, that counts. The route cuts through the centre of the Parque Natural and climbs as high as you can in the area. The roads are quiet and the views and cycling are breathtaking.

From the centre of El Bosque retrace yesterday's stage, climbing all the way. After a short distance turn left, signed to Grazalema. The climb continues but contours along the pine-covered southern valley side above the Río de El Bosque. At Benamahoma the road converges with the river but continues its relentless climb. From this point on there are numerous picnic sites and car parks, many of which have short signposted walks. The road climbs out of one valley only to emerge high along the northern valley side of the Río Tavizna. The gradient is even but the climb is long. To the south is the steep-sided valley and to the north the equally steep pine-covered Sierra del Pinar.

The Puerto del Boyar (1110m) is followed by a steep twisting descent for a couple of kilometres before taking the left turn towards **Zahara de la Sierra**. The road is narrow and poorly maintained. It has non-stop spectacular views to the north and west as it clings to the precipitous rocky slope. ◀

This is a good place to see the goat-like Spanish ibex on the craggy hillside, occasionally posing on prominent rocks. Also expect to see many eagles and buzzards, and the odd vulture. It is so quiet here that you can hear the gentle 'whoosh' of their occasional wing-beats.

Soon the Puerto de las Palomas (1183m) is reached. The Michelin map identifies its height as 1157m, but the Spanish maps and some guides claim 1357m. This would of course make it higher than Monte Prieto that overlooks it. Numbers are not important: but the views are.

The descent is spectacularly contorted, which is why it features as a climb in the Tour of Spain race. The road zigzags through countless bends, meandering through olive groves round hill and valley so that height is lost gradually. Eventually the road straightens and levels off near **Zahara**, a white town plastered onto an unbelievably steep hillside. For the centre take the first turn on the left, climbing past the ruined Moorish castle at the top of the

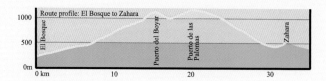

town, followed by a steep descent into its centre. The central cobbled plaza/street in Zahara is the Calle San Juan.

STAGE 5
Zahara to Teba

Distance	76km (47.1 miles)
Type	High plateau and hills
Climb	964m (3163ft)
Cycling time	4hr 40min

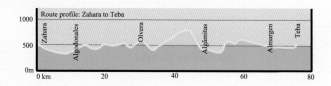

Starting from the centre of Zahara, head downhill and pick up the former main Ronda to Algodonales road that skirts to the east of the town. Turn left, heading north alongside the Embalse de Zahara. Past the dam wall the road drops and crosses the river. Take the first right (passing over the town's bypass) and head into the centre of **Algodonales**. The town sits on the south side of the Sierra de Líjar, so the road in is a climb. Enter the long open central plaza via a side road, turning right to head east out of town, climbing all the way. Join the town bypass heading towards **Olvera**.

This stage is a transition from mountains to plain. Olive groves start to predominate. The route deliberately avoids the quicker A-384 which has been upgraded over the last few years and so attracts a lot of fast heavy traffic.

71

After less than ½km on the main Olvera road turn right towards Ronda. After a couple of kilometres turn left signed to Setenil. Keep to this road through fields and olive groves as it drops to the Arroyo Bermejo, climbs then drops again only to climb and drop to the Río Guadalporcún. The climb from this leads into the centre of Olvera after having gone under the bypass. In the centre follow the many signs for Pruna. Leaving town there is a long descent followed by a climb up to **Pruna**.

Pass through the town and at the roundabout turn right to Algámitas. The sinuous climb levels off on the approach to the Puerto del Zamorano at 777m. There is an excellent descent into **Algámitas**. Pass through town keeping left signed to El Saucejo. On entering **El Saucejo** fork right immediately after the green tourist sign down the Calle Majadahonda. At the end turn right continuing straight ahead climbing out of town into olive groves. Follow the signs for Almargen at all times. Enjoy the fast undulating ride. Pass under the A-384, and at the small roundabout turn left and enter **Almargen**. Follow the Avenida Del Saucedo to its end in front of the railway. Turn right then sharp left, cross the railway and again turn sharp left to parallel the track. Follow this narrow and often potted lane towards Teba. At the T-junction with the wide road turn left. At the roundabout turn right and climb up into **Teba**.

STAGE 6
Teba to Antequera

This stage is relatively short, allowing plenty of time to explore Antequera or stop off at the Laguna Dulce or de la Fuente de Piedra with their flamingos and other waterfowl.

Distance	43km (26.7 miles)
Type	High plateau
Climb	215m (705ft)
Cycling time	2hr 30min

From the centre of Teba retrace the previous stage down the hill, going straight ahead, right then straight ahead

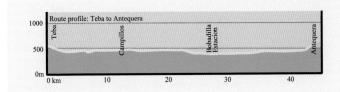

again at the three roundabouts to **Campillos**. Head straight through Campillos, circumnavigating the plaza in a clockwise direction then turning right at the main A382 road.

Around 11km from Campillos take the right turn to Bobadilla Estación. Follow the signs to Antequera, turning right in front of the railway station. Pass through Bobadilla and keep to this road all the way to Antequera. Enter **Antequera** passing the bullring.

For the Laguna del la Fuente de Piedra from Campillos, turn left on the A-384 then right signed to Sierra de Yungas. Turn into Sierra de Yungas and follow the road through before picking up the signs for Fuente de Piedra.

For the Laguna Dulce turn right at the A-384 towards Granada and Antequera. Just past the junction with the A357 and adjacent to the road is the laguna. It has a hide and car park. From here flamingos and other waders can be seen feeding. The small size of the laguna, combined with the sun from the south, makes birdwatching here more rewarding than at the better known and more developed Laguna de la Fuente de Piedra.

Staying on in Antequera

Washington Irving stayed here on his way to Granada where he wrote *Tales from the Alhambra*. For modern visitors the Turismo is located at Plaza San Sebastián, 7 (tel: 952 70 25 05). The town is packed with churches and convents, and rewards a pleasant wander. It is constrained to the south by the hills on which the Alcazaba (Moorish castle) is built, and from which there is a fine view of the town. There are also recently excavated Roman baths.

Around Antequera

To the north-east of the town in a small park are two 4500-year-old dolmens. Entry is free and information leaflets are available. The most impressive is the spacious Cueva de Menga roofed with 180-tonne stones. As would be expected, during the summer solstice the rays of the sun penetrate the chamber, having risen over the very distinct La Peña de los Enamorados (Lovers' Rock). Also in the park is the smaller Cueva de Viera. Further out on the Granada road is signposted the newer Cueva del Romeral.

STAGE 7
Antequera to Málaga airport

Located 12km south of Antequera is the Parque Natural de El Torcal, an optional excursion on this stage. The park is a high limestone plateau carved into fantastically shaped towers and pinnacles by wind and rain. It is the home to 30 species of orchid and has waymarked paths and a visitor centre.

Distance	66km (40.9 miles)
Type	Hilly then river valley
Climb	520m (1706ft)
Cycling time	4hr 40min

Retrace the previous stage's route as far as the bullring. Take the left turn from the roundabout signposted to Torcal and Álora, heading south. The road climbs round the south-west of the town, giving panoramic views. After 2km take the turn towards **Torcal**. This road dips, climbs and curves around the soft rounded sandstone hills. The sheer-sided limestone massifs of the Sierras de Chimenea and Pelada, complete with scree, rise to the south. As the road climbs the grandeur of the area becomes more apparent.

Route profile: Antequera to Málaga Airport

Shortly after the large right-hand bend the road reaches its highest point. To the right is the turn for the road to **Torcal**. The visitor centre is some 3.5km from and 240m above this point. As the road climbs above the sheer cliffs the extent and stark beauty of Torcal is revealed. This excursion is highly recommended.

From the Torcal junction the road descends through fields and pasture, leaving the limestone heights behind. In Villanueva turn right to leave the town heading west. The road continues its descent through fields with the odd olive and almond grove, and excellent views to the east. The road climbs over a rocky red sandstone ridge before again descending to the white town of **Almogía**, which is skirted to the east. From here the road descends to **Málaga** with only the occasional short climb. The Embalse Casasola is passed in its steep-sided valley before crossing the Río Campanillas. The road becomes twistier as it descends through the steep spur-and-gully terrain of the sandstone hills.

Torcal de Antequera

As Málaga is approached, particularly after passing under the motorway, the level of development increases. From Puerto de la Torre onwards the route is urban. The road continues into the centre of **Málaga** from where the road to the airport is well signposted from the railway station. Start by following the signs for the Alcazaba then for the Puerto. Nearing the Puerto signs for the railway station and the airport can be found. The airport is 8km from the centre of Málaga.

Staying on in Málaga

Málaga is a great place in which to spend either a few hours or a whole day. It has an Alcazaba, Roman theatre, a park full of palm trees and cycads, a cathedral, Moorish quarter and many elegant squares in which to relax over a meal or just a coffee outside Picasso's birthplace. The Turismo can provide advice: its address and contact numbers are given under the accommodation list.

Time to spare at Málaga airport

If you get to the airport early you could go and have a look at the coast. Arriving from the Málaga direction go as far as the roundabout on the airport link road, and double back as if returning to Málaga. San Julián is signed from on the flyover. Head west through the village turning left after the Restaurante El Kiosko, through the fields and under the motorway. Enter the coastal strip town and keep heading west to reach the coast close to the mouth of the Río Guadalhorce.

ACCOMMODATION ON OR CLOSE TO ROUTE 2

Please note that this is not an exhaustive list. Hotel guide prices are in Euros, based on a double room with an en suite bathroom at high season. Rooms without en suite are typically 20% cheaper, as are single rooms. Please note that hotels are constantly opening, closing or being refurbished; it is always advisable to book ahead. Prices (where known) are indicated as follows: (1) up to 50 Euros; (2) 50–75 Euros; (3) 75–100 Euros; (4) over 100 Euros.

Montes de Málaga

Álora
(2) Pensión Don Pera, Veracruz, 39 (tel: 952 49 96 75)
(1) Durán, La Parra, 9 (tel: 952 49 66 42)
(1) Valle de Sol, Carambuco, 27 (tel: 952 49 73 47)

Carratraca
(1) Casa Pepa, Calle de los Baños, 18 (tel: 952 45 80 49)

Ardales
(2) La Posada del Conde, Bariada Conde de Guadalhorce, 16–18 (tel: 952 11 24 11)
(1) Pensión El Cruce, Ctra. Ardales-Campillos 2 (tel: 952 45 90 12)
Camping Parque Ardales, Bariada de los Embalses, s/n (tel: 952 11 24 01)

El Burgo
(2) La Casa Grande del Burgo, Mesones, 1 (tel: 952 16 02 32)
Hotel Sierra de los Nieves, C/ Real Comandante Benítez, 26 (tel: 952 16 01 17)

Ronda
(4) Polo, Mariano Soubirón, 8 (tel: 952 87 24 47)
(4) San Francisco, María Cabrera, 18–20 (tel: 952 87 32 99)
(3) El Tajo, Cruz Verde, 7 (tel: 952 87 40 40)
(3) El Espejo, Ctra. Del Cuco, s/n (tel: 952 16 60 40)
(2) Marcías, Pedro Romero, 3 (tel: 952 87 42 38)
(2) Virgin de los Reyes, Lorenzo Borrego, 13 (tel: 952 87 11 40)
(2) Royal, Virgin de la Paz, 42 (tel: 952 87 11 41)

Almogía

(1) Andalucía, Avda. Martinez, 19 (tel: 952 87 54 50)
(1) Berlanga, Genal, 16 (tel: 952 87 56 26)
(1) Arunda II, José Marío Castello Madrid, 10 (tel: 952 78 25 19)
(1) Morales, Sevilla, 51 (tel: 952 87 15 38)
(1) Colon, Pozo, 1 (tel: 952 87 00 80)
(1) Arunda I, Tabares, 2 (tel: 952 19 01 02)
Camping El Sur, Ctra. Algeciras, km 1.5 (tel: 952 87 59 39)
Camping El Abogao, Ctra. Campillos km 5 (tel: 952 87 58 44)

Grazalema
(2) Peñon Grande-Grazalema, Plaza Pequeño, 7 (tel: 956 13 24 34)
Casa de las Piedras, Las Piedras 32 (tel: 956 13 20 14)
Camping Tajo Rodillo, Ctra. El Bosque, km 49 (tel: 956 13 24 18)

Villaluenga del Rosario
(2) La Posada, Calle de la Torre, 1 (tel: 956 12 61 19)

Benaocaz
(4) Los Chozos, Senda Ojo del Moro, s/n (tel: 956 23 41 63)
(1) San Antón, Plaza de San Antón, 5 (tel: 956 12 55 77)
(1) Pensión El Parral, Laderas del Parral, 1 (tel: 956 12 55 65)

El Bosque
(2) Las Truchas, Avenida Disputacíon 1 (tel: 956 71 60 61)
(2) Enrique Calvillo, Avenida Disputacíon, 5 (tel: 956 71 61 05)

(1) La Bodeguita, Avenida Disputacíon, 11 (tel: 661 63 02 02))
Casa Gil, Avenida Disputacíon, 13 (tel: 956 71 60 08)
Camping La Torrecilla, Ctra. El Bosque-Ubrique, km 1 (tel: 956 71 60 95)

Benamahoma
Camping Los Linares, Prolongacíon del Nacimiento, s/n (tel: 956 71 62 75)

Zahara de la Sierra
(2) Arcos de la Villa, Camino Nazavi, s/n (tel: 956 12 32 30)
(1) Marqués de Zahara, San Juan 3 (tel: 956 12 30 61)
(1) Los Tadeos, Po de la Fuente, s/n (tel: 956 12 30 96)

Algodonales
Alameda, Avda. Constitución, 7 (tel: 956 13 72 29)
Sierra Lijar, Ronda 5 (tel: 956 13 70 65)
El Cortijo, Ctra. Jerez-Antequera, km 82 (tel: 956 13 81 36)

Olvera
(2) Sierra y Cal, Avenida Nuestra Señora de los Remedios, 2 (tel: 956 13 03 03)
(2) Mesón Fuente del Pino, Ctra. N342, km 97 (tel: 956 13 02 32)
Medina, Sepulvedra, 6 (tel: 956 13 01 73)
Camping Pueblo Blanco, Ctra. 384 , km 69 (tel: 956 13 00 33)

Ventas de Zafarraya and its fertile hinterland (Route 3)

Almargen

(1) El Cuarterón, Avda. Del Saucejo, 111 (tel: 952 18 21 62)

Teba

(3) Molino de las Pilas, Ctra. Vieja de Ronda, km 2 (tel: 952 74 86 22)

(3) Posada Los Olivos, Avda. Flores, 1 (tel: 951 19 16 28)

(3) Cortijo El Puntal, Lugar Zona El Puntal, s/n (tel: 952 30 61 45) houses for rent

Campillos

(2) Los Chopos, Ctra. N342 km 135 (tel: 952 72 27 70)

(1) Hostal San Francisco, Real, 36 (tel: 952 722 056)

Fuente de Piedra

Camping La Laguna de Fuente de Piedra, Calle Campillos, 88–90, (tel: 952 73 52 94)

Antequera

(3) Lozano, Polígono Industrial A6 y 7 (tel: 952 84 27 12)

(3) Las Villas de Antikaria, Ctra. Córdoba, 3 (tel: 952 84 48 99)

(2) Plaza San Sebastian, Plaza San Sebastian, 4 (tel: 952 84 42 39)

(2) Coso Viejo, Encarnación, 5 (tel: 952 70 50 45)

(2) Las Pedrizas, Ctra. Madrid-Málaga km 527 (tel: 952 73 08 50)

(1) Los Dolmenes, Cruce El Romeral (tel: 952 84 59 56)

(1) Nuevo Infante, Calle de Infante Don Fernando, 5 (tel: 952 70 02 93)

(1) Pensión Colón, Infante Don Fernando, 29 (tel: 952 84 00 10)

(1) Hostal Número 1, Lucena 40 (tel: 952 84 31 34)

Villanueva de la Concepción

(4) Posada del Torcal, Partido de Jeva, s/n (tel: 952 03 11 77)

Málaga

With some 65 hotels and pensiónes accommodation should not be a problem. The Turismo in Pasaje de Chinitas near to the cathedral should be able to help (tel: 951 30 89 11, fax: 951 30 89 12, email otmalaga@andalucia.org).

ROUTE 3
LAS ALPUJARRAS AND THE SIERRA NEVADA

ROUTE SUMMARY

From	To	km	Type	Cycling time
Almería airport	Alhama de Almería	31	Rolling desert hills	2hr 20min
Alhama de Almería	Bayárcal	64	Climbing valley side	5hr 15min
Bayárcal	Capileira	76	Climbing valley side	5hr 25min
Capileira	Granada	84	Long climb & descent	5hr 55min
Granada	Alhama de Granada	52	Rolling plains, some hills	3hr 20min
Alhama de Granada	Colmenar	57	Rolling plains & mountains	4hr 20min
Colmenar	Málaga airport	42	High ridges & descents	2hr 50min
Option 1 Bayárcal	Granada	112	Mountains & plains	7hr 45min
Option 2 Pampaneira	Alhama de Granada	95	Valley side & hills	6hr 30min

This tour combines an exploration of Spain's turbulent past with its geographical extremes. It would be difficult to devise any other seven-day cycling route that so completely encapsulates the country.

Following in the footsteps of the original Iberians, who landed here, the route starts from the coast at Almería before heading inland to the Alpujarras. Here the Moors settled after being defeated at Granada by Los Reyes Católicos and before being expelled from Spain. Granada is reached by climbing over the highest road pass in Europe, La Carihuela (3180m). The route to Málaga follows through the fertile Vega and Axarquía before descending into the strip of high-rise hotels that mark the modern Costa del Sol. The whole area was split during the Civil War.

In landscape terms the route starts in the desert hinterland of Almería before climbing up the increasingly fertile valley between the Sierra de Gádor and the Sierra Nevada. By the time the southern flank is replaced by the Sierra de la Contraviesa irrigation has made much of the land fertile and lush. Climbing over

ROUTE 3: CLIMATE DETAILS

	Jan	Feb	Mar	Apr	May	Jun	Jul	Aug	Sep	Oct	Nov	Dec
Almería												
av min temp °C	8	9	11	13	15	18	21	22	20	16	12	9
av max temp °C	16	16	18	20	22	26	29	29	27	23	19	17
rainfall mm	31	21	21	28	18	4	0	6	16	25	27	36
Granada												
av min temp °C	2	3	5	7	10	14	17	17	14	10	6	3
av max temp °C	12	14	16	19	23	29	34	33	29	22	17	12
rainfall mm	54	49	62	53	44	8	3	8	25	49	48	70
Málaga												
av min temp °C	8	9	11	13	15	19	21	22	20	16	12	9
av max temp °C	16	17	18	20	23	27	29	30	27	23	20	17
rainfall mm	61	51	62	46	26	5	1	3	29	64	64	62
sunrise	08:28	08:18	07:47	08:02	07:23	07:00	07:01	07:22	07:48	08:12	07:41	08:12
sunset	18:10	18:40	19:11	20:38	21:05	21:38	21:39	21:22	20:46	20:00	18:21	18:02
Best time												
Main		–	–	–	G	VG	G	–	G	VG	G	–
Option 1 (Stage 7)	–	G	G	VG	VG	G	–	–	G	VG	G	G
Option 2 (Stage 7)	G	G	G	VG	VG	G	–	–	G	VG	VG	G

(G = good time to go; VG = best time to go)

the Sierra Nevada alpine vegetation takes over above the treeline. These mountains are a naturalist's paradise, with many rare plants, animals and birds. By contrast, between Granada and Málaga areas of intense fertility are found between the barren hillsides and are heavily exploited.

In addition to crossing Europe's highest road pass under the peninsula's highest mountain, Mulhacén (3482m), the route passes through Spain's highest village, Trevélez, home to the finest air-dried hams. Granada has the Alhambra with its Nasrid palace and the Generalife gardens, some of the country's 'must see' attractions.

The route is described in seven stages, so making use of a seven-day return charter flight. However, serious consideration should be given to staying longer and exploring the area in more depth on foot and by bike. There are numerous off-road and circular day rides, and a network of paths and drovers' roads. This is a popular part of Spain, and there is plenty of accommodation throughout.

This ride is covered by the Instituto Geográfico Nacional 1:200 000 Mapas Provinciales of Almería, Granada and Málaga. The Michelin 1:200 000 map no 124 Zoom Costa del Sol is recommended but it does not extend much beyond east of the route. Editorial Penibetica have produced two highly recommended 1:40 000 maps covering the Sierra Nevada; these are very detailed and show a number of off-road cycling itineraries. Available locally, through many map shops or from the publisher direct: www.penibetica.com. Accompanying guidebooks describe these itineraries and the western map is excellent for the Capileira to Granada stage. The *Rough Guide to Andalucía* gives good coverage of the area.

Granada is cooler and wetter than Almería during winter, but warmer and just as dry in summer. Málaga is slightly warmer than Almería in the summer, but wetter the rest of the year. Inland is usually warmer than the coast. Remember that the temperature drops approximately 1°C for every 100m of climb, and the mountains are generally wetter than the coast. Much of the ride is above 1200m and the highest point reached is 3180m. As

Public holidays
Andalucía: 28 February
Almería: 25 August and 26 December
Granada: 2 January and Corpus Christi
Province of Málaga: 9 August and 8 September

Granada basks in warm sunshine, snow and hail can be falling at that altitude. The table Climate details table will help you work out the best time to go.

For those who might find the ride over La Carihuela on the Veleta road too much of a challenge, but would still like to visit Granada, an alternative route is described. This departs from the main route at Bayárcal and approaches Granada via Guadix, famous for its cave dwellings. If La Carihuela and Granada are not of interest, another alternative to see more of Las Alpujarras is to continue westward from near Capileira through Lanjarón picking up the main route near to Alhama de Granada.

Caution. The road from Capileira to Granada rises from 1436m to 3180m over 33km before descending some 41km to Granada at 685m. This is well above the ski slopes. The first 12km of the descent are still exposed and lacking in support facilities. The 33km climb is on a very good mountain track but will take a minimum of 4 hours' cycling time and is far from support and habitation. Do not expect to get food or drink en route. The weather may be treacherous at any time of the year, and mountain storms can appear out of nowhere. When trying out the route Capileira and Granada basked in 30°C temperatures under clear blue skies, whereas we were hit by savage hailstorms and lightning near the Laguna de Río Seco. The road is often blocked by snow from November to May. Assume that help will not arrive quickly so be prepared for all eventualities and do not travel solo. Check the weather forecast before setting off, and if necessary delay the ride until conditions improve. Remember that you are responsible for your own safety.

Getting to and from Almería and Málaga

Both are conveniently located close to airports with good schedule and charter services. While flying into one and out of the other is possible it is rarely a cheap option. Consider instead a return trip to either Málaga or Almería and arrange a one-way car rental between airports. The drive is 230km and takes 3hr. Although cyclable the coast road is extremely busy and not as scenic as could be expected. There are two places of particular interest on route: Nerja, with its painted caves, and Almuñécar, from which point the Moors finally left Spain, and where the writer Laurie Lee was stranded during the Civil War.

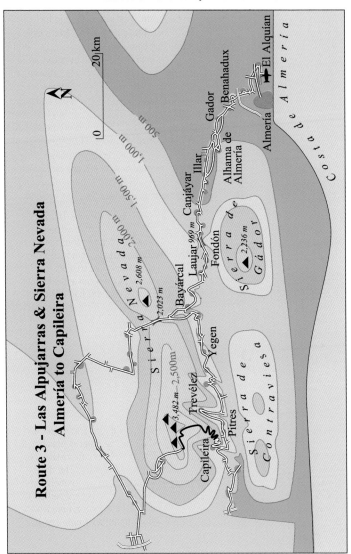

Route 3 - Las Alpujarras & Sierra Nevada
Almeria to Capileira

STAGE 1
Almería airport to Alhama de Almería

Distance	31km (19.25 miles)
Type	Rolling desert hills
Climb	530m (1739ft)
Cycling time	2hr 20min

Almería airport is small. Join the road outside the terminal building as shown in Appendix 5 and head east. Keep in the right-hand lane and follow the road to leave the airport. At the main road turn right, which is signposted to El Alquián. In **El Alquián** turn left up the Avenida de la Guardería immediately after the divided section of road, turning left at the top heading for Viator. Pass under the main road and continue under the elevated road after the river bed. ◀

The road turns north and parallels the Río Andarax. Continue straight past Viator and under the motorway. From Viator irrigated citrus groves predominate. At Pechina turn west by taking a slip road off to the right and doubling back under the bridge. The river is crossed by a causeway rather than a bridge; this should not be a problem as the river rarely runs. The wide, dry, sandy riverbeds, a feature of this part of Spain, are often used as roads. At the T-junction turn right and continue over the railway and into **Benahadux**. In the centre cross the N340 main road and climb up

This arid, flat coastal plain is the delta of the Río Andarax. The innumerable polythene greenhouses here and along the coast are used to grow salad crops, watered by springs from the coastal mountain ranges.

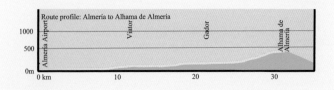

Desert terrain, Almería

the cutting past the cement factory to gain more level ground. Even for first-time visitors the country here can be familiar: the 'spaghetti Westerns' were filmed 12km north of Benahadux. From this point a new road continues directly to Alhama de Almería, but the route instead turns right and contours into **Gádor**. At the far side of town the road begins its gradual climb out of the dry valley bottom. The country is sandy desert cut by steep-sided flat-bottomed dry valleys, the cliffs and hillsides eroded into fantastic shapes. Having completed a steeper stretch of climb the route passes the innocuous-looking yet important archaeological site of Los Millares. ▶

Ignore the Sta Fe de Mondújar turning to the right and continue upwards. At the junction turn left and climb steeply uphill again. At the main road turn right and follow it to **Alhama de Almería**. Take the first left turn from the bypass and cycle up into town where the Hotel San Nicolás can be found by keeping to this road as it skirts the Moorish district. The Hostal is a large white building on the far side of the town centre.

The chalcolithic fortified settlement of Los Millares dates from 2700BC. It is open most mornings and some afternoons; check with the Turismo in Parque San Nicolás Salmerón, Almería (tel: 950 175 220, email: otalmeria@ andalucia.org).

87

Staying on in Alhama de Almería

The town was established in Moorish times as evidenced by the tight network of narrow streets around the town centre and occupying its higher ground. This makes for a pleasant exploration. The San Nicolás is a gem. Its central patio is (surprisingly) planted with mature palm trees, and its basement houses the thermal baths – still in use – for which the town is famed. The style is Moorish, but the treatments are modern with bathing, douches and inhalations.

STAGE 2
Alhama de Almería to Bayárcal

Distance	64km (39.7 miles)
Type	Climbing along valley side
Climb	1190m (3904ft)
Cycling time	5hr 15min

From the Hotel San Nicolás head downhill to join the main road that bypasses Alhama and turn left. Very shortly take the turn right to Galachar, ignoring the left fork immediately after the turn. The road gradually descends the hillside in long loops with sharp bends through olive groves. At the bottom turn left at the main road and follow it up the valley. The road soon drops and crosses the Río Andarax by a bridge. After a short climb take the left turn for the road that keeps to the valley bottom. Ignore the right turn to Santa Cruz and cross the Río Nacimiento. Pass below the villages of Terque

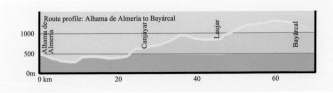

and Bentarique, sitting high on terraces, safe from possible floods.

From Bentarique the road climbs to rejoin the main valley road, the A348, at **Illar**. Turning into and cycling through Illar saves a little climb. Turn right to join the A348 heading west along the valley; the vegetation becomes more lush the further west you go. The road descends to rejoin the valley bottom, passing Instinción and Rágol before the long steady climb up to **Canjáyar**, from where there are excellent views back down the valley. ▶

Beyond Canjáyar the climb continues, but more gradually. Staying high above the valley floor pass above Padules and into Almócita though olive, almond, apple and pomegranate trees. On a hot day the cascading irrigation channels come as a refreshing shock, chilling the air and introducing an alien sound to the hills. From the col at 969m there is an extended sinuous descent before turning right into **Fondón** where the valley broadens out. Pass straight through Fondón and climb gently through Fuente Victoria to Laujar de Andarax. At **Laujar** turn right, taking the road signed to Paterna del Río, climbing up through almond trees, olive groves and patches of pine trees. As the road climbs the vegetation becomes sparser with grasses and rosemary dominating. There has been much replanting of pine trees.

A short distance out of Laujar, where the road climbs round a large spur, the route passes from the watershed of the Río Andarax (that reaches the coast at Almería) to that of the Río Adra (that flows south to Adra). The road drops to cross the Río de Paterna where there is a picnic area and the Fuente Agria. The water is apparently drinkable but has a foul metallic taste. For refreshment continue up into Paterna del Río where there is a fountain on the right, set back from the road, that dispenses cool sweet water. You may have to queue with the locals. The road continues on upward rounding a large spur before contouring into **Bayárcal**. There are a couple of places to stay and the most convenient, with clean, simple rooms, is the Hostal above the Bar Sol y Nieve. Go up the stairs and call out to announce your arrival.

Oranges, lemons and grapes flourish on the irrigated river banks and hillside terraces around here, while everywhere else the light brown sandy soil supports little vegetation. The rivers are constrained by man-made river banks so that when water does flow crops and soil are not washed away. At Terque the riverside resembles a seaside promenade, with benches overlooking a particularly sandy stretch of river bed.

STAGE 3
Bayárcal to Capileira

This stage contours along the southern slopes of the Sierra Nevada at an altitude ranging from 800m to 1500m. There are panoramic views to the south over the Sierra de la Contraviesa. The road skirts the gorges and valleys that cut the convex slopes of the Sierra Nevada.

Distance	76km (49 miles)
Type	Climbing valley side
Climb	1222km (4008ft)
Cycling time	5hr 25min

Starting from the centre of Bayárcal, head uphill towards the Puerto de la Ragua. After 1km turn left down an unmarked tarmac road that drops steeply into a beautiful wooded valley, cross the Río Bayácaral at the bridge and climb out of the valley. This is a rare short cut across the deep gorges that cut into these Sierras and does not appear on all the maps listed in the introduction. As the road levels out the province of Almería is left behind as Granada is entered. The underlying rock type is now shale, an important factor in Alpujarran architecture (described below).

At the main road turn left, which is straight on in reality, and continue downhill to Laroles. At Laroles turn right and skirt above the town. Continue along this road crossing the Río Laroles, passing the Júbar turn and below Mairena. The road drops to Mecina Alfahar, after which turn right at the T-junction. From here the route gradually climbs all the way through Valor to **Yegen** and beyond.

The road descends into the gorge of the Río Mecina and is followed by a climb up to and through

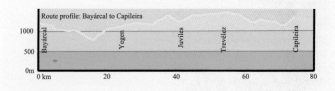

Route profile: Bayárcal to Capileira

Mecina-Bombarón. The road continues upward before descending towards Cádiar. However, well before Cádiar turn right to Alcútar and Bérchules, crossing the Río Chico and climbing briskly towards the two villages, both of which are passed without entering. The road continues in and out of valleys through to Juviles and on to **Trevélez**, ignoring the turns for Nieles and Cástaras. ▶

The valley of the Río Trevélez is broad and abundantly wooded towards the bottom with poplar, eucalyptus avenues and plantations of chestnut, oak and pine.

The trees hereabouts are mostly fig, chestnut, almond, pine, oak and olive, mixed in with crops of grapes, raspberries, maize and strawberries. It was in Yegen that Gerald Brenan wrote *South of Granada*.

Pampaneira in the Poqueira gorge, with Capileira and the Pico Veleta beyond

In spring the valley sides are a rich green, but by late summer have become tan coloured.

Trevélez (1476m) is said by many to be the highest town in Spain, a height beaten by many Teruel towns and most notably by Valdelinares (1694m). It is undoubtedly renowned for its air-dried hams, and certainly has the feel

Alpujarran architecture

The characteristic two-storey box-like houses of the Alpujarras are unique to Spain but identical to those built by the Berbers of the Atlas Mountains, who at one time colonised the area. The walls are made of uncut stone, plastered on the inside and rendered on the outside; traditionally only the inside was whitewashed. The roof is made from wooden beams that span the entire width of the property, and these in turn are crossed by slats of split chestnut. On top of this framework a layer of flagstones or sometimes brushwood is built. The whole ensemble is waterproofed by a layer of the shaley clay, dug from the river beds. This clay is known as *launa* and must be laid during the waning of the moon. The roofs project beyond the walls to protect them, and a spout is made to carry away the rainwater. Many of the houses have an attic built on the roof terrace, open on one side and used for air drying crops. If there is no attic an open gallery can often be found on the first floor for the same purpose. The chimneys are also distinctive, being tall and either circular or square in cross-section, with vent holes near to the covered top. The houses usually run into each other, producing narrow, disjointed and picturesque streets.

Staying on in Capileira

The Poqueira gorge is an outdoor lovers' paradise, with walks of all grades, numerous off-road cycle routes, horse riding and, in winter, cross-country skiing. The area abounds with unique flora and fauna. Self-catering accommodation is available either directly with the owners or through agents such as Rustic Blue; they are based in Bubión and can also arrange other activities (www.rusticblue.com, tel: 958 76 33 81, fax: 958 763134). Nevadensis (tel: 958 76 31 27) in Pampaneira is another gateway to accommodation and outdoor activities.

of a mountain town. As a major hillwalking centre it has all the expected facilities in terms of hotels and restaurants. From the centre of Trevélez the road climbs out along the valley side before settling down to more or less level. A couple of kilometres before Busquístar the Acequia de Busquístar is crossed. This is one of the many irrigation canals built by the Moors, and one of the reasons why this area is so fertile and lush. From Busquístar the road continues through Pórtugos and **Pitres** ignoring all turn-offs.

Soon the Poqueira gorge is encountered. This is one of the Alpujarras' most spectacular features, a huge gash in the Sierra Nevada containing the three unbelievably pretty villages of Pampaneira, Bubión and Capileira, each hanging precariously onto the valley side. This is naturally a tourist hotspot. At the petrol station take the right turn uphill. It is a hard 4km of cycling to **Capileira**, even though the gradient is no steeper than elsewhere on this route. The villages of Bubión and Capileira gradually reveal themselves but Pampaneira remains hidden behind the curve of the hillside. At Bubión there is a water tap outside the supermercado.

STAGE 4
Capileira to Granada

Distance	84km (52.2 miles)
Type	Long climb & descent
Climb	1850m (6070ft)
Cycling time	5hr 55min

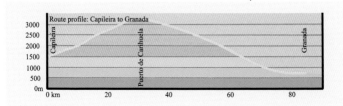

93

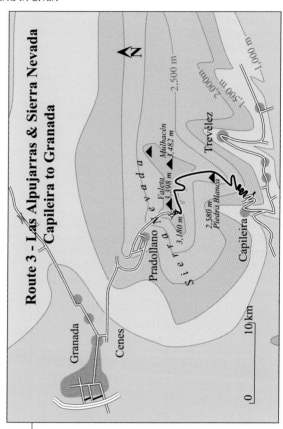

Route 3 – Las Alpujarras & Sierra Nevada
Capileira to Granada

The route is largely exposed so sufficient warm, water-proof clothes should be carried. An early start is required; note that hotels generally start breakfast around 09:00, which is when the shops open.

Leave Capileira by continuing on the road that climbs through the village. Settle down to the continuous uphill. Keep to this road, ignoring the turn to the power station on the second hairpin and the forest road on the third. At the fourth hairpin the asphalt gives way to a good-quality forest road. The route is well used and easy to follow. There is a public car park ahead and a number of service buses ply the route. Keep to the main forest road as it climbs up through blocks of forest and pasture. Above hairpin six the road crosses the Acequia Baja, which even in late summer has a good flow of clear mountain water destined for the fields around Pórtugos. At hairpin eight the Acequia Alta is crossed. Just beyond hairpin 10 is the car park, picnic site of Hoya del Portillo and control point of the Sierra Nevada. Pass the barrier and shortly reach the 2200m contour, having cycled 12km.

Open pasture is soon reached, and at hairpin 11 the last of the pine trees are left behind. From hairpin 12 the Refugio Poqueira can be seen up the valley on the 2500m contour. From this point the mountain ridge from Mulhacén to Carihuela, including Veleta, can also be seen. Here the worst of the Sierra's convex slopes have been overcome and there are no more hairpins. There is a lofty feeling of mountain cycling with fine views all round. The road continues to climb, skirting to the east of Prado Llano (2577m) before flattening off for a while.

At the Mirador de Trevélez (2700m) the end of the road is reached for the mountain buses. The road steepens again and the surface become rockier as it climbs around the west flank of Mulhacén. The road retains this roughness until the top. It is cyclable but requires greater effort and concentration. A second barrier is reached after 22km at an altitude of 2825m. The road continues its climb before levelling slightly to enter Caldera, even dropping towards the Laguna de la Caldera. To the east of the laguna on a low ridge north of the road is the unmanned Refugio Vivac La Caldera with 12 places. The ground cover is now predominantly broken rock from the abundant cliffs.

The road turns south and climbs round the spur of Loma Pelá to a height of 3100m. It retains this height as it heads north, then west, passing below the sharp edge of the Crestones de Río Seco. Passing through a cut in the rocky ridge, Veleta dominates the skyline ahead. The road continues to skirt the hills, passing under Veleta

Cycling in Spain rarely is as tough or rewarding as this stage. It is a day ride amongst big mountains so take the necessary precautions (see 'Caution' box, introduction to Route 3). The road climbs for 33km from Capileira (1436m) to the Puerto de Carihuela (3180m) on forest and mountain roads, followed by a 41km descent towards Granada. There are no shops, bars or restaurants until well after Carihuela, so ensure your food and fluid stocks are adequate.

Prado Llano, road to Puerto de Carihuela

before climbing via a couple of hairpin bends to the Puerto de Carihuela. For the last few kilometres the road is particularly rocky and the odd push may be required. At this altitude expect to feel tired from any exertion. There is another unmanned refuge, the Refugio Vivac La Carihuela, on the ridge just north of the pass. At this point you will have cycled 33km.

The views all round are breathtaking, although the ski-lift machinery is a blot on the landscape. The next 41km are downhill to Cenes de la Vega, with only a couple of flat sections at 28 and 37km, so wrap up well to keep the wind chill at bay. The asphalt road surface improves as height is lost, but the views remain through-out. There are countless bends that require care and the odd barrier across the road to stop motor traffic. About a kilometre from the pass a cyclable road off to the right leads to the top of Veleta (3398m). Keep to the road past the observatory and the Albergue Universitario, ignoring the turn left to Pradollano, and turn left after the Albergue Militar. The road levels before dropping down to the main road, the A395, where the route turns right. This becomes a wide sweeping descent. The road is well-signed towards Granada passing a number of bars and restaurants.

In the valley bottom, 41km from the top, take the right turn to cross the Rio Genil into Cenes where a left turn is taken to **Granada**. There are more than 87 hotels listed in Granada; the Turismo will help you out with lists and a detailed city map. Follow this road into the centre of Granada, ignoring the turns for La Alhambra. This road turns into the park-like Paseo de la Bomba, which in turn becomes the Paseo del Salón. At the end turn right and north along the Acera del Darro. At the end turn right into the Calle Reyes Católicos. There is a plaza in front of the Ayuntamiento from which the Turismo is signposted. The Turismo (tel: 958 24 82 80, email: contacta@granadatur.com) is located in the Corral de Carbón, a building unique in Spain. The entrance is a carved Moorish arch, and the inside a galleried court-yard with rooms off that were used for accommodation and storage by travellers.

Decoration, the Alhambra, Granada

Granada is a pleasant city of quiet plazas, worth exploring. The Albaicín district on a hill to the north of the Alhambra is the old Moorish town, characterised by narrow winding streets and stunning houses in various states of disrepair, with the odd view across the city.

Staying on in Granada

The big draw is the Alhambra, perched above the city. Its main attraction is the Moorish palace built by the Nasrids, who settled here having been forced out of Toledo during the Reconquest. After defeat in 1492 the Nasrids again moved south to the Alpujarras. The 'palace' is actually a wonderful collection of palaces and patios, pools and fountains. Many visitors miss the equally impressive Generalife gardens, which are not very conveniently placed. The gardens are their creator's view of paradise, a shady place with refreshing fountains and pools. The Alcazaba and the out-of-place toroidal (ring-shaped) Palacio of Carlos V are worth a look. Access to the Moorish palace is time controlled, and as tickets cover the whole complex there is a limit to the numbers available. To avoid disappointment book tickets in advance: www.alhambra-tickets.es, Tel: 902 88 80 01 (in Spain) or 00 34 934 92 37 50 (abroad).

STAGE 5
Granada to Alhama de Granada

Distance	52km (32.2 miles)
Type	Rolling plains, some hills
Climb	745m (2444ft)
Cycling time	3hr 20min

Starting from outside the Ayuntamiento, head southwest along the Calle Reyes Católicos. At the junction with the Acera del Darro bear slightly right of straight head along the Calle de los Recogidas. Continue without deviation to the roundabout under the motorway, go three-quarters of the way round, re-emerging on the Granada side. Take the cycle-path on the right heading south; it parallels the motorway. At the end of the cycle-path turn right along the road, and just before the flyover turn left along another cycle-path. At the main road turn right to **Armilla**. In Armilla fork right where signed towards Alhama de Granada. This road soon quietens. The Sierra Nevada has now been left behind. The Vega de Granada is fertile and once supplied Granada's half

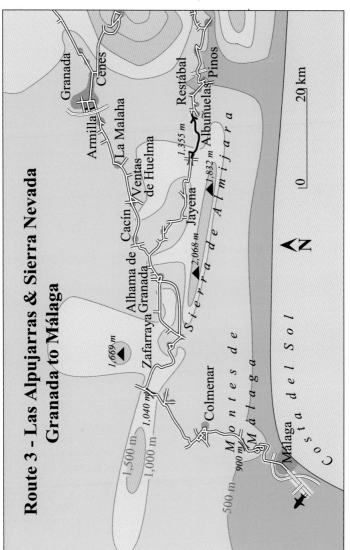

Route 3 - Las Alpujarras & Sierra Nevada
Granada to Málaga

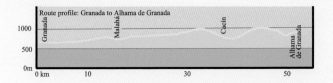

million population with food. Grains are grown on the flatter areas, while almond and olive groves protect the hilltops and slopes. This is sparsely populated country-side. After descending into **La Malahá** (named variously on maps as Malá and La Malatía) the road crosses a very wide cultivated bowl with low-lying hills to the east, south and west.

Leave the A338 by taking the right turn at **Ventas de Huelma**. Pass straight through the town before climbing the rounded hills planted with olives and almonds. Ochíchar is shown on many maps but is barely noticeable on the ground. The road drops into **Cacín** before crossing the lush and fertile valley of the Río Cacín. Turn left at the T-junction and pass through irrigated poplar woods. Take the next right turn for a stiff climb towards **Alhama de Granada**. At the top of the climb turn right at the main road and bear left at the junction 3.4km further on. Cross the Río Alhama and climb into town.

Staying on in Alhama de Granada

This is a quiet and very pleasant town for walking around. It has a Moorish centre built over a precipice, with many old houses lining an irregular net-work of narrow streets. The Turismo and town library are in the refurbished Hospital de la Reina. There are impressive churches aplenty and a town trail; a walk along the gorge leads to the bird reserve. On the way in the route passed a *puente Romano* along with *baños Arabes*.

STAGE 6
Alhama de Granada to Colmenar

Distance	57km (35.4 miles)
Type	Rolling plains & mountains
Climb	475m (1558ft)
Cycling time	4hr 20min

Leave Alhama de Granada from the Plaza de la Constitución. Take the road to the left of the Caja Rural and keep left when it forks. Join the town bypass, heading uphill at the town's outskirts, for a very short distance. Take the first right turn heading west. The route is on a newly constructed road to the north of the hill of La Torrecilla and is missing from most maps. The old road further south is mapped and is also an acceptable route. The road climbs very steeply out of Alhama for 1km before dropping through cereal fields, only to climb again to a high plateau where maize, tomatoes and peppers are grown. Another climb, this time over a very rocky limestone ridge with much exposed pavement scattered with olive and oak trees, gives way to views of **Ventas de Zafarraya**. The road drops sharply to the fields, across the flat and into the town. Ignore the road to the left that is the southern road.

There are two options to **Colmenar**. One enters the province of Málaga through the gash and passes through the beautiful area known as the Axarquía. The route

Ventas de Zafarraya is located at a spectacular gash in the mountains that separates the Sierras of Alhama and Almijara. Equally impressive is the farmland in a natural bowl in the barren mountains; the rich brown soil supports tomatoes, runner beans, lettuce, artichokes, kale, peach and lemon trees. Such fertility is hard to believe.

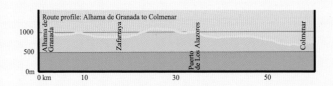

101

Campo de Zafarraya, with irises and fruit trees in flower

Cazalla–Pintado loop
(Route 4)

described stays in the mountains and is slightly shorter, with less climb but fewer towns.

In Ventas de Zafarraya turn right and across the plain to Zafarraya, skirting its centre to the south. Continue across the plain on the A341 in a north-west direction. The climb soon starts. In spring the pastures are full of dwarf blue irises. The road climbs up a valley through limestone mountains with scattered oaks to 1100m before dropping to the Loja road. Turn left, signed to Alfarnatejo, to double back before climbing through a limestone chasm to the Puerto de los Alazores (1040m). Here the province of Málaga is entered, and the descent through olive groves to Colmenar starts with only one short climb after the junction for Alfarnate and Alfarnatejo (ignore this junction). Turn left at the T-junction to **Colmenar**, passing over the town's bypass. The town itself is a collection of white houses around squares with a prominent church all built on a hill.

STAGE 7
Colmenar to Málaga airport

Distance	42km (26.1 miles)
Type	High ridges & descents
Climb	210m (689ft)
Cycling time	2hr 50min

Almonds are harvested by covering the ground with netting and beating the branches with sticks. The sound carries for miles as families go about their work.

The route takes the road due south out of Colmenar, signed 'Málaga lugar pintoresco and Hotel Humaina'. The road climbs gradually through a series of bends and continues high on a ridge. Soon the Parque Natural de los Montes de Málaga appears on the right, dominated by Mediterranean pines. On the left are almond trees as far as the eye can see. ◀

Ignore the right turn to Olías and climb to the Puerto del León (900m). From here the route is downhill all the way to Málaga. The descent is a treat through mature pine forest with views along the coast to Torremolinos, and includes a corkscrew section where the road passes under itself twice. The road is dotted with bars and restaurants serving the Malagueños who come out in droves at weekends. The road continues into the centre of **Málaga**, from where the road to the airport is well signposted from the railway station. Start by following the signs for the Alcazaba then for the Puerto. Nearing the Puerto signs for the railway station can be found. The airport is 8km from the centre of Málaga.

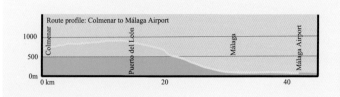

Staying on in Málaga
See Route 2, Stage 7.

Time to spare at Málaga airport
See Route 1, Stage 5.

OPTION 1
Bayárcal to Granada

Distance	112km (69.5 miles)
Type	Mountains & plains
Climb	1246m (4088ft)
Cycling time	7hr 45min

Although this option is designed to provide an alternative to the high climb over the Puerto de Carihuela, which can be either blocked by snow or be more of a challenge than is called for, it is worthy in its own right. The option crosses the Sierra Nevada at the Puerto de la Rauga at 2000m and so is clear of snow for a far longer period than Carihuela at 3180m, thus allowing an extended touring season in this part of Spain. Following a descent into Guadix with its cave dwellings the route continues into Granada through some of the prettiest countryside imaginable.

This is the only route or option that allows cycling from Almería to Málaga via Granada wholly on asphalt roads. The option is described as one stage but an overnight break at Guadix is recommended.

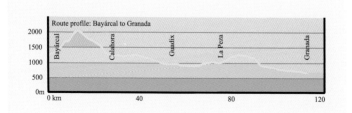

Route profile: Bayárcal to Granada

105

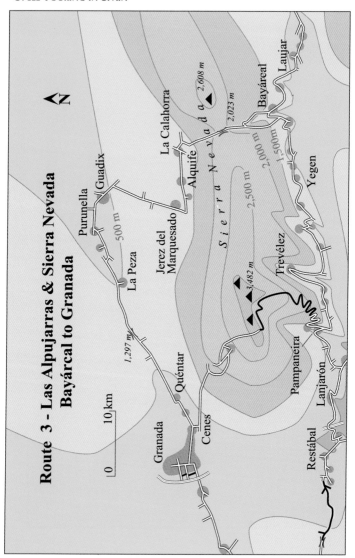

Route 3 – Las Alpujarras & Sierra Nevada
Bayárcal to Granada

From the centre of Bayárcal take the through road heading north and uphill out of town. One kilometre out of town ignore the road to the left (this is the turn for the main route). The road continues its climb on the east side of the steep-sided valley, twisting up through scrubby oak woodland. Eventually the road levels slightly before crossing the Río Bayárcal at the Posada de los Arrieros and doubles back. After a short climb turn right at the T-junction to join the road that has come up from Laroles. Continue the climb to Ragua, set in pine wood-land, where there is a mountain refuge offering accom-modation, as well as public toilets and picnic sites.

The road now descends through pine forest (becom-ing very bendy in places) to **La Calahorra** (also known as Calahorra and Lacalahorra). Ignore the road coming in from the right to Ferreira as the plain starts. La Calahorra is on the plain of the Marquesado de Zenete and has a squat square castle on a round hill. In La Calahorra turn left at the T-junction before shortly turning right to **Alquife**. Pass through Alquife, pass to the north of Lanteira and skirt round to the west side of **Jerez del Marquesado** over a flat sandstone plain, with deeply incised valleys support-ing crops and fruit trees. From Jerez the road continues roughly north for 12km to the Almería to Guadix road. The road has fortunately been bypassed, making it fairly quiet. At this road turn left towards **Guadix**. Pass straight through Guadix, ignoring the major right turn in the cen-tre. Head out of town in a north-west direction. Pass the right turn to the motorway, and in **Purunella** take the left turn towards La Peza and Los Baños. ▶

Characteristic of this area are the troglodyte houses – cave dwellings dug out of the soft sandstone hills.

Cross the Río Alhama and ignore the turns to Cortes and Graena and pass through Los Baños. Turn right to **La Peza** where signed, crossing the narrow valley before passing between steep hills and then turning left at the T-junction. The road descends through a deep cutting that reveals the underlying structure of the hills. Pass by the Embalse de Franco Abellán. Here the valley floors are fertile and well managed. The road skirts to the north of **La Peza** and starts an extended climb alongside the Río Morollón. The route is very scenic with crags, oak and pine forest combining to give a different view at each turn. The constantly changing profile of the valley adds to the effect. The Puerto de los Blancares (1297m) has picnic sites. The route to Granada is now all downhill. Keep to the road, ignoring the left turn to Tocón and then the right turn to El Molinillo.

The valley narrows to become a canyon holding the Embalse de Quéntar, then widens before the road passes round the village of **Quéntar**. Pass through Dúdar. At the T-junction in the valley bottom turn right to **Cenes** and **Granada**. In Cenes the main route is joined by the road from the Sierra Nevada coming in from the right.

For details on Granada see Stage 4.

Staying on in Guadix

Guadix is famous for the cave district known as the Barrio Santiago. Several thousand people live in caves carved out of the soft sandstone hills; the exposed surface of the sandstone soon hardens. Chimneys, television aerials and electricity supply poles stick out of what otherwise appear to be grassy knolls. There is a museum to the troglodytes. Also worth a look are the cathedral, built on top of the mosque, and the Moorish castle.

OPTION 2
Pampaneira to Alhama de Granada

Distance	95km (58.9 miles)
Type	Valley side & hills
Climb	1527m (5010ft)
Cycling time	6hr 30min

This option changes the route into an all-year traverse of the Alpujarras. The off-road section is on a *pista forestal* (forest road) which is steep and badly broken in places. One time constraint would be the summer heat. The option passes through some very empty country with limited accommodation.

As with Option 1 it is described as one stage, but because of the distance and climb is best done in two. Think about making the break in Lanjarón, leaving some 70km and most of the climb to be done in one day, and adjust the previous stage. For example, end the stage from Bayárcal at Trevélez, and ride Trevélez to Lanjarón as one stage.

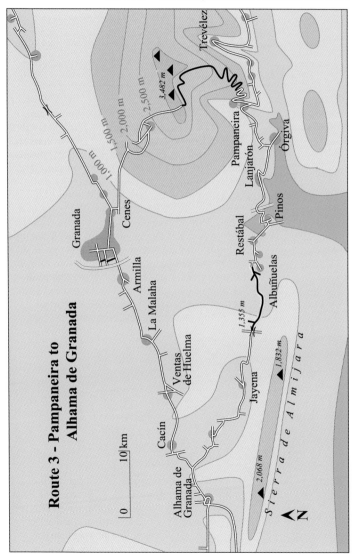

Route 3 - Pampaneira to
Alhama de Granada

Route profile: Pampaneira to Alhama de Granada

The route starts overlooking the Poqueira Gorge at the road junction some 4km before Capileira on Stage 3. The petrol station is a good checkpoint. Instead of turning right towards Capileira, keep to the main road that descends into and through **Pampaneira**. Cross the Río Mulhacén in the bottom of the gorge. The road continues downhill for 15km to Órgiva through groves of olive, orange, lemon and almond. At the T-junction on the outskirts of **Órgiva** (also spelt 'Ójiva') turn right and uphill to **Lanjarón**, the largest town in the area and the last sizeable place before Alhama de Granada. Lanjarón is famous for its water, both bottled and therapeutic. Pass through town and after a section of bends the road straightens before crossing over the A-44. Take the turn for Pinos del Valle, descending to cross the

Olive groves, Cacín

dam wall before the climb to **Pinos**. In Pinos turn right at the road's zenith, then right again at the T-junction.

Descend to **Restábal**, and on the right-hand bend turn left to Saleres and Albuñuelas. In Saleres, 1.7km from the turn in Restábal, fork right up a steep hill and continue climbing towards **Albuñuelas**. Just 1.8km from the Saleres junction turn right heading north. This junction is readily identifiable as the road sign for straight ahead reads 'Albuñuelas 600m'. Another 300m north along this road is a left turn at the pillar signed 'Distrito Forestal, Monte Puerto de la Toba 45'. Take this uphill side road and fork right after 800m onto the gravel track. This is after a final pass under the electricity pylons. Pass a large house on the left. Keep to this gravel track ignoring the left turn after 1.2km and the right turn after a further 0.2km.

Albuñuelas can be seen to the south, overlooking its own river in a gorge. As height is gained the gravel road enters mountain forest on craggy hillsides. There are fine views back to the Alpujarras. The road surface is particularly poor on the steeper parts making the odd push necessary. Where the grit road levels, ignore the right turn to Herreros and continue across the plateau to a four-way junction at the main road. Take the asphalt road straight across, heading west. The extended descent passes through **Jayena**. Beyond Jayena ignore the left turn to Fornes, but turn left 3km further on. Keep to this poorly maintained road past the Bermejales camping site and into Poblado del Embalse, turning left at the main road. This road continues without significant turns into **Alhama de Granada**. The road climbs from the *embalse* and at its highest point joins the main route where the road staggers in from the left. Continue downhill and bear left at the junction 3.4km further on. Cross the Río Alhama and climb into town.

Staying on in Alhama de Granada
See Stage 5.

ACCOMMODATION ON OR CLOSE TO ROUTE 3

Please note that this is not an exhaustive list. Hotel guide prices are in Euros, based on a double room with an en suite bathroom at high season. Rooms without en suite are typically 20% cheaper, as are single rooms. Please note that hotels are constantly opening, closing or being refurbished; it is always advisable to book ahead. Prices (where known) are indicated as follows: (1) up to 50 Euros; (2) 50–75 Euros; (3) 75–100 Euros; (4) over 100 Euros.

Almería

There are some twenty two hotels and pensiónes in Almería. Only those known to cost less than 75 Euros are listed.

(2) Embajador, Calzada de Castro, 4 (tel: 950 25 55 11)

(2) Mirabel, Avda. Federico García Lorca, 153 (tel: 950 23 51 73)

(2) Sol Almería, Ctra. Ronda, 193 (tel.: 950 27 18 11)

(2) Delfín Verde, García Cañas, 2 (tel: 950 26 79 27)

Camping La Garrofa, Ctra. N340, km 4 dirección Aguadulce (tel: 950 23 57 70)

Alhama de Almería

(3) San Nicolás, Baños, 2 (tel: 950 64 13 61)

Pensión Chiquito, Pablo Picasso, 5 (tel: 950 64 02 31)

Laujar de Andarax

(1) Almírez, Ctra. Laujar-Berja km 1.6 (tel: 950 51 35 14)

Pensión Nuevo Andarax, Calle de Canalejas, 27 (tel: 950 51 31 13)

Camping La Molineta, Paraje El Batán (tel: 950 51 43 15)

Bayárcal

(3) Posada de los Arrieros, Ctra. Bayárcal-Puerto de la Ragua (tel: 950 52 40 01)

(1) Hostal Bar Sol y Nieve, Granada, 3 (tel: 950 512 813)

Laroles

(2) Hotel Rural Real De Laroles, Calle del Malcoba, 51 (tel: 958 76 0058)

Refugio de Nevada, Ctra. de Mairena, s/n (tel: 958 76 03 20)

Camping Alpujarras, Carretera. Puerto de la Ragua km.1, (tel: 958 76 02 31)

Mairena

(2) Real de Laroles, Real, 46 (tel: 958 76 00 58)

Ugíjar

Pensión Vidaña Ctra. Almería, s/n (tel: 958 76 70 10)

Válor

(2) Hostal Las Perdices, Torrecilla, s/n (tel: 958 85 18 21)

(2) Los Arcos, Pl. de la Iglesia, s/n (tel: 659 44 84 25)

Yegen
(1) Bar la Fuente, Calle de Real, s/n (tel: 958 85 10 67)
El Tinao, Carretera, s/n (tel: 958 85 12 12)

Mecina Bombarón
(2) La Bombarón, Calle de San Rafael, s/n (tel: 958 85 11 13)

Cádiar
(2) Alquería de Morayma, Ctra. A-358, km 50 (tel: 958 34 32 21)
Hostal Montoro, San Isidro, 20 (tel: 958 76 80 68)
Pensión Nuevo Cadi, Real, 21 (tel: 958 76 80 64)

Bérchules
(2) Los Bérchules, Carretera, s/n (tel: 958 85 25 30)

Juviles
Hostal Tino, Altillo Bajo, s/n (tel: 958 76 91 74)

Trevélez
(2) Fragua II, Posadas, s/n (tel: 958 85 86 26)
(1) La Fragua, San Antonio, 4 (tel: 958 85 86 26)
(1) Fernando, Pista Barrio del Medio (tel: 958 85 85 65)
Camping Trevélez, Ctra. Trevélez-Órgiva 1 km (tel: 958 85 87 35)

Busquístar
(4) Alcazaba, Ctra. Órgiva-Lujar km 37 (tel: 958 858 687)

Pórtugos
(3) Nuevo Malagueño Ctra. Órgiva a Trevélez (tel: 958 76 60 98)
Pensión Mirador, Pl. Nueva, 5 (tel: 958 76 60 14)

Pitres
Camping Balcón de Pitres, Ctra. Órgiva-Ugíjar km 51 (tel: 958 76 61 11)

Bubión
(4) Villa de Bubión, Barrio Alto, s/n (tel: 958 76 39 73)
(1) Terrazas de la Alpujarra, Placeta del Sol, s/n (tel: 958 76 30 34)

Capileira
(3) Finca Los Llanos Ctra. Sierra Nevada, s/n (tel: 958 76 30 71)
(2) Cascapeñas, Carril, s/n (tel: 958 76 30 76)
(1) Mesón Poqueira, Doctor Castilla, 6 (tel: 958 76 30 48)
(1) Atalaya, Perchel, 3 (tel: 958 76 30 25)
(1) Moraima, Ctra. de la Sierra, s/n (tel: 958 76 31 80)

Güejar-Sierra

Camping Las Lomas Ctra. Güejar-Sierra, km 6,5 (tel: 958 48 47 42)
Camping Cortijo Balderas, Camino de Padules km 5 (tel: 958 34 05 50)

Sierra Nevada

There are some 15 hotels in the ski resort and surrounding villages. They are not detailed here.

Granada

There are more than 100 hotels and pensiónes, and three campsites listed in Granada. The Turismo will provide you lists and a detailed city map (tel: 958 24 82 80, email: contacta@granadatur.com).

Armilla

(2) Los Galanes, Ctra. Bailén-Motril km 136 (tel: 958 55 05 08)
(2) Ibis Granada, Ctra. de Armilla, s/n (tel: 958 18 42 50)
(1) Pensión Etap, Parque Comercial San Isidro, s/n (tel: 958 12 31 88)

Alhama de Granada

(4) Balneario Alhama de Granada (tel: 958 35 00 11)
(2) San Jose, Constitución, 27 (tel: 958 35 01 56)
Ana, Ctra. Granada, 8 (tel: 958 36 01 08)

Ventas de Zafarraya

Pension Aquí te Quiero Ver, Delicias, 21 (tel: 958 36 20 01)
Pensión Casa Bartolo Buenos Aires, 12 (tel: 958 36 20 12)
Al-Andalus, Pilas de Algaida, 13 (tel: 958 36 21 39)

Colmenar

(2) Venta Los Arrieros, Ctra. Casabermeja-Colmenar km 8 (tel: 952 73 10 66)
(2) Arco del Sol, Fresca, 18 (tel: 952 73 01 98)
(2) Belén, Avenida De los Montés, 11 (tel: 952 75 05 78)
(2) Balcón De Los Montes, Calle Serranía de Ronda (tel: 952 73 05 30)

Málaga

With some 65 hotels and pensiónes accommodation should not be a problem. The Turismo in Pasaje de Chinitas near to the cathedral should be able to help (tel: 951 30 89 11, fax: 951 30 89 12, email otmalaga@andalucia.org).

OPTION 1

La Calahorra

(3) Hospederia del Zenete, Ctra. de la Ragua, 1 (tel: 958 67 71 92)
(1) Labella, Ctra. de Aldeire, 1 (tel: 958 67 70 00)
Pensión La Fuente, Pedro Antonio de Alarcón, 4 (tel: 958 67 71 76)

Guadix

(3) Hotel Comercio, Mira de Amezcua, 3 (tel: 958 66 05 00)

(2) Mari Carmen, Avenida Mariana Pineda, 61 (tel: 958 66 15 00)

(2) Hotel Mulhacén, Avenida Buenos Aires, 41 (tel: 958 66 07 50)

Purullena

(1) El Caminero, Avda. Andalucía, 30 (tel: 958 69 01 54)

Pensión Ruta del Sur, Ctra. De Granada, 2 (tel: 958 69 01 67)

Cortes Y Graena

(2) Montual, Ctra. de la Peza, s/n (tel: 958 67 07 35)

(1) El Mirador, Ctra. Granada, s/n (tel: 958 68 00 04)

Quéntar

(2) Quentarhotel, San Sebastian, s/n (tel: 958 48 54 26)

OPTION 2

Pampaneira

(4) Estrella de las Nieves, Huertos, 21 (tel: 958 76 39 81)

(2) Pampaneira, Avda. de la Alpujarra, 1 (tel: 958 76 30 02)

Pensión Barranco del Poqueira, Cercado, 10 (tel: 958 76 30 04)

Órgiva

(3) Taray, Ctra. A348 km 18 (tel: 952 78 45 25)

(1) Mirasol I, Avenida González Robles, 5 (tel: 958 78 51 08)

Camping Órgiva, Vega de Órgiva – Valle del Guadalfeo (tel: 958 78 43 07)

Camping Puerta de la Alpujarra, Ctra. de Lanjarón-Órgiva, s/n (tel: 958 78 44 50)

Lanjarón

(3) Nuevo Manolete, San Sebastián, 3 (tel: 958 77 07 73)

(3) Castillo Lanjarón, Granada, 1 (tel: 958 77 07 12)

(3) Alcadima, Francisco Tarrega, 3 (tel: 958 77 08 09)

(2) Miramar, Avenida Andalucía, 10 (tel: 958 77 01 61)

(2) Nuevo Palas, Avenida de la Alpujarra, 24 (tel: 958 77 00 86)

(2) Central, Avenida de Andalucía, 21 (Tel: 958 77 01 08)

(2) España, Avenida Andalucía, 42 (tel: 958 77 01 87)

(2) El Sol, Avenida Andalucía, 32 (tel: 958 77 01 30)

(1) Lanjarón, Pérez Chávez, 7 (tel: 958 77 00 94)

(1) París, Avenida Andalucía, 23 (tel: 958 77 00 56)

(1) Paraíso, Avenida Alpujarra, 18 (tel: 958 77 00 12)

The Río Bembézar valley, Sierra Morena

ROUTE 4
SIERRA MORENA

ROUTE SUMMARY

From	To	km	Type	Cycling time
Sevilla	Almadén	65	Rolling plain then hilly	4hr 20min
Almadén	Cazalla	47	Hills and valleys	3hr 25min
Cazalla	Ojuelos Altos	87	Hilly	5hr 40min
Ojuelos	Hornachuelos	57	Hilly	3hr 45min
Hornachuelos	Córdoba	83	Hilly	5hr 20min
Option 1				
El Pedroso	Hornachuelos	90	Plain and low hills	5hr 35min
Option 2				
Cazalla–El Pintado loop		72	Plain and hills	4hr 30min

The Sierra Morena is Spain's longest mountain range. Stretching from the Portuguese border in the west to the Desfiladero de Despeñaperros in the east it occupies Andalucía's northern border. The Sierra is wide and relatively low lying, and for the most part lacks the characteristics of a mountain range apart from the centre, an area of close-packed hills and ridges.

The area is not only interesting for its landscape features but also for the local flora and fauna. The valleys are full of alder, eucalyptus and willow, while the hillsides are covered in holm, gall and cork oak, pine and olive trees. Raptors are common: buzzards, imperial and royal eagles, griffon, and Egyptian and rare black vultures are often seen either soaring on thermals or looking for carrion. Hoopoes, owls, bee-eaters and black storks can be found in the valleys. Mammals include deer, boar, otter, lynx, mongoose and wolf. Apart from lizards and other reptiles, turtles may be seen walking along the sandy banks of the quieter rivers. The rivers swarm with trout. Man is largely absent, but has made his mark through mining for zinc, copper, silver and mercury, now just about finished. Towns and villages tend to be spread well apart.

The route starts on the plain of the Río Guadalquivir at Sevilla and finishes on the plain at Córdoba. Both cities are worth a visit in their own right. Railway stations are used as the start and finish points because they are easily accessible. Both

ROUTE 4: CLIMATE DETAILS

	Jan	Feb	Mar	Apr	May	Jun	Jul	Aug	Sep	Oct	Nov	Dec
Sevilla												
av min temp °C	6	7	9	11	13	17	20	20	18	14	10	7
av max temp °C	15	17	20	24	27	32	36	36	32	26	20	16
rainfall mm	66	61	90	57	41	8	1	5	19	70	67	70
sunrise	08:37	08:27	07:56	08:10	07:30	07:04	07:04	07:27	07:53	08:19	07:48	08:19
sunset	18:15	18:45	19:16	20:44	21:12	21:38	21:47	21:33	20:55	20:09	18:28	18:07
Best time	G	G	VG	VG	G	–	–	–	–	G	VG	G

(G = good time to go; VG = best time to go)

Public holidays
Andalucía: 28 February
Province of Sevilla: 30 May and Corpus Christi (varying dates)
Province of Córdoba: 8 September and 24 October

cities connect to Málaga, with both trains and inter-city coaches. One-way car hire between Málaga and the start and finish points is another possibility. Sevilla's airport can be found to the north-east of the city, while Córdoba's is to its south-west. Direct flights are rare, and connecting flights can by very time-consuming.

The cities have plenty of accommodation, but this can be scarce in the country. There are many campsites, and wild camping is an option if long days in the saddle are to be avoided. Do not wild camp in national parks, and elsewhere it is polite to ask for permission first. For those averse to camping or extended cycling the El Pedroso to Hornachuelos option can be used. The El Pintado loop gives an extra day of cycling from Cazalla de la Sierra. The area is sparsely populated and the asphalt roads are less maintained than elsewhere, so parts of the route use grit roads.

This route is covered by the two Instituto Geográfico Nacional 1:200 000 Mapas Provinciales

Sierra Morena

of Sevilla and Córdoba. The Michelin 1:400 000 map no 578 Andalucía, covers the area. The 1:100 000 Mapa Guía Parque Natural Sierra Norte is highly recommended. Please note that with the odd exception the quality of maps leaves a great deal to be desired in relation to roads and tracks. Not all roads on the ground are on the map, and some roads on the map have never been built. The route described does exist. The *Rough Guide to Andalucía* gives limited coverage of the area.

Sevilla is in the hottest part of Spain in the summer and the winters are mild. Sevilla is almost at sea level, and most of the Sierra Morena is at 400 to 600m so there is little cooling effect. However, the heat is fairly dry. Please see the 'Climate details' table (left) for a guide to the best time to visit the area.

This is a very empty part of Spain. Visitors are not that common, with the exception of hunters who take advantage of the wildlife. This route gets about as far away as is possible from the 'madding crowd'.

Caution

The area between the towns of Alanís, Argallón, Villaviciosa de Córdoba and Hornachuelos is crossed by an extensive network of cyclable forest roads, many made to service the now abandoned mines. Many of the tracks are mapped, but many are not, and some on the map cannot be found on the ground. In addition the prominence of the tracks shown on the maps does not correlate well with those on the ground. Map reading can be very difficult.

The area is large and very sparsely populated (for example, on an exploratory 86km ride – not described in this book – only two occupied and three unoccupied buildings were passed). One junction, prominently marked on the map, was missed, and 8km covered on an excellent track that was not on the map. Relocation was only possible by the use of two maps, a GPS and an orienteering compass. As it turned out the intended route was impassable because an uncrossable gate blocked the track. Explorers should be prepared for all eventualities, but will be rewarded with some excellent rides.

There is one area out of bounds. The village of El Cabril, and all approach roads in the immediate vicinity, are closed to public access as Spain stores its nuclear waste in nearby disused mines.

STAGE 1
Sevilla to Almadén de la Plata

Distance	65km (40.3 miles)
Type	Rolling plain then hills
Climb	570m (1870ft)
Cycling time	4hr 20min

The route starts at the Estación Santa Justa in Sevilla. Leave the railway station main entrance straight ahead bearing south-east. Turn left at the traffic lights to join Avenida de Kansas City heading north-east. Ignore the first junction, and after 800m on the Avenida take the left turn signed to Huelva. This requires a right fork before turning left round a discontinuous roundabout again towards Huelva in a north-west direction.

Cross over the railway and go straight ahead at the first set of traffic lights which involves a slight bend to the right. Continue heading towards Huelva: go straight

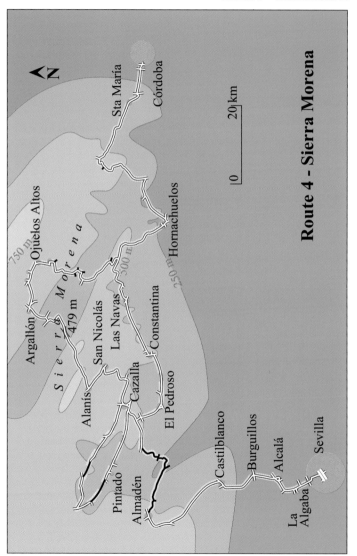

Route 4 - Sierra Morena

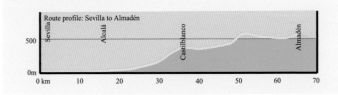

Route profile: Sevilla to Almadén

ahead at the second, third and fourth sets of lights. Pass the two metal columns in the central reservation and continue straight on at the fifth and sixth sets. Go straight ahead at the large roundabout heading for the Carrefour column, passing to its left, and straight ahead at the second, smaller roundabout. Turn left at the third roundabout onto Ronda Tamarguillo and straight ahead at the next, passing to the left of the white church. At the next roundabout turn right on the Calle Navarra heading west of north to **La Algaba**. Leave Sevilla by the flyover that crosses a dual carriageway and railway.

The route continues through low-lying country planted with orange groves. Continue straight on at the roundabout before crossing the wide brown Río Guadalquivir. At the next roundabout continue straight ahead, passing to the east of **La Algaba**. At the next roundabout stay in the right hand lane to Alcalá del Río. Continue on this road through Alcalá del Río towards Córdoba before turning right to **Burguillos**, heading north on a straight road. Pass through Burguillos and straight ahead at the roundabout in its centre.

North of Burguillos the undulating road provides views in all directions, and the vegetation becomes more wooded with olives, vines and *dehesa*. South of **Castilblanco de los Arroyos** continue straight ahead at the roundabout before passing through the town of low white buildings with bumpy cobbled streets. At the town's northern edge turn left to Almadén de la Plata on the SE-5405. The road climbs through rolling *dehesa* before joining a broad flat *dehesa*-covered ridge with the odd planting of eucalyptus. At the next junction turn right to **Almadén de la Plata**. This former mercury mining centre has a museum of amphibians.

Staying on in Sevilla

With a history dating back to pre-Roman times there is more to Sevilla than oranges! Most of the places of interest are located to the west of the railway station. The 'must-see' attraction is the Giralda, a former minaret, which along with the Patio de Naranjas is all that remains of the mosque that was demolished to make way for the Gothic cathedral. The Alcázar is again Moorish, based on Roman foundations but with later rebuilding. For details of the other numerous attractions contact the Turismo at Avenida de la Constitución, 21B (tel: 954 78 75 78, email: otsevilla@andalucia.org).

STAGE 2
Almadén de la Plata to Cazalla de la Sierra

Distance	47km (29.2 miles)
Type	Grit road; hills and valleys
Climb	605m (1985ft)
Cycling time	3hr 25min

Of the maps listed in the introduction the Mapa Guía Parque Natural Sierra Norte represents the stage best. The Michelin map is acceptable though.

The route described is on good-quality grit and clay tracks. Expect dust or mud (depending on the weather) but forget about bars, restaurants or shops en route so take necessary supplies. Distances are measured from the exit of Almadén.

At the eastern edge of town turn right turn right into a road that drops downhill and after 150m becomes a grit road with a 50kmph sign post. The turn is signed 'Centro de Vistantes Cortijo El Berrocal 5km'.

Soon all traces of the town are left behind. The road descends to join the Arroyo de la Calzadilla. The topography is of steep-sided oak-covered valleys, and the road is a good-quality grit track. At 4.5km ignore the track to the right just before a large plantation of eucalyptus, signed 'Centro de Vistantes Cortijo El Berrocal 100m'. At 6.6km cross the *arroyo* and again at 8.4km,

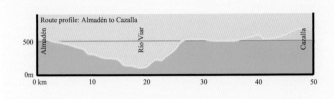

climbing over a grassy ridge and crossing another *arroyo*. From here the country opens up into a broad-bottomed fertile valley. In addition to the signs marking reserved hunting there are also signs reserving the collection of mushrooms and asparagus. The clay road continues descending, this time paralleling the Arroyo de la Barra through fields and pasture with good views of the surrounding hills.

At 15.5km, just before the large gates, take the left fork, heading just south of east. Skirt south of the farmhouse and at 19.6km cross over the Embalse de Melonares. Turn immediately left uphill and at 20.8km cross a small river. The grit road now starts a sinuous climb up through sparse but mature pine forest with excellent views to the south and west. At 23km continue straight ahead at the junction. The road continues to climb but soon levels off, passing through *dehesa* and pasture. Farmhouses become more frequent.

At 30.3km turn right at the T-junction on the asphalt road no A-450. A sign declares that the route has passed through the 'Dehesa de Upa'. The road continues through walled-off *dehesa*, keeping level before dropping steeply into the Arroyo de San Pedro, where at 39.1km there is a right turn for El Pedroso. This is the start of Option 1 (see below).

The route continues straight on. Ignore the left turn to El Pintado, and at the next junction turn left before climbing into **Cazalla de la Sierra**.

Staying on in Cazalla de la Sierra

Cazalla is the urban centre for the area, and has long been a staging post for those travelling north from Sevilla. Today it is a centre for the production of *aguardiente* (brandy). A walk round town reveals quiet squares, churches of mixed styles and fine renaissance mansions.

Around Cazalla de la Sierra

Cycling: there are some excellent day rides from the town including the Pintado loop described in Option 2.

Walking: for those wishing to explore on foot there are a number of way-marked walks described in *Cuaderno de Itineraries del Parque Natural Sierra Norte de Sevilla*, published in Spanish by the Consejería de Medio Ambiente, Junta de Andalucía. This guidebook is available from the Turismo, located close to the Posada del Moro. One of the walks is from town and another from the railway station. There are further walks from El Pedroso, Constantina, San Nicolás, Cerro del Hierro and two from Almadén. A number of walks can be picked up on the way through or be mixed into day rides. The Cerro del Hierro walk can be combined with the Vía Verde de la Rivera del Huéznar.

STAGE 3
Cazalla de la Sierra to Ojuelos Altos

Distance	87km (54 miles)
Type	Hilly
Climb	1140m (3740ft)
Cycling time	5hr 40min

This stage crosses the empty centre of the Sierra Morena.

From the centre of Cazalla head north on the main through road and take the first major right turn, signed to the station and Villa Turística. The road drops steeply past the Villa Turística to the station through pasture

125

There is no accommodation listed between Alanís and Hornachuelos at the end of Stage 4. This section is broken into two stages for narrative convenience. For those prepared to rough camp the route can be followed; others may consider leaving the route at Argallón to continue north to Fuente Obejuna where there are a couple of Hostales and a campsite. There is a direct road from Fuente Obejuna to Ojuelos Altos to rejoin the route. The two days' cycling are certainly worth any logistic inconvenience.

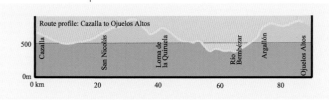

and olive groves. Beyond the station in the valley bottom turn left to cycle upstream beside the Rivera Huesna (also spelt Huéznar). The river babbles its way through the lush valley under deciduous trees: a significantly different landscape from the last couple of stages. There are numerous campsites and picnic spots. After a while the disused railway (Vía Verde) makes an appearance and is cyclable for 15km from Cazalla to San Nicolás. The road continues to climb, passing disused water mills. At the T-junction on the northern side of **San Nicolás** turn left to **Alanís**. The climb continues but is now through *dehesa*, olives and open fields. Alanís's castle, standing proud on its hill, announces the town well in advance. ◀

Please note: Alanís is the last place to stock up on food and drinks for a long way.

In the centre of town turn right in the small plaza, going uphill on Calle Nueva for a short distance before turning right again to head east then north-east. The climb continues, and soon hills, valleys, deciduous oak and pine dominate the landscape as the empty and rugged part of the Sierra Morena is entered, this part of the range being eroded by the Río Bembézar and its tributaries. Four kilometres from Alanís the Lomo del Aire is crossed, at 757m the highest point on the entire route.

A descent and climb lead to the Loma de la Quiruela (645m). ▶

The road drops through many bends before crossing the Río Onza and climbing up to the Puerto de Martín Alonso (479m), the boundary between the provinces of Sevilla and Córdoba. The road again descends with good views through replanted pine forest and bare hills. Cross the Arroyo de la Onzuela and enter *dehesa*. The knoll and spur terrain is incredibly pretty and each turn presents a refreshing vista. A gradual climb leads to the Mina de Valdeinfierno (Mine of the Valley of Hell) before a descent to the Río Bembézar which has cut a wide rocky gorge. This is a good picnic spot. The road again climbs, this time to **Argallón**. Ignore the left turn to Azuaga and then the futile right turn to El Cabril. The roads here are much improved, no doubt to service the waste repository at El Cabril.

At Argallón turn right and east to stay on the route, or continue straight ahead for Fuente Obejuna with its campsite and Hostales. A short distance after the right turn fork left. Approaching Cañada del Gamo turn right at the T-junction to pass to the south of the town. Continue east and pass south of **Ojuelos Bajos**. A further 2.5km turn right and into Ojuelos Altos, passing the village.

The ridge attracts countless numbers of raptors, including black vultures, who use the thermals to climb and glide over the deep, wide valley: a sight that enhances the whole experience of this part of the route.

STAGE 4
Ojuelos Altos to Hornachuelos

Distance	57km (35.4 miles)
Type	Hilly
Climb	505m (1657ft)
Cycling time	3hr 45min

Leave Ojuelos Altos on the main through road heading south. This is the start of a 500m descent over the next 25km (ignoring the odd minor uphill). Pass through the hamlet of Los Morenos and on entering La Cardenchosa

This stage crosses the centre of the Sierra Morena, empty of people but not wildlife. In terms of navigation the route from Ojuelos Altos to Hornachuelos is straightforward; roads are asphalt and there are only two junctions, one of which is barred, but the single-track road surface is very poor in places. There are no shops or bars en route.

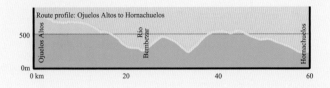

Route profile: Ojuelos Altos to Hornachuelos

turn right at the roundabout to San Calixto, bending sharp right to leave town. The road twists its way in a southerly direction through replanted lollypop and Christmas tree pine forest. The views are excellent with the countless hills and ridges lending a pleasing shape to the land. Many grit roads lead further into the wilderness and with time, the right maps and GPS, these are worthy of a lengthy but careful exploration.

At the bridge across the Río Bembézar, ignore the right turn to the barred road to El Cabril. Cross the river. The steep climb from the bridge is through a deep wooded valley. Pass through scrubby pasture before more replanted forest where the road peaks. The descent is on a straight road, for a change, to the blandly named Arroyo de Baja. Another climb leads to the Lomo de los Peñones. From here to Hornachuelos the predominant tree cover is oak and cork oak forest. After a short descent bend left at the T-junction. It is here that the Option 1 route comes in from the right.

From the junction the route to Hornachuelos is mostly downhill, twisting and turning through *dehesa* over ridges and round hills. As the town nears small olive groves appear and gradually increase in number. The through road skirts to the south of the centre of **Hornachuelos** and passes the two hotels. The municipal campsite is also signed from this road.

STAGE 5
Hornachuelos to Córdoba

Distance	83km (51.5 miles)
Type	Hilly
Climb	845m (2772ft)
Cycling time	5hr 20min

This stage takes a final look at the Sierra. The cycling is through quiet hills before entering Córdoba through the back door and going straight to the railway station.

Rejoin the through road heading south-east. At the outskirts of town turn left, and cross the Río Bembézar just below a dam wall. At the junction 600m beyond the river take the left turn heading roughly north towards Villaviciosa de Córdoba. The road climbs up a ridge through thick scrubby oak with occasional pasture. As height is gained the view of the Guadalquivir plain opens to the south. The road levels where the scrub becomes mature hilly *dehesa* before a small descent to the next junction.

At the T-junction turn right. A left turn would lead to the Embalse de Bembezar. The road gradually climbs through *dehesa* and passes disused silver mines. After crossing a low ridge descend to a T-junction. Turn left heading north; the road climbs onto and then along a ridge. The country is very pretty and the views excellent. Pigs graze in the oakwoods. After 4km the road climbs over and around spurs, gaining height all the time. Pine and eucalyptus trees take over. The steep climb from the Arroyo del Pajaroncillo ends on a very broad wooded spur. At the highest point is a white building set in pasture

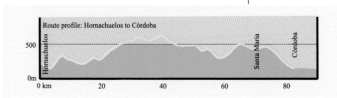

Route profile: Hornachuelos to Córdoba

The Mezquita and Puente Romano, Córdoba

next to the road; opposite is a forest road leading to a car park, from which a number of waymarked paths head off through the woods. The route continues straight on.

The road soon drops and skirts around the head of a large valley before a gentle climb out. About 4km from the white building turn right to **Santa María de Trassierrra**.

The road gradually descends through a mixture of pasture and scrubby *dehesa*. The area has a feel of desolation reinforced by the numerous abandoned buildings and lichen-covered oaks. Cross the Río Guadiatillo and climb steeply to an unnamed pass for an extended sinuous descent to the much larger Río Guadiato. Cross the river and again climb before a gentle descent into **Santa María**. Continue straight through to Córdoba. Half a kilometre from Santa María continue straight ahead at the roundabout. A right turn leads to the ruins of Medina Azahara, a Moorish palace covering some 2km² that is open to the public.

The road to **Córdoba** descends across the side of the last hill, and the Sierra Morena is left behind. The road continues across the plain of the Río Guadalquivir. At the edge of Córdoba continue straight ahead at the roundabout and again at the second, heading directly to the city centre. At the third the station is clearly visible to the right.

Staying on in Córdoba

With a history dating from the time of the Phoenicians, this city is one of Spain's great attractions. The rare beauty of the Mezquita, the finest mosque built by the Moors, brings a lump to the throat. It is famous for its forest of columns topped by horseshoe arches, its mihrab and the fact that there is renaissance cathedral built incongruously in the middle. To the south are the river and the Puente Romano, while the surrounding streets form an attractive maze. More information from the Turismo at Torrijos, 10 (Palacio de Congresos) (tel: 957 35 51 79, email: otcordoba@andalucia.org).

OPTION 1
El Pedroso to Hornachuelos

This option significantly shortens the main route and is described in its entirety, leaving the reader to decide where to stop overnight in lieu of Cazalla. It can be used to take a day out of the tour by stopping at Constantina, or to give a couple of days' easy cycling by stopping at El Pedroso and then Constantina. The option leaves the main route short of Cazalla, and rejoins it before Hornachuelos.

Distance	90km (55.9 miles)
Type	Plain and low hills
Climb	665m (2182ft)
Cycling time	5hr 35min

Starting at the junction as described in Stage 2, turn right heading south-east, paralleling the Arroyo de San Pedro and descending a steep wooded valley. The road flattens, then climbs only to flatten again as it swings around to the south of the Sierra de El Pedroso. The vegetation is olive groves and *dehesa* with numerous rounded granite boulders and outcrops on the plain. At the outskirts of El Pedroso keep right where the road forks at the hermitage. Outside the hermitage is the Cruz del Humilladero, made in 1540 from a single piece of granite. Keep straight on, bearing left at the far side of town. Leave town heading east, paralleling the railway on the right towards Cazalla and Constantina.

About 4km from El Pedroso, having crossed the railway, turn right to **Constantina**. The road is through *dehesa*, and descends to clip an extension of the Embalse de Huesna with its picnic site before an undulating climb to Constantina. Turn left at the roundabout at Constantina's southern end. Pass through the town centre, heading north, and take the right turn to

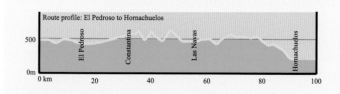

Las Navas de la Concepción. Ignore the road off to the left and continue to **Las Navas** through *dehesa*. The road, which is in good condition, gently undulates over ridges and *arroyos*.

In Las Navas turn right in the main square, then turn left onto the SE159 to San Calixto while still in town. The road to Hornachuelos is mostly single carriageway and in generally very good condition, and it is very pretty. From Las Navas the road crosses a number of fields before entering the *dehesa*. The climb is followed by a decent to the Río Retortillo, where the Parque Natural Sierra Norte is left and that of the Sierra de Hornachuelos entered. The road again climbs, bends and undulates before becoming level and straight before the junction at which it joins the main route. From the junction continue as described in Stage 4 to **Hornachuelos**. From Las Navas it is worth keeping an eye on the sky as there are often dozens of Egyptian vultures soaring above the larger isolated hills.

Dehesa, El Pedroso

OPTION 2
Cazalla–El Pintado loop

An excellent day ride from Cazalla round the Embalse de El Pintado, taking in open hilly terrain which gives a different experience of the Sierra Morena from what will follow on the main route.

Distance	72km (44.7 miles)
Type	Plain and hills
Climb	595m (1952ft)
Cycling time	4hr 30min

From the centre of Cazalla head north out of town on the main through road. Ignore the right turn signed to the Villa Turística (the route of Stage 3). Turn left at the roundabout heading north-west through cork oakwood. The road undulates through *dehesa* and pasture. After 6.6km on this road turn left signed to Hoya de Sta María on the SE-7100. The road descends to a valley, crossing one of the arms of the *embalse* where the Rivera de Benalija enters it. From here there are very few trees. There is a gentle climb up to a low ridge where the road surface changes from asphalt to grit. Descend to and over the Arroyo Del Moro, where the province of Extremadura is entered. The grit road climbs to T-junction with an asphalt road that is missing from many maps. At the T-junction turn left for an excellent curving descent to the Río Viar.

From the bridge the road climbs viciously towards **Puebla del Maestre** with a couple of undulations near the top where pines have been replanted. Short of Puebla del Maestre, at the T-junction turn left towards La Hoya de Sta. María for a steep descent to the Río Vendoval.

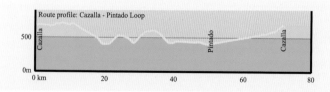

Route profile: Cazalla - Pintado Loop

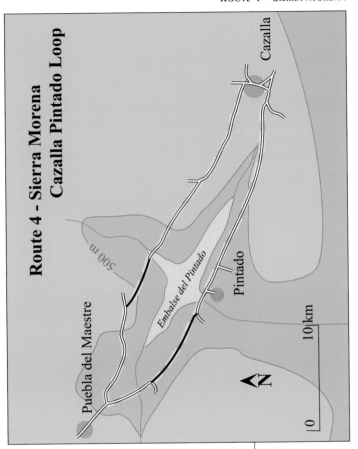

Route 4 - Sierra Morena
Cazalla Pintado Loop

While checking this the route this river was teeming with huge trout. After a short climb, where the road bends sharply to the right, take the grit road straight ahead. The grit road is in a wide wooded valley separating two ridges. The road climbs gently before levelling. There are a couple of steep drops and climbs just as Andalucía is re-entered. A descent leads to a T-junction with an asphalt road. Turn left to the *embalse*.

Cazalla–Pintado loop

The road crosses the dam wall with a deep gorge below it. The village of **El Pintado** lies beyond the dam down a short road; there is a bar but little else. Ignore the turn to El Pedroso and continue straight on. Ignore the right turn for La Ganchosa. The road climbs all the way to Cazalla through *dehesa* and open pasture in the valley of the Arroyo del Valle. At the T-junction turn left and follow the road back into Cazalla and the start of the ride.

ACCOMMODATION ON OR CLOSE TO ROUTE 4

Please note that this is not an exhaustive list. Hotel guide prices are in Euros, based on a double room with an en suite bathroom at high season. Rooms without en suite are typically 20% cheaper, as are single rooms. Please note that hotels are constantly opening, closing or being refurbished; it is always advisable to book ahead. Prices (where known) are indicated as follows: (1) up to 50 Euros; (2) 50–75 Euros; (3) 75–100 Euros; (4) over 100 Euros.

Sevilla
With more than 140 hotels and pensiónes accommodation should not be a problem; contact the Turismo at Avenida de la Constitución, 21B. 41004 Sevilla (tel: 954 78 75 78, email: otsevilla@andalucia.org)

La Algaba
(4) Torre de los Guzmanes, Ctra. A-8006. km 18.9 (tel: 955 78 91 75)

Alcalá del Río
(3) Ancla, Plaza de los Pescadores, 1 (tel: 955 65 02 18)
(2) El Chaparral, Avda. de Andalucía, 101 (tel: 955 65 07 97)
Pensión Venta, Avenida de Andalucía, 113 (tel: 954 78 00 85)

Castilblanco de los Arroyos
Pensión, Finca Linde de Escardiel, 1 (tel: 680 40 15 41)
Hotel Castillo Blanco, Ctra. Cazalla de la Sierra, 0 km 32–34 (tel: 955 73 40 34)

Almadén de la Plata
(2) Hotel El Romeral, Calle de Antonio Machado, 57 (tel: 954 73 5 4 53)
Pensión Camino de la Plata, La Cruz, 8 (tel: 954 73 50 43)
Las Gateras, Paseo del Reloj, 1 (Tel: 954 73 53 09)

Cazalla de la Sierra
(4) Hospedería la Cartuja, Ctra. de la Estación 3km (tel: 954 88 45 16)
(3) Vega de Cazalla, Durillo, 16 (tel: 954 88 46 80)
(2) Posada del Moro, Paseo del Moro, 46 (tel: 954 88 48 58)
Hostal Castro Martinez, Virgen del Monte, 36 (tel: 954 88 40 39)
Hostal Casa Kini, Plaza Juan Carlos I, 12 (tel: 954 88 44 83)

San Nicolás del Puerto
Pensión El Salud, Avda. Huéznar, s/n
Camping El Marinete, Ctra. Estación de Cazalla, km 12 (tel: 955 88 65 33)
Camping Batan de los Monjas, Av. el Huéznar, 14 (tel: 955 88 65 98)

Alanís
(2) Adriano, Barrionuevo, s/n (tel: 954 88 59 15)
Pensión Alanís, Calle de Juan Castellanos, 41 (tel: 617 13 97 62)

Fuente Obejuna
(2) Hotel Rural Romero Torres, CO-8405, 1 (tel: 957 58 46 31)
(1) El Comendador, Luis Rodrígues, 25 (tel: 957 58 52 22)
Camping Pozo Canito, Camino del Pozo Canito (tel: 957 58 40 48)

Hornachuelos
(2) El Alamo, Ctra. de San Calixto, s/n (tel: 957 64 04 76)
(1) El Kiosko de los Angeles, Esplanada del Kiosko (tel: 957 64 04 30)

Villaviciosa de Córdoba
Camping Puente Nueva, Ctra. A-433, km 8.5 (tel: 957 36 07 27)

Santa María de Trassierra
Hotel Villa De Trassierra, Calle de la Encina, 7, (tel: 957 73 00 29)

Córdoba
The city has more than 60 hotels and pensions; contact the Turismo at Torrijos, 10 (Palacio de Congresos) (tel: 957 35 51 79, email: otcordoba@andalucia.org)
Camping El Brillante, Avda. del Brillante, 50 (tel: 95740 38 36)
Camping Los Villares, Ctra. Los Villares, km 7.5 (tel: 957 33 01 45)

OPTION 1

El Pedroso
(2) Casa Montehuéznar, Avenida de la Estación, 15 (tel: 954 88 90 00)

Constantina
(3) San Blas, Miraflores, 4 (tel: 955 88 00 77)
(3) Las Erillas, Sendero de los Castañares, s/n (tel: 955 88 17 90)
(2) Casa Grande, Ctra. Constantina-Cazalla km 1 (tel: 955 88 16 08)
(1) Albergue Inturjoven Constantina, Avda. Del Dr. Larrauri, s/n (tel: 902 51 00 00)

Las Navas de la Concepción
Los Monteros, Calle Virgen de Belén, 65 (tel: 955 88 50 62)

Sierra Morena

ROUTE 5
SIERRAS DE GREDOS AND GUADARRAMA

ROUTE SUMMARY

From	To	km	Type	Cycling time
Airport	Navalcarnero	61	City then rolling plain	3hr 50min
Navalcarnero	Piedralaves	69	River valley then wooded hills	5hr 10min
Piedralaves	Burgohondo	75	Mountainous	5hr 25min
Burgohondo	Ávila	37	Mountainous	2hr 50min
Ávila	Segovia	75	Rolling plain then hills	4hr 40min
Segovia	Cercedilla	43	Mountains	4hr 20min
Cercedilla	Airport	70	Hills then rolling plain	4hr 10min

Central Spain takes some beating for the sheer variety of cycling available. South of Madrid is the flat plain of La Mancha, and to the west and the north are the mountains of the Sierras de Gredos and de Guadarrama. The granite Sierras are very scenic and offer very rewarding cycling. In addition to the numerous towns and villages worth a visit in their own right this route includes the walled city of Ávila and Segovia, famous for its Roman aqueduct. An exploration of Madrid can be made by breaking Stage one, or as a day trip from Cercedilla.

This route requires at least two of the 1:200 000 maps from the Instituto Geográfico Nacional. The options are the Mapa Guía Madrid y su Entorno and the Mapa Provincial of Ávila, or the three Mapas Provinciales Madrid, Ávila and Segovia. The Michelin 1:400 000 map no 576, Extremadura, Castilla-La Mancha, Madrid, is good, as is their 1:170 000 map, 121 Madrid y Alrededores, in the Zoom series but it does not cover the very western end. The *Rough Guide to Spain* gives reasonable coverage of the area too.

The climate of central Spain can be summarised as lots of sunshine, wet and freezing cold winters and baking hot summers. By late summer the plants die back leaving a dry, barren scene. The route is centred on Madrid at 650m above sea level. The route peaks at 1800m, and so based on the 1°C drop per 100m ascent rule expect temperatures there to be considerably colder. Winter snow may linger on the higher hills into March and April. See below for a guide to the best time to go.

The route is described in seven stages, but consideration should be given to spending more time exploring the cities and countryside. This route is a concentrated cycling and cultural feast.

Public holidays
Communidad de Madrid: 2 May
City of Madrid: 15 May and 9 November
Province of Ávila: 22 June and 15 October
Province of Segovia: 29 June and 25 October

ROUTE 5: CLIMATE DETAILS

	Jan	Feb	Mar	Apr	May	Jun	Jul	Aug	Sep	Oct	Nov	Dec
Madrid												
av min temp °C	2	2	5	7	10	14	17	17	14	9	5	2
av max temp °C	9	11	15	18	21	27	31	30	25	19	13	9
rainfall mm	39	34	43	48	47	27	11	15	32	53	47	48
Ávila												
av min temp °C	-2	-1	1	3	6	10	13	13	10	6	2	0
av max temp °C	7	8	11	14	17	23	28	27	22	16	10	7
rainfall mm	22	13	29	37	62	36	13	19	36	33	36	35
Madrid												
sunrise	08:37	08:24	07:48	07:58	07:14	06:47	06:48	07:11	07:42	08:11	07:45	08:20
sunset	17:57	18:30	19:06	20:38	21:10	21:39	21:48	21:29	20:48	19:57	18:13	17:50
Best time	–	–	VG	VG	VG	–	–	–	G	VG	–	–

(G= good time to go; VG = best time to go)

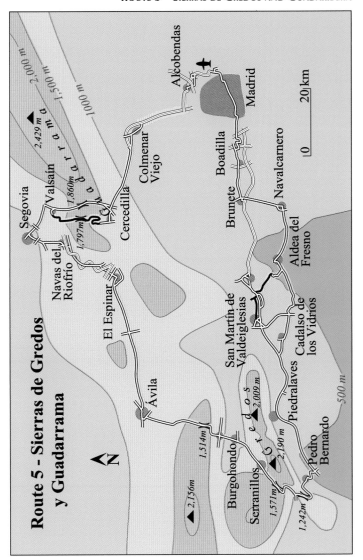

Route 5 - Sierras de Gredos y Guadarrama

STAGE 1
Madrid–Barajas airport to Navalcarnero

Distance	61km (38 miles)
Type	City then rolling plain
Climb	390m (1280ft)
Cycling time	3hr 50min

Madrid airport is not ideally situated for cyclists. The majority of connecting roads are either motorway, or of motorway standard, where cycling is either not permitted or not recommended. For those heading west without excessive deviation, this means passing through the centre of Madrid. The route is fairly obvious and the experience is more like cycling through a large town than a capital city. The standard of driving is generally courteous, while at the same time being the worst in Spain! Be cautious and plan ahead. Remember: the city will recede and rural Spain will take over.

Follow the route out of the airport as described in the revised Appendix 5 to the Avenida de Logroño. At the T-junction with the Avenida turn right to head north. At the combination of traffic lights and roundabout double back to head south. At the motorway roundabout with chapel continue straight ahead keeping to the Avenida de Logroño. Pass under the railway then continue straight ahead at the roundabout under the motorway. Continue straight ahead at the roundabout over the A2 autopista and join the Calle de Alcalá heading southwest. The Calle de Alcalá is a cañada or drover's road and is still used so do not be too surprised if you come across the odd flock of sheep.

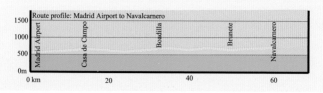

Route profile: Madrid Airport to Navalcarnero

1500
1000
500
0m

Madrid Airport
Casa de Campo
Boadilla
Brunete
Navalcarnero

0 km   20   40   60

Keep to the Calle de Alcalá into the centre of Madrid. Pass the Plaza de Toros and the Parque de Eva Peron.

Unfortunately the road goes underground near to the Parque del Buen Retiro. To avoid this turn sharp right onto the Calle de Velázquez then turn first left and then turn third left to rejoin the Calle de Alcalá at the Puerta de Alcalá. The Puerta is one of the remaining medieval gates of the city. Its appearance is that of a large stone arch. Continue straight ahead at the Plaza de Cibeles and shortly fork right onto the Gran Vía at the Metropolis building.

At the park like Plaza de España turn left at the near side and descend into the underpass at the far side of the Plaza. At the subterranean roundabout continue straight ahead bearing southwest then west. Fork right and climb up to the roundabout with a monument to avoid another underpass. At the roundabout take the second exit (Paseo de la Virgin del Puerto) which should be signed to the Casa del Campo. Continue south before turning right (Paseo de Extremadura) then right again (Paseo de la Virgin del Angel) before entering the Casa del Campo.

Motor vehicles are now banned from most of the Casa del Campo. Pass the Metro station and at the roundabout turn left (Paseo de los Castaños). Follow the road west though the park and fork left at the Y-junction towards the Zoo. Continue straight on taking the right fork at the second Y-junction. No longer towards the Zoo. Continue straight on at the roundabout and exit the park at the Puerta de Rodajos.

Upon leaving the park take the second exit at the roundabout (Avda de Rodajos). At the next roundabout turn left and pass over the M502. Continue straight ahead (Calle Prado del Rey) at the next 2 roundabouts. At the third turn left (Paseo de la Finca) and continue straight ahead at the next two. At the third bear right (Calle Cañada de las Carreras) and then straight on at the next. At the second turn right and north to parallel the **M40 autopista**. At the next roundabout turn left and cross over the M40. Turn right onto the unsurfaced road (Calle Cañada de las Carreras) and continue northwest to the M513. Turn left at this roundabout heading towards Boadilla del Monte. ▶

Note: there is a cycle shop in the centre of Boadilla – 'Rider Bike'. (tel: 916 33 38 42)

143

Continue west on the well signed M513 with its many roundabouts bypassing **Boadilla del Monte**, pass Guadamonte and approach **Brunete**. All the time Madrid recedes. Turn left and south on the M600 and follow it to **Navalcarnero**. Follow the signs to the centre of town.

STAGE 2
Navalcarnero to Piedralaves

This stage cuts across the western extremity of the Sierra de Guadarrama before traversing the south side of the Sierra de Gredos. Between the mountain chains there is the option to experience some off-road riding in the peaceful beauty of the Spanish countryside.

Distance	69km (42.9 miles)
Type	River valley then wooded hills
Climb	813m (2667ft)
Cycling time	5hr 10min

From the centre of Navalcarnero leave town following the signs to Aldea del Fresno M507. Cross the bypass. The route is through undulating farmland before entering a shallow valley around Villamanta. Staying on the M507 pass through **Aldea del Fresno** and cross the Río Alberche. Pass the Presa de Picadas turnoff where the Option route starts.

Beyond Villa del Prado the country starts to change. The road becomes hillier, twistier and there are more trees. Soon we will be sweeping and swooping through mature pine forest on a rollercoaster of a ride. Exhilarating stuff! At the N403 continue straight across. The excellence continues but this time with granite exposed as huge boulders, tors and cliffs. The road climbs to **Cadalso de los Vidrios**. This is a smashing village to overnight in. It has a superb

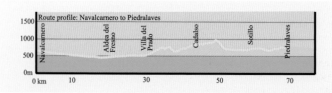

144

location and its own wine. In Cadalso turn left keeping on the M507 to Rozas de Puerto Real. Another hilltop village. Pass through and descend to the Tiétar valley.

At the M501 turn left heading west to Piedralaves. The M501 now skirts the southern limit of the **Sierra de Gredos**, the imposing mountain range to the north. This is very pleasant cycling and allows rapid progress. Pass through the villages of Santa María del Tiétar, Sotillo and La Adrada which has a ruined castle well worth a visit for its views over the mountains.

Piedralaves has the feel of a mountain village. Its buildings are constructed largely of granite and most have balconies. The streets are narrow and squares small. It is very picturesque with the Gredos as a backdrop. There are several hotels in town but only the Hostal Mainz on the main through road seems to be open all year. It has a bar, good value restaurant and takes care of bikes. It is highly recommended.

OPTION 1

Navalcarnero to Piedralaves
via the Vía Verde del Alberche and
San Martin de Valdeiglesias

Distance	71km (44 miles)
Type	Quiet waterside and forest tracks then river plain
Climb	474m (1555ft)
Cycling time	4hr 40min

From the main route turn right at the Presa de Picadas junction. Continue on this road following the signs for Presa de Picadas. After the houses it starts to climb, narrows and the surface deteriorates.

After 3km keep left and away from the Ermita de Santa Teresa. After a further 500m, by the house, keep straight on. Descend and cross the dam. Pass the buildings and the barrier at the end of the road.

This option detours from the main route for those who enjoy a bit of gentle off road action. It follows the disused railway line firstly alongside the Embalse de Picadas then through pinewoods to San Martin de Valdeiglesias.

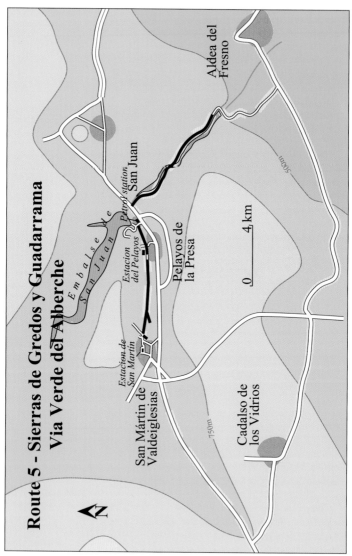

Route 5 – Sierras de Gredos y Guadarrama
Via Verde del Alberche

Vía Verde, San Juan

From here the route continues as a well consolidated hardcore track alongside the embalse crossing over where it narrows. After the kayaking centre in the fenced compound bear right and downhill leaving the old trackbed. Keep straight on and after a short climb turn left at the main road for a climb and descent to San Juan.

Continue straight ahead at the roundabout then turn right immediately after the petrol station to take the road signed to the **Embalse de San Juan**. The road at first dips slightly then climbs, ignore the gravel road to the left. The road swings first right and then left. Just before it straightens slightly there is a broad, flat, level and fairly wide grit road off to the left. Take it, this is the Vía Verde, expect no signs. This former railway track has an excellent riding surface with a slight incline to San Martín. The route is easy to follow, just follow your nose. Cross the asphalt road, pass the **old station** for Pelayos de la Presa.

The track becomes asphalt for a few hundred metres as it passes through the north of town. Ignore all junctions until San Martín is approached. At the crossroad continue straight ahead on the asphalt road and again where a cobbled road cuts the road at an angle. With a kink to the left the road leads to the **former station**.

San Martín de Valdeiglesias is worth at least a brief look around. It has a cycle shop, food shops, restaurants and hotels and a town walk. From the station simply head downhill through town to pick up signs for the M501.

Rejoin the M501 heading west to Piedralaves. The next eleven kilometres are undulating with a gradual height gain before entering the valley of the Río Tiétar with the main route coming in from the left.

Staying on in San Martín de Valdeiglesias

There is a pleasant town walk taking in the town hall, parish church (16th century), hermitages, bullring and castle. Details are available from 'La Estación', the former railway station.

Around San Martín de Valdeiglesias

Cycling: a short ride takes you north out of town to the western end of the Embalse de San Juan, a very pretty and peaceful spot.

STAGE 3
*Piedralaves to Burgohondo
via the Collado de Serranillos*

Distance	75km (46.6 miles)
Type	Mountainous
Climb	1219m (3998ft)
Cycling time	5hr 25min

Two passes over the Sierra de Gredos lead to Burgohondo. The Puerto de Mijares is the higher (1572m) but shorter route. The more interesting, longer way, is over the Puerto de Serranillos (1571m). This is a great day's cycling.

Rejoin the M501 and head west out of Piedralaves. There is a gentle descent for 21km; very agreeable cycling through very pretty countryside. Turn right and climb to **Pedro Bernardo**, leaving behind grazing cows and passing through olive groves and cultivated fields. This 7km stretch, much of which is hard going, gives the chance to perfect gear-changing techniques and to adjust pace after a few days on benign roads.

Pedro Bernardo is a pleasant mountain village that caters for its visitors in a quiet way. Its Balcón de Tiétar provides views to the south and west and is a welcome place to rest. However, although the cobbled streets may be attractive to the eye they are painful to the rest of the body!

Continue on the through road and leave Pedro Bernardo. The road climbs relentlessly through pine forest for 12km to the Puerto de Pedro Bernardo (1242m and unnamed on most maps). The Puerto is a good place to stop, eat and water. The far side has views over to the

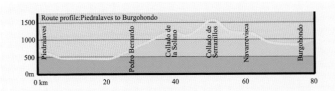

Route profile: Piedralaves to Burgohondo

Puerto del Pico from Collado de la Solano

Puerto del Pico (1395m) on the main Ávila to Talavera road. The air here is a lot cooler than in the valley bottom, having gained 800m of height. From the pass the road drops steeply for 3km to the San Esteban junction; put on some windproof gear for the descent, otherwise the wind-chill effect can make things painfully cold.

Turn right at the T-junction to restart the climb: 480m of ascent in 9km. The only respite is where bridges span streams to give short sections of almost level road. As height is gained the valley widens and the roadside vegetation becomes tougher and less penetrable. All too soon the climb ends at the Puerto de Serranillos, either 1571m or 1575m (road sign). Prepare for the downhill by donning warm and windproof clothes. The ride down is excellent; the scenery is superb, often with snow-clad mountains (up to 2190m) on either side. Surprisingly, after passing through the small village of **Serranillos** oakwoods appear.

The road continues directly to **Burgohondo** via Navarrevisca. The countryside is bleakly stunning, especially when the broad valley of the Río Alberche is joined. There are granite tors and boulders, and patches of deciduous and coniferous woods on the hillsides above the river.

In Burgohondo the Hostal El Alberche provided a welcome overnight stay, with the ground floor bar/restaurant providing food.

STAGE 4
Burgohondo to Ávila

Distance	37km (22.9 miles)
Type	Mountainous
Climb	726m (2382ft)
Cycling time	2hr 50min

Following on from the effort required to cover Stage 3, the ride to Ávila is a lot shorter but still has the Puerto de Navalmoral to contend with. There will be plenty of time to explore Ávila.

Leave Burgohondo on the main through road heading north to Navalmoral. The road gently climbs through more granite boulder country. The fields on the right are well looked after and quite lush by contrast those on the left that have been abandoned. The drystone walls are made of single-width granite blocks split along natural fissures caused by land movements long after the mountains were formed. Pass straight through Navalmoral and straight ahead at the crossroads. Navalmoral is the last shopping opportunity before Ávila.

Although the Puerto de Navalmoral is high (1514m) the climb is well graded (this stage did start at 840m), and is not too long or tiring. As height is gained cultivated fields are left behind and boulder-covered rough pasture is encountered. The pass is 8km from Navalmoral. A high stone wall surrounds the Hermitita de San Cristoba and provides shelter in poor weather. From the pass it is downhill all the way to Ávila; warm and windproof clothes are recommended to avoid wind chill. Near Aldea del Rey Niño the country changes dramatically from boulder-strewn mountain to fertile plain and the road suddenly levels off.

The classic approach to **Ávila** is from the west at sunset when the sandstone city walls turn gold in the last rays of light. The lack of development west of the city increases the effect, which unfortunately cannot be replicated by an easterly exit early in the morning. There are plenty of places to stay within the walled part of the city. The popular restaurant behind the bar of Casa Felipe in the Plaza de la Victoria provides an excellent tourist menu.

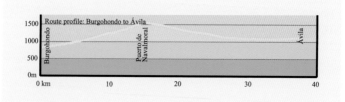

Staying on in Ávila

Try the Turismo in the Casa de las Carnicerías, San Segundo, 17 (tel: 920 21 13 87) for an up-to-date town map and details of things to do. The walls – with 88 towers – enclose the old city, and were built by Muslim prisoners after the city's Reconquest in 1090. Exploring them makes a pleasant walk. The town itself is worth exploring, with its myriad of medieval streets, compact squares and stork-inhabited Romanesque churches.

What to see in Ávila

Saint Teresa sites: Saint James and Santa Teresa are the joint patron saints of Spain. Three convents – de Santa Teresa, de la Encarnación and de San José – and Los Cuatro Postes make up the Santa Teresa sites.

Cathedral: this wonderful creation, built into the city walls, is a mix of styles with no regard for theme or continuity. When viewed from the plaza it is obvious that granite is not the prettiest of building materials. The southern tower is incomplete and seems to have a brick-built lean-to on the top. The nave is Gothic, the pointed windows letting in plenty of light, while the older, darker altar end is Romanesque, with rounded window arches. There is an intricately carved trascoro (screen behind the choir), showing the adoration of the Magi, murder of the innocents and presentation in the temple. In contrast the trasaltar (screen round behind the altar) is a much later and

Doorway, Ávila Cathedral

poorer work, in which it is hard to find any religious significance. The cathedral museum is worth a look and includes works by El Greco and Jose Ribero.

STAGE 5
Ávila to Segovia

There are two roads
between Ávila and
Segovia, the direct
N110 or the quieter
SG500 to the south.
The route takes the
quieter option.

Distance	75km (46.6 miles)
Type	Rolling plain, then hills
Climb	355m (1165ft)
Cycling time	4hr 40min

Leave the walled city heading north of east, and pick up
the signs for Segovia via the N110. Follow these signs
and ignore the right turn for El Escorial via the CL-505.
Pass under the railway and turn right at the roundabout
signed 'Bernúy-Salinero' – this is the AV-500. The road
bends left. At the roundabouts continue straight ahead to
El Espinar. The road skirts the south side of modern Ávila
and soon the city is left behind.

The terrain is undulating and the road straight; the
initial *dehesa* is replaced by prairie. This is an excellent
ride in the sunshine with a tail wind (and the opposite
in the cold rain with a chilling headwind!). There are
dolmens signed from Bernúy-Salinero. The undulations become more pronounced and the straight road
makes no effort to contour round them. After crossing
the Embalse de Serones on a causeway continue straight
ahead at the crossroads. Enter the province of Segovia.
After 8km the road stops its gradual ascent; the gentle
descent is through lush cattle-grazed pasture interspersed with woodland.

El Espinar is at the halfway point and is the only substantial town on this stage. It provides a welcome break,
though the downside is its location – on top of a hill.
At the bottom of the hill on the approach to El Espinar
turn left where the main road swings right. Climb into
the town on the narrow road. At the top of the hill turn right
and descend to the centre of town. There are numerous
places to eat and drink. The church is unusual in that
storks have built nests on the roof of the nave rather than
on the tower.

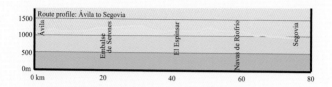

Segovia

Leave El Espinar, following the signs towards Segovia NVI and the Estación de Espinar. Pass under the NVI and then under the AP-6. Ignore the right turn for the Estación de El Espinar. Descend then climb to the N603 having passed under the AP-61. Turn left at the T-junction towards Segovia. The road is busy and climbs steeply, interweaving with the AP-61. Although the road continues to Segovia the route detours north. About 2km beyond Rivera de los Molinos on the main road, turn left

155

towards the palace and deer park of Riofrío. Turn right at the crossroads immediately after the railway crossing and pass through the village of **Navas de Riofrío**. The road drops into and climbs out of a very steep-sided valley (a high price to pay for the peace and quiet!).

Continue straight ahead at the crossroads and right at the T-junction. Pass Hontoria and under **Segovia**'s bypass. Follow the road into the city and from the outskirts follow the road signs for the 'Centro histórico'. The route leads downhill past what looks like the end of a low wall made of granite blocks with a small house on top. This 'wall' starts next to a set of traffic lights on the main road. The road continues downhill, then bends left into the valley that gave the walled city a defensive helping hand. Rounding the bend the city's Roman aqueduct is revealed in all its glory. That 'wall' has grown, and now spans the valley in a series of layered arches topped by a water channel.

There are plenty of places to stay and eat within the walled city. By evening most of the trippers will have gone, and the city regains its quiet medieval peace and beauty.

Segovia Cathedral

The Roman Aqueduct, Segovia

Staying on in Segovia

The city's history goes back to 192BC when the Romans defeated the Celtiberian inhabitants. There is masses to see and do. Most of the visitor attractions are located inside the city walls that ring a limestone plateau, rising out of the plain. The clichéd view is the galleon of Segovia sailing on a sea of wheat, with the Alcázar as the bow, the cathedral the main mast and the aqueduct the rudder. The Turismo in the Plaza Mayor gives out excellent city maps that can be supplemented by more detailed multilingual guides available at the specific sites.

What to see in Segovia

The Alcázar (castle): this stands on its own platform slightly detached from the city, and from the 12th century was occupied by a series of Castilian kings. A fire in the 19th century and its subsequent restoration led to its current appearance, with round fairy-tale towers with pointed slate roofs. Inside there is a museum which includes a fine collection of armour. Well worth a visit.

The cathedral: the last Gothic cathedral to be built in Europe, it is extremely ornate on the outside but somewhat plain on the inside.

The aqueduct: world famous, with 20,000 free-standing granite blocks making up the 166 arches and 120 pillars. It is 28m tall at its highest point, and was part of a system that carried water underground from the Riofrío for 14km, then over the 1.2km-long aqueduct and into the city.

STAGE 6
Segovia to Cercedilla

This stage is an excellent ride and provides the highest point of the main route, the Puerto de la Fuenfría (1797m). The route detours from the main road and provides the best route though the mountains and most scenic entry into the province of Madrid. The off-road section is suitable for reasonably robust bikes. An alternative road route goes via the higher Puerto de Navacerrada (1860m).

Distance	43km (26.7 miles)
Type	Mountain, significant section off-road
Climb	804m (2638ft)
Cycling time	4hr 20min

Return to the Plaza del Azoguejo where the aqueduct is at its highest. With the aqueduct on your left head south. At the no entry sign duck under the arches and continue on the pavement until it is safe to rejoin the road. At the end of the aqueduct join the main road and head south towards La Granja and Navacerrada. Continue straight ahead at all the roundabouts and under the new bypass. The road continues to climb to the Bourbon palace of San Ildefonso La Granja, built to rival Versailles, and its surrounding village. There are many picnic spots in the woods either side of the road, but stop before the Embalse Ponton Alta as just beyond is the local sewerage works. At La Granja turn right at the roundabout, staying

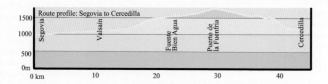

on the CL601. The road climbs through mature deciduous woodland.

At Pradera de Navalhorno the route leaves the main road for the Puerto de la Fuenfría. (The alternative is to continue on the main road as described below.) Turn sharp right to Valsaín and cross the river. Climb to **Valsaín**, ignore the first left turn and turn right at the crossroads. Pass the wooden sheds on the right and turn left immediately before the fenced builders' yard. Pass the village cemetery on the right.

After the initial steep climb the route joins the route of the Roman road between Cercedilla and Segovia. A number of yellow arrows indicate that you are on the Camino de Santiago from Madrid. South of the Puerto the route joins up with a forest road system that is open to and popular with walkers and cyclists.

Pass the barrier and enter the forest. The asphalt road is narrow with a stiff climb at the outset. Initially the woodland is scrubby deciduous with cattle pasture over the fence on the left. In the open pasture ignore the turn to the right and continue the climb. From the pasture there is a good view back over Segovia which can clearly be seen 'sailing' across the plain. The forest soon changes to mature coniferous trees which continues for almost the entire stage. The road climbs over the ridgeline. The valley to the right contains the Riofrío on its 'over ground' way to Segovia. As the road climbs the surface becomes more broken and patched. This is more than compensated for by the beauty and

159

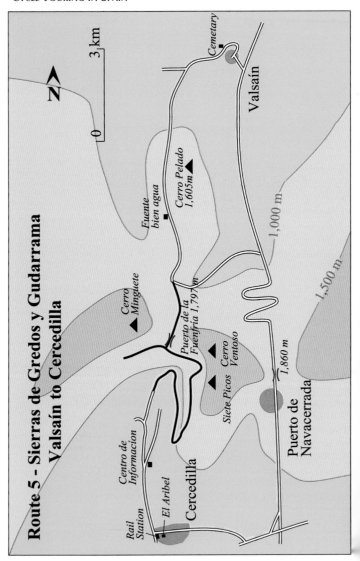

Route 5 - Sierras de Gredos y Gudarrama Valsaín to Cercedilla

Puerta de la Fuenfría

tranquillity of the forest, the sound of birds and the absence of traffic. ▶

Shortly after passing though a large clearing there is a road junction. The asphalt road drops sharply down and returns to the CL601. Take the unsurfaced forest road to the right, which climbs for a further 3km to the Puerto. The road is well graded and perfectly rideable, and may be the course of the old Roman road. Only snow would cause a problem. Pass through the gate immediately before the crossroads of the Puerto de la Fuenfría (1797m). The right turn leads nowhere.

Straight ahead is La Calzada Romana (Roman road) with many of the original stones still in place. This road has many sharp bends as it zigzags its way up the hillside, making one wonder how a legion could march in step on a hairpin bend – do not even think about cycling down it. Turn left, heading east of south. At first the grit road is rough with many fist-sized loose stones which are surprisingly black – this is still granite country. After a couple of kilometres the surface improves and is most acceptable by the time the Pradera de Navarrulaque is passed. If the road is wet, clags of gritty clay are thrown up which grind down brake blocks better than any power sander. At the mirador

About 8km from Valsaín is the 'Fuente bien agua', a spring of cold, invigorating water, drunk from several times without ill effect.

161

*Fuente bien agua,
Sierra de Guadarrama*

on the big bend there are poems painted onto the rocks. The road continues downhill past a couple of barriers and via the one-way system in the car parks to the asphalt road to **Cercedilla**. Pass the Centro de Información which gives out free guides to walks in the valley.

The alternative route is to stay on the CL601 at Pradera de Navalhorno and enter the province of Madrid via the **Puerto de Navacerrada** (1860m). The Puerto has all the feel of an out-of-season ski resort (which is what it is for most of the year). Staying on what is now the M601 follow the signs to **Cercedilla** from the outskirts of the town of Navacerrada. The Hostal El Aribel can be reached by continuing through the town to the railway station.

The Hostal El Aribel is just uphill from the station. Bikes are stored in the kitchen along with those of the owners. It also has a hose out the back for rinsing off the clag.

Staying on in Cercedilla

Cercedilla is a popular spot with the *Madrileños* who come to escape the city heat in the summer. At weekends the town and surroundings are busy with walkers and mountain bikers.

Around Cercedilla

Cycling: El Escorial is an easy if not-too-pleasant bike ride away. El Escorial is the stern palace, built by Felipe II, from where he ruled the Spanish Empire. En route is the Valle de los Caídos, Franco's memorial to the dead of both sides in the Civil War. There is an entrance charge.

Visit Madrid: there are frequent trains into the city from the station next to the hotel.

Walking: return to the Valle de la Fuenfría to the Centro de Información and pick up a guide, in English or Spanish, to local walks. There are six waymarked routes, including one up La Calzada Romana. However, do not expect to be alone.

STAGE 7
Cercedilla to Madrid–Barajas airport

Distance	70km (43.3 miles)
Type	Hills then rolling plain
Climb	207m (679ft)
Cycling time	4hr 10min

From the Hostal El Aribel climb up to and pass through the centre of Cercedilla. Leave in the direction of Navacerrada. The first 3km are uphill but make up the only real climb of the day. At the T-junction turn left to join the M-614, which soon becomes the M-607, all the way to **Colmenar Viejo**. The road becomes a pleasant descent, and by Cerceda the foothills of the Sierra de Guadarrama are left behind. Not that the road is flat or level; the mountains that rise so dramatically out of the undulating plain gradually recede.

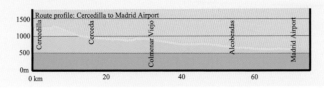

On reaching the start of the dual carriageway turn right and follow the road through the centre of **Colmenar Viejo**. This is about halfway and provides a convenient break point. Continue through the town to join the M607 dual carriageway heading south towards Madrid. As far as dual carriageways go this is a good one; at the junction there are signs to alert motorists to the presence of cyclists and the cycle lane is a smooth-topped track on which the going is easy. The cycle lane starts off beside the dual carriage way but soon changes into a two-lane segregated cycle lane. The views to the right are quite pleasant.

After about 14km the cycle lane crosses over the M607 just before the motorised vehicle junction for Alcobendas. Once over the M607 keep right, pass under the spur road and turn left to parallel the spur road. At the roundabout, after 4.4km of this dual carriageway, take the exit signed 'Calle Marqués de la Valdavía'. Continue straight on heading east. Ignore every sign for 'all directions', as they lead to motorways. After 2.6km a T-junction is reached where the road becomes a one-way system. Turn right and descend to the kidney-shaped roundabout.

From the kidney-shaped roundabout take the third exit (Bulevar de Salvador Allende). Turn right and downhill immediately after the Hostal Fronton. Turn left at the next roundabout (Avda Olimpica) then right at the next (Calle de Anabel Segura). Continue straight ahead at the dual carriageway, the roundabout and pass under the A1 autovía where the road continues uphill as the Camino Ancho. Go straight ahead at the roundabout. Ignore the Paseo Conde de los Gaitanes turn on the right but after 100m turn left into the road of the same name heading east. Continue straight on to the large roundabout over the M12 autopista. Take the second exit signed Antigua M110 and Barajas.

Keep on this remarkably quiet dual carriageway heading south. Signing is virtually non-existent, expect the odd one for 'Urbanazación sur' or 'Barajas'. Pass to the right of the Repsol service station. Those returning to T4 follow the signs for Salidas at the third roundabout. South of T4 at a larger than usual roundabout keep with the dual carriageway as it turns left and east before continuing straight ahead at the next two roundabouts. At the third larger roundabout take the fourth exit signed Zona Industrial Aeropuerto and T3 T2 T1. This little road will take you to the roundabout with the pink infil on the Barajas map.

From there follow the signs to your terminal.

ACCOMMODATION ON OR CLOSE TO ROUTE 5

Please note that this is not an exhaustive list. Hotel guide prices are in Euros, based on a double room with an en suite bathroom at high season. Rooms without en suite are typically 20% cheaper, as are single rooms. Please note that hotels are constantly opening, closing or being refurbished; it is always advisable to book ahead. Prices (where known) are indicated as follows: (1) up to 50 Euros; (2) 50–75 Euros; (3) 75–100 Euros; (4) over 100 Euros.

Boadilla del Monte
(4) Partner Boadilla Palacio, Plaza de la Concordia, s/n (tel: 916 33 31 15)
(4) Husa Prado de Boadilla, Labradores, s/n (tel: 916 32 46 80)
(4) Antiguo Convento, De las Monjas, s/n (tel: 916 32 22 20)

Brunete
(2) La Ermita, Miguel Cervantes, 2 (tel: 918 12 49 10)
(1) Brunete, Paseo de Ronda, 14 (tel: 918 15 80 81)
(1) Casa Mae, Paseo de Ronda, 6 (tel: 918 15 97 75)
(1) Brunetex, Paseo Ronda, 4 (tel: 918 16 37 95)
Julián, Paseo Ronda, 2 (tel: 918 15 84 35)

Navalcarnero
(3) Villa de Navalcarnero, Paseo Alpararache, 19 (tel: 918 10 16 45)
(2) El Labrador, Ctra. Extremadura, km 36.8 (tel: 918 13 94 20)
(2) Casa Julián, Pozo del Concejo, 59 (tel: 699 05 29 66)
(2) Cruz Verde, Calle Cruz Verde, 3 (tel: 918 10 10 03)
(1) La Mansion de Navalcarnero, Jacinto Gonzáles, 24 (tel: 918 10 12 50)

Aldea del Fresno
(3) El Jardin, Ctra. Madrid, 12 (tel: 918 63 68 34)

Villa del Prado
(1) El Extremeño, Avda. Generalisimo, 78 (tel: 918 62 24 28)

Pelayos de la Presa
Camping La Enfermería, Ctra. San Ramon (tel: 918 64 52 25)
Camping El Pinar de Pelayos, Av de Nicasio Hernández Redondo, 25 (tel: 918 64 52 25)

San Martín de Valdeiglesias
(2) Casa de Labranza, Arco, 3 (tel: 918 61 16 53)
(1) Las Conchas, Ancha, 7 (tel: 918 61 00 33)
(1) San Martín, Anchuelas, 5 (tel: 918 61 02 82)
Plaza del Pilar, Plaza Pilar, 1 (tel: 918 61 51 14)
La Corredera, Calle de la Corredera Alta, 28 (tel: 918 61 10 84)
Camping Ardilla Roja, Pantano de San Juan (tel: 918 64 41 19)

Cadalso de los Vidrios
(3) Ermita de Santa Ana, El Coso, 32 (tel: 918 64 06 28)
(1) San José, Dr. Menéndez, 2 (tel: 918 64 01 57)
(1) Cadalso, Ronda de Sangre, 2 (tel: 918 64 10 11)

Santa María del Tiétar
(2) La Posada Del Tietar, Calle Calvo Sotelo, 23 (tel: 918 66 23 29)

Sotillo de la Adrada
(1) Chico, Los Guijuelos, 11 (tel: 918 66 82 67)

Piedralaves
(2) Almanzor, Progresso, 2 (tel: 918 66 50 00)
(2) Mainz, Avda. Castilla y Leon, 9 (tel: 918 66 56 12)
(2) Posada Quinta San José, Avda. De Castilla y Léon, 82 (tel: 918 66 55 11)
Posada Trastamara, Calle Muñoza, 49 (tel: 918 66 64 00)

Casavieja
Niágara, Del Puerto, 26 (tel: 918 67 85 81)
El Corralón, Paraje El Corralón, s/n (tel: 918 67 85 63)
Camping Paraje Fuente Helecha, Paraje Fuente Helecha (tel: 918 67 84 87)

Mijares
(2) Barbacedo, Miguel Gallego, 2 (tel: 920 38 50 07)
Casa Ligia, Travesía Ayuntamiento, 7 (tel: 670 48 42 48)
La Posada, Calle Esquinilla, 9 (tel: 920 38 53 74)

Gavilanes
Mirador del Tiétar, Risquillo, 22 (tel: 920 38 48 67)

Pedro Bernardo

(2) La Gatera, Medio, 35 (tel: 920 38 72 23)
(1) El Cerro, Avda. Duperier, 55 (tel: 920 38 91 03)
Camping Balcón del Tiétar, A 2 km, (tel: 920 38 71 82)

Burgohondo

(2) El Alberche, Ctra. Ávila-Casavieja, 39 (tel: 920 28 30 34)
(2) Posada Real El Linar del Zaire, Ctra. Ávila-Casavieja, 42 (tel: 920 28 40 91)

Navalmoral

(2) Arpa, Avda. de Gredos, 1 (tel: 920 28 00 66)

Ávila

There are over 20 hotels in Ávila, only those costing less than 90 Euros and located within or very close to the city walls are listed.
(3) Hostería de Bracamonte, Bracamonte, 6 (tel: 920 25 12 80)
(3) El Rastro, Plaza del Rastro, 1 (tel: 920 21 12 18)
(3) Palacio De Los Velada, Plaza de la Catedral, 10 (tel: 920 25 51 00)
(3) Las Leyandas, Francisco Gallego, 3 (tel: 920 35 20 42)
(2) Don Diego, Marqués de Canales y Chozas, 5 (tel: 920 25 54 75)
(2) El Rincon, Pl. Zurraquín, 3–4, (tel: 920 21 31 52)
(2) San Segundo, San Segundo, 28, (tel: 920 25 25 90)
(2) Ray Niño, Pl. de José Tome, 1 (tel: 920 25 52 10)
(1) Bellas, Caballeros, 19 (tel: 920 21 29 10)
(1) Casa Felipe, Plaza Mercado Chico, 12 (tel: 920 21 39 24)
(1) Alcántara, Esteban Domingo, 11 (tel: 920 22 50 03)

El Espinar

(2) La Viña, Ctra. Segovia, 4 (tel: 921 17 17 94)
(2) Siete Picos, Martí Estévez, 10 (tel: 921 18 10 84)
(1) La Cigüeña, Antonia Machado, 3 (tel: 921 18 23 88)
(1) Marino, Marqués de Perales, 11 (tel: 921 18 23 39)

Segovia

There are 20 hotels in Segovia, only those costing less than 90 Euros and located within the city walls or close to the aqueduct are listed.
(3) Las Sirenas, Juan Bravo, 30 (tel: 921 46 26 63)
(2) Fornos, Infanta Isabel, 13, 1ºA (tel: 921 46 01 98)
(2) Plaza, Cronista Lecea, 11 (tel: 921 46 03 03)
(2) La Hostería Natura, Colon, 5 (tel: 921 46 67 10)
(2) Don Jaime, Ochoa Ondategui, 8 (tel: 921 44 47 87)
(2) Don Jaime II, Ochoa Ondategui, 11 (tel: 921 44 47 87)
(2) Aralso II, Teniente Ochoa, 8 (tel: 649 80 42 20)
(1) Juan Bravo, Juan Bravo, 12 (tel: 921 46 34 13)
(1) Taray, Cuesta de San Bartolomé, s/n (tel: 921 46 30 41)

(1) El Hidalgo, José Canalejas, 3–5 (tel: 921 46 35 29)
(1) Hidalgo II, Juan Bravo, 21 (tel: 921 46 35 29)
Camping Acueducto, Avda. Don Juan de Borbón, 49 (tel: 921 42 50 00)

La Granja

(4) San Luis, Barco, 8 (tel: 921 47 21 21)
(2) Roma, Guardas, 2 (tel: 921 47 07 52)
(2) El Jardín de la Hilaria, Carretera de Villalba Madrid, (tel: 921 47 02 92)

Valsain

(4) Casa de Navalhorno, Carretera de Villalba Madrid, 41 (tel: 652 09 18 88)

Puerto de Navacerrada

(3) Pasadoiro, Ctra. Madrid M-601, 6 (tel: 918 52 15 11)

Cercedilla

(4) Casa Lafora, Camino Majavilán, 3 (tel: 918 52 10 50)
(4) Los Frutales, Ctra. Dehesas, 33 (tel: 918 52 02 44)
(2) El Aribel, Emilio Serrano, 41 (tel: 918 52 15 11)
(1) La Maya, Carrera Señor, 2 (tel: 918 51 12 67)

Navacerrada

(3) Hacienda Los Robles, Avda. De Madrid, 27 (tel: 918 56 02 00)
(2) Nava Real, Las Huertas, 1 (tel: 918 53 13 00)

Manzanares El Real

(2) Hostal El Yelmo, Avda. Pedriza, 67 (tel: 918 53 06 55)
(2) Parque Real, Padre Damián, 4 (tel: 918 53 99 12)
(2) El Tranco, Tranco, 4 (tel: 918 53 00 63)
Camping El Ortigal, La Pedriza (tel: 918 53 01 20)

Colmenar Viejo

(2) El Chiscón, Frailes, 91 (tel: 918 45 28 47)
Chabeli, Calle Boteros, 6 (tel: 918 45 11 65)

Tres Cantos

(1) Tres Cantos, Avenida Viñuelas, 39 (tel: 918 03 71 17)

Alcobendas

(3) Frontón, Bulevar Salvador Allende, 16 (tel: 916 52 34 37)
(3) Grand Prix, Bulevar Salvador Allende, 10 (tel: 916 52 46 00)
(2) Arba, Huesca, 37 (tel: 916 54 34 12)
(1) Los Ángeles, Miño, 14 (tel: 916 51 50 06)
(1) Miraflores, Miraflores, 9 (tel: 916 63 97 17)

ROUTE 6
MADRID TO BILBAO
VIA THE SIERRA DE LA DEMANDA

ROUTE SUMMARY

From	To	km	Type	Cycling time
Madrid airport	Cogolludo	93	Undulating plains	5hr 15min
Cogolludo	Galve de Sorbe	50	Steady climb through hills	3hr 25min
Galve de Sorbe	San Esteban	57	Undulating descent	3hr 35min
San Esteban	Quintanar	66	Undulating plain and hills	4hr 10min
Quintanar	Anguiano	71	Hills and extended valley	4hr 25min
Anguiano	Miranda	72	Plain and hills	4hr 25min
Miranda	Amurrio	53	Plain and hills	3hr 20min
Amurrio	Bilbao	37	Valleys	2hr 20min
Option 1				
Najerilla valley	Santo Domingo	59	Mountains and plain	4hr 10min
Option 2				
Sierra de la Demanda loop		94	Plain and mountains	6hr 25min

In any country cycling from the centre to the coast has its own appeal. This route is for those who prefer scenery to spectacle; those who are happy with hills but prefer to cycle between mountains rather than over them. Apart from the reduced physical challenge there are no other compromises. The roads are quiet, the towns small and friendly, and the countryside very pretty.

The route starts at Madrid airport on the central plain before heading north over the gentle hills of Guadalajara and the wooded ranges of Soria. The valley of the Río Najerilla is used to avoid crossing over the Sierra de la Demanda. Continuing north the route crosses the plain of the Río Ebro before catching the eastern end of the Cordillera Cantábrica and descending through wooded valleys into Bilbao. The route ends in the centre of Bilbao at its main railway station rather than its rather stylish airport. Much effort has gone into finding a safe route between the city and its airport but this has proved futile. Fortunately buses to the airport will carry bicycles subject to a small charge. The railway station is the focus for many of the car rental agencies.

ROUTE 6: CLIMATE DETAILS

	Jan	Feb	Mar	Apr	May	Jun	Jul	Aug	Sep	Oct	Nov	Dec
Soria												
av min temp °C	-2	-1	1	3	6	10	12	12	10	5	1	-1
av max temp °C	7	9	12	15	18	24	28	27	24	16	11	7
rainfall mm	49	48	46	51	65	54	30	32	51	48	48	57
Santander												
av min temp °C	7	7	8	10	11	14	16	16	15	12	10	8
av max temp °C	12	12	14	15	17	20	22	22	21	18	15	12
rainfall mm	119	88	78	83	89	63	54	84	114	733	125	129
Madrid												
sunrise	08:37	08:24	07:48	07:58	07:14	06:47	06:48	07:11	07:42	08:11	07:45	08:20
sunset	17:57	18:30	19:06	20:38	21:10	21:39	21:48	21:29	20:48	19:57	18:13	17:50
Best time	–	–	G	G	VG	VG	–	–	VG	VG	G	

(G = good time to go; VG = best time to go)

Public holidays

Communidad de Madrid: 2 May
City of Madrid: 15 May and 9 November
Province of Guadalajara: 8 and 14 September
Province of Soria: 28 June and 2 October

Province of La Rioja: 9 June
Álava Guipúzcoa and Vizcaya: Easter Monday
Bilbao: 31 July and first Friday after 15 August

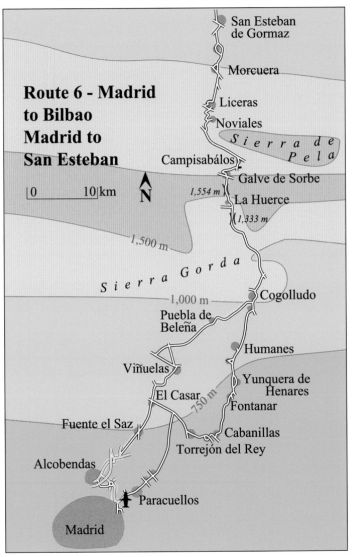

Michelin Regional 1:400 000 maps 576 Extremadura, Castilla-La Mancha, Madrid, 575 Castilla y León and 573 La Rioja, País Vasco/Euskadi are required for the entire route. The Instituto Geográfico 1:200 000 Mapas Provinciales Madrid y su entono, Soria, La Rioja and Álava Guipúzcoa & Vizcaya also cover the route. Although it also passes through the provinces of Segovia and Burgos the maps listed contain sufficient detail for navigation. Readily available guidebooks provide scant coverage, and the *Rough Guide to Spain* is as good as any.

The route moves from the centre of Spain, with low rainfall, freezing cold winters and baking hot summers, to the north coast with its mild winters, warm summers and plentiful rain. This route starts in Madrid, some 650m above sea level, and peaks at 1500m. Based on the 1°C per 100m rule expect temperatures to be cooler than Madrid but not that much colder than Soria (1063m). The 'Climate details' table will help you work out the best time for your trip.

STAGE 1
Madrid–Barajas airport to Cogolludo

This first stage is long but relatively flat. Those who get away from the airport late should consider breaking the stage into two.

Distance	93km (57.8 miles)
Type	Town then mesa with some steep valleys
Climb	849m (2786ft)
Cycling time	5hr 15min

Those starting at T1, T2 or T3 should use the map in Appendix 5 and make their way to the roundabout with the pink infil. From there exit heading north immediately passing under a flyover. Follow this road as it parallels the M13 Autovía. After two small roundabouts and one large there is a large and busier fourth. Take the second exit. The first exit is signed M111 to Paracuellos. At the

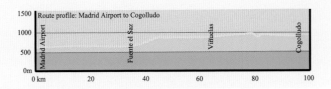

time of writing our turn has only one sign and that is a 5m height restriction. Keep on this dual carriageway to the outskirts of Alcobendas. No doubt the poor sign-posted is to encourage use of the motorway system but this does not help us cyclists. There are occasional signs for 'Alcobendas' and 'Urbanazación norte'. At the third roundabout turn right and north. Continue straight ahead at the next but at the one after bear left of straight ahead. Keep heading north at all roundabouts including the one by the Repsol service station.

Those starting at T4 should head for the multi-storey car parks opposite; make their way to the ground floor and exit turning right and north. After the pay booths continue straight ahead. Take the right fork immediately before the flyovers and again fork right after them. At the roundabout next to the Repsol service station turn right onto the dual carriageway to join the route from the other terminals.

At the large roundabout over the motorways, some 9km from the pink roundabout, take the second exit signed La Moraleja. Continue west on this suburban road (Paseo Conde de los Gaitanes) and at the end turn right (Camino Ancho). After 100m fork right to stay on the Camino Ancho which becomes the Calle de Anabel Segura. Continue north and straight ahead under the Autovía, over the roundabout, the dual carriageway with the wide grassed centre and climb to the next roundabout. Here turn left (Avda Olimpica) and at the next turn right. Turn right onto the dual carriageway (Bulevar de Salvador Allende) next to the Hostal Fronton. Continue straight ahead and northeast on this road which becomes the Avda de Europa.

Seven kilometres from the Hostal Fronton pass under the A1 Autovía and at the roundabout turn right towards Algete. At the large roundabout turn left signed M111 Fuente el Saz and almost immediately bear right to leave it. At the roundabout take the first exit signed Urbanazación Prado Norte. Keep on this road to and then through Fuente el Saz. At the roundabout take the M117 to El Casar. All the while the hustle and bustle of Alcobendas fades behind as the emptiness of Castile takes over. There is even a bit of a climb up to El Casar.

At the national road turn right and the immediately left towards Mesones. However, before Mesones bear right to Valdenuño-Fernández and then Viñuelas. Here the cycling in on high but level mesas at an altitude of around 900m which is good making headway and for big panoramas. There are arroyos cut into the mesa which means it isn't all easy going. At the far side of Viñuelas turn left then right to Villaseca de Uceda. Pass through the village. At the cross roads with the CM1001 turn right and keep on this road all the way to Cogolludo.

The cycling is good as are the views. Apart from one arroyo the road is fairly flat as far as Puebla de Beleña from where the road becomes more interesting. Some might say hilly. A few kilometres before Cogolludo turn left at the T-junction and then follow the road into town.

Cogolludo is a charming and interesting village. It has an enormous colonnaded 14th-century Plaza Major complete with medieval snow hole, 16th-century churches one of which was built over a Roman temple, a 15th-century Palacio de los Duques de Medinaceli, quiet squares, a ruined castle and a couple of hotels. A lot of history for the towns 600 residents.

STAGE 2
Cogolludo to Galve de Sorbe

Distance	50km (31 miles)
Type	Steady climb through hills
Climb	763m (2503ft)
Cycling time	3hr 25min

Return to the main road. Turn left at the roundabout and cycle round the outside of the village before dropping to the river. Ignore the left turn to Tamajón. The road climbs a steep hill with pine forest on top; having reached the trees the climb eases.

Turn left at the roundabout, heading west. The road remains level for a while before descending in a cutting through pine forest. Cross the Arroyo Hondo and climb steeply at first onto a broad ridge. Ignore all turns. The views to the north and east are excellent. Descend into the extended but gentle dip before the climb to an unmarked coll at 1333m. Continue along the forested eastern side of the Río Sorbe valley; there are good views to the west with the Sierra de Ayllón prominent. The soil is poor and the vegetation scrubby, with rocks and crags breaking through.

Ignore the Tourist Route left turn towards Valverde. Continue the climb and leave the forest before passing above the villages of **La Huerce** and Valdepinillos. Enter more pine forest and cross the Sierra de Alto Rey

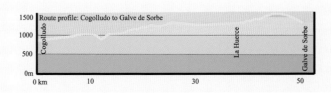

(1554m). Descend to **Galve de Sorbe**, which is set in open pasture.

Galve de Sorbe is a small and isolated village. However, it does have a ruined 14th-century Castillo de los Zúñigas, a 16th-century church, two hermitages, an antique four-spout fountain and a hotel.

STAGE 3
Galve de Sorbe to San Esteban

A second short day of cycling with only a couple of hills. Enjoy the relaxed pace.

Distance	57km (35.4 miles)
Type	Undulating descent
Climb	269m (883ft)
Cycling time	3 hours 35 minutes

Leave Galve de Sorbe on the narrow road leading out of the north-west corner of the village square, heading towards the castle. Turn right immediately before the castle. The road gently bends right to head north-east through rich pasture in a broad valley surrounded by limestone ridges. Ignore the grit road turn to the left. ◀

It was along this stretch of road that I saw my first Spanish fox. It was larger and stouter than its British cousins, and its coat brown and grey rather than red.

Turn left at the crossroads next to the sports pitches. The road climbs up a limestone scarp. Ignore the left turn. This is lovely limestone country with rocky ridges, crags and dry valleys covered with scrub and lush green pasture in between. Continue into **Campisábalos** with its 12th-century Romanesque church of San Bartolomé

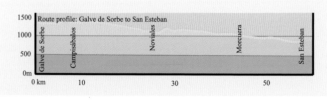

Limestone country, Galve de Sorbe

containing a chapel to San Galindo. Leave the village heading north, and at the T-junction with the main road turn left.

Continue heading approximately north-west on this fairly level road. The flat pine *dehesa* to the south is home to wild boar. To the north are the limestone ridges of Sierras de Pela and Grado. The province of Segovia is entered, but not for long. Ignore the left turn to Grado and in approximately 3km turn right towards Noviales.

The road enters Soria. After initial scrub the road passes through big fields of red soil. **Noviales** is a tightly packed red sandstone hamlet. Approaching the village turn left at the T-junction to Liceras. This leads away from the village. Cross the Río Pedro and diagonally climb the steep bare sandstone scarp slope. This line of sandstone stretches either side as far as the eye can see and the views from the top are excellent.

From the top the road descends to Liceras. Approaching **Liceras** turn left at the crossroads before turning right towards San Esteban. The road bypasses the village. Climb the second steep scarp slope. From the top the road descends to the end of the stage. Continue north across the undulating plateau of rocky fields, *dehesa*, scrub and natural pine forest. Turn left at the T-junction and pass through more of the same, but this time with the odd fertile field. At the second T-junction turn left. The road continues directly to San Esteban though big fields located on the top of eroded scarp slopes, and the rocky areas support oak trees. Divert through **Morcuera** and Atauta as you please for a little variety. Cross the Canal de Inés and ignore the road to the right. Turn right at the T-junction with the main road. Cross the Río Duero on the 16-arch medieval bridge to enter **San Esteban de Gormaz**.

San Esteban established its place in history in AD883 during the Reconquests, when Duero became the established boundary between the Moors and Christians. North of the town are several steep sandstone hills, one of which houses the remains of a castle. There is a smashing town square with colonnaded and galleried buildings reached through the town arch. The 11th- and 12th-century churches of San Miguel and Nuestra Señora del Rivero are striking in both appearance and location.

Noviales and Sierra de Grado

STAGE 4
San Esteban to Quintanar

This stage takes in the popular Parque Natural Cañón del Río Lobos as well as the lonelier pine-forested ridges of Los Pinares. Expect a very good day's riding.

Distance	66km (40.9 miles)
Type	Undulating plain and hills
Climb	549m (1801ft)
Cycling time	4hr 10min

From the north side of the medieval bridge head west on the main road towards Aranda de Duero. Turn right after 0.5km and pass under the town's northern bypass, heading north. Cross the gently undulating flood plain of the Río Duero.

At **Matanza de Soria** ignore the left turn into the village and continue on its bypass to where the through road rejoins the bypass. Turn right onto the Camino Rurales and head north-east (do not take the earlier Camino Rurales halfway round the bypass which heads east). These Camino Rurales are well-made grit roads and are perfectly suitable for cycling. The road passes through undulating fields some with vines. Continue straight on and ignore any turns.

At Berzosa continue straight ahead crossing the two roads, bend left at the cross-roads at the start proper of the village, keeping to the asphalt road heading north-east. Continue straight ahead through flat countryside in a shallow valley. Continue straight ahead ignoring the left turn for Valdealbín. Turn left at the T-junction to **Rejas de Ucero**. In the village turn right beside the church. Turn left

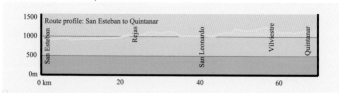

Route profile: San Esteban to Quintanar

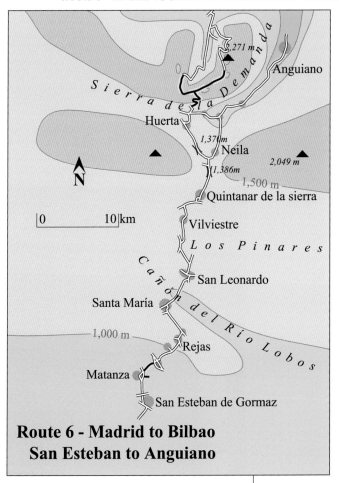

Route 6 - Madrid to Bilbao
San Esteban to Anguiano

at the next T-junction and pass through Nafría de Ucero. The road is fairly level, with a dominant wooded ridge paralleling it 1km to the north. An area of pine *dehesa* is encountered as Santa María de las Hoyas (of the Holes) is neared. Pass through the eastern side of **Santa María** and

There are numerous waymarked tracks through the forest on which bikes are welcome as long as pedestrians are given priority. These are an excellent way to explore this beautiful forested canyon with its spectacular rock formations.

at the T-junction with the main road turn right, heading north-west. Climb over the bare limestone scarp. The top is pine forest with lovely views over the Parque Natural. A bendy descent leads to the wide valley floor where there is an information centre and picnic sites. ◀

Cross the Río Lobos heading north in a wide, open valley surrounded by wooded hills. The exit from the canyon is not the expected steep climb. Past Arganza continue straight ahead at the roundabout before turning left at the T-junction and left again at the second T-junction, this time in **San Leonardo de Yagüe**, in front of the church. Turn right immediately behind the church,

Los Pinares, San Leonardo de Yagüe

182

keep to this one-way road as it bends left and continue under the railway where the road has become two-way. The town borders mature pine forest with fantastic rock formations. Head north in a steep-sided valley set out with picnic areas. Bend left 2.7km from town to pass through a delicious mix of spur and valley topography. Enter the province of Burgos before turning right at the T-junction towards Palacios. At the next junction turn right to Vilviestre del Pinar. The road continues to climb over a couple of low summits before descending to **Vilviestre del Pinar**, set on a hillside amongst pasture.

Pass through Vilviestre, cross the Río Arlanza and turn right at the T-junction. After 3.8km turn left and climb up to **Quintanar de la Sierra**, a pleasant mountain resort with swimming pool, campsite and hotels.

STAGE 5
Quintanar to Anguiano

Distance	71km (44.1 miles)
Type	Hills and extended valley
Climb	458m (1503ft)
Cycling time	4hr 25min

This is a long stage, but the climb comes early on and well over half the total is along the valley of the Río Najerilla: at worst very pretty, at best quite awesome.

Leave Quintanar heading north-east on the main through road. Ignore the right turn to the Necropolis. Climb into mature pine forest high above the river to the east. As height is gained the road becomes more twisty and crags protrude as the trees become more sparse.

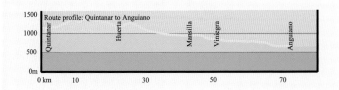

Route profile: Quintanar to Anguiano

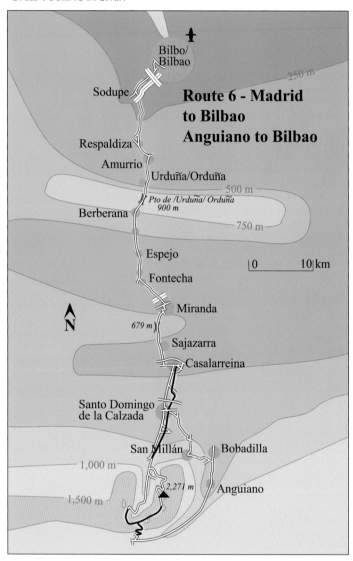

Bilbo/ Bilbao

250 m

Sodupe

Route 6 - Madrid to Bilbao Anguiano to Bilbao

Respaldiza

Amurrio

Urduña/Orduña

500 m

Pto de /Urduña/ Orduña 900 m

Berberana

750 m

Espejo

| 0   10| km

Fontecha

Miranda

↑ N

679 m

Sajazarra

Casalarreina

Santo Domingo de la Calzada

San Millán

Bobadilla

1,000 m

2,271 m

Anguiano

1,500 m

0

At the Puerto del Collado ignore the left turn. Descend steeply, leaving the forest for a short time. At the next junction turn left and climb back into the forest. (Continuing straight ahead through **Neila** would cut the stage short.) Continue over a couple of colls and descend to **Huerta de Arriba**, set in a steep-sided valley amongst scrubby hills. Continue through the village, and at the far end turn right to double back. Fork left at the next junction and follow the sign for Logroño located behind the church. Pass through pasture, then climbing and descending through mature pine and beech forest. Enter the province of La Rioja. Turn right at the T-junction with the main road. After a very short distance there is a left turn. This is the start of the Najerilla valley to Santo Domingo option.

Hemmed in by the Sierra de la Demanda to the north and the Sierra de Castejón to the south, the route takes the easy downhill option. Ignore the left turn. Heading east then swinging north, the route stays on this road all the way to Anguiano. Enter the limestone Najerilla valley and pass the villages of Canales and Villavalayo before following the north shore of the Embalse de Mansilla. The road swings round inlets made by the tributary valleys, many of which are sheer-sided gorges.

Beyond the *embalse* enter a steep-sided wooded gorge that continues to **Anguiano**. The eroded limestone bedding planes have formed interlocking spurs around which the river has cut its tortuous path. The road tries to follow the river. After the road crosses the river the gorge widens with fields in the bottom. Anguiano is framed by a pair of narrow sandstone ridges that act as gates to the town.

Apart from its spectacular setting **Anguiano** is a pretty town, famous for its stilt dancers. In late July they carry an icon of Mary Magdalena from the church down the Cuesta de los Danzadores to a shrine, and on the last Saturday in September dance the icon back again.

STAGE 6
Anguiano to Miranda

Distance	72km (44.7 miles)
Type	Plain and hills
Climb	469m (1539ft)
Cycling time	4hr 25min

Leave Anguiano on the main through road, heading north. Pass the fantastic sandstone cliffs, buttresses and razor-sharp ridges. As the flood plain of the Río Ebro is approached the gorge widens. Ignore the turns to Pedroso and Ledesma. On the approach to **Bobadilla** turn left to San Millán. Ignore the left turn to Matute. The country is fertile eroded sandstone hills. Pass north of Villaverde de Rioja, through San Andres and north of Estollo. Cross the Río Cárdenas and turn right at the T-junction to bypass **San Millán de la Cogolla**. Continue straight through Berceo, ignoring the right turn. Turn left at the roundabout, pass through Villar de Torre and continue straight on, ignoring the turns for Villarejo and Manzanares. Pass through Cirueña with its hop fields. Turn left at the first roundabout, continue straight ahead at the second and again at the third, entering the industrial fringe of **Santo Domingo de la Calzada**. The town has a medieval centre; the cathedral has a detached ornate bell tower, built apart from the main building after the first one fell down and the second threatened to. The town is certainly worth a visit, and is the start point for the Sierra de la Demanda option. ◀

Santo Domingo is also an important stop on the pilgrim route to Santiago. The Camino de Santiago passes through the town and is well marked with scallop shell motifs.

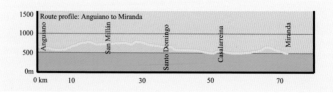

The route uses the Vía Verde, built on the former railway line from Ezcaray to Casalarreina. The Vía Verde crosses the road east of the town proper where the road forks right to skirt north of the centre. The 'beware of cyclists' road sign is the indicator. Turn right just before the fork and pass round to the rear of the prefabricated steel bullring set up on waste ground. Head north on a well-consolidated grit track. Pass under the town's bypass and bend right, then left, to parallel the Santo Domingo to Casalarreina road. The Vía Verde passes through flat fields. Approaching **Casalarreina** cross the town's eastern bypass. The Vía Verde terminates on a road of little consequence in town. Turn left at the T-junction and then left again at the main road. Continue west through the town centre.

Pass through Tirgo and turn right on the west side of the Río Tirón to head north. Continue straight on, ignoring all turn-offs. Pass the lovely village of **Sajazarra** with its golden stone-built houses, churches and quaint castle. The road gently climbs to a low pass where the province of Burgos is entered. Descend into **Miranda de Ebro**. On the outskirts of town turn left at the T-junction then turn right at the roundabout, right again then bend left approaching the river in response to the one-way system. Cross the Río Ebro. Turn immediately left and parallel the river. Take the left fork and pass under the railway. Follow the road as it bends to the right. Take the second exit from the roundabout to join the main road that passes through town. Shortly there is a second major roundabout where the next stage begins.

STAGE 7
Miranda to Amurrio

Distance	53km (32.9 miles)
Type	Plain and hills
Climb	445m (1460ft)
Cycling time	3hr 20min

The two remaining stages could be combined for one long, but not too hilly, day.

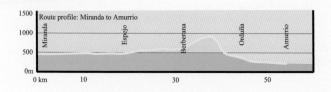

Start from the centre of Miranda at the roundabout described at the end of Stage 6. Leave the city heading north-west, paralleling the Río Ebro to the south. The road is flat but not too scenic. Ignore all turns to either side and pass through **Fontecha**. At the T-junction next to the dammed Ebro turn right to head north. Ignore the left turn to Sobrón and pass through the villages of Bergüenda, **Espejo**, Osma and **Berberana** in a rising wide shallow valley. The undulating fields are rimmed by small wooded limestone hills to the east. To the west the limestone mountains of the Cordillera Cantábrica are clearly visible.

From Berberana the road climbs more steeply through country with limestone pavement, oak trees and lush pasture. The tree cover increases with altitude. The road peaks at the **Puerto de Orduña** (900m). Descend the 450m limestone cliff in zigzags through the trees. On both sides the cliff line can be seen stretching into the distance. The fields become more fertile as you descend. Pass under the railway before continuing straight ahead at the roundabouts passing east of **Urduña/Orduña**. Pass through Saratxo before shortly turning left into **Amurrio**.

STAGE 8
Amurrio to Bilbao

Distance	37km (22.9 miles)
Type	Valleys
Climb	197m (646ft)
Cycling time	2hr 20min

From the centre of Amurrio head west towards Balmaseda on the main road. Ignore all turn-offs. At **Respaldiza** ignore the first right turn signed to Luiaondo and Bilbao. Take the third right turn at the allotments into the village. The road loops back to the main road. At the top of the hill turn right onto the unsigned road heading north and downhill. Cross the Río Izalde and turn right at the T-junction. Continue downhill to the bottom of a fairly steep-sided lush valley with lots of forestry plantations. The houses are generally stone with low-angled roofs and big eaves. Ignore the turn to Okondo; continue straight ahead at the roundabout under the dual carriageway and climb into **Sodupe**.

Turn right at the T-junction and keep on this old main road. Although now bypassed this road is busier than those ridden on for the last few days. It passes down a steep-sided narrow wooded valley. Pass through Alonsotegi, straight ahead at the roundabout and under the motorway. At the next roundabout take the last exit signed for Zorrotza on the BI-3742. The road parallels the railway and passes a steel works on the left. Pass under the motorway next to Zorrotza railway station. Turn right at the T-junction onto the Avenida de Montevideo and head into the centre of the **Bilbo/Bilbao**. Pass the Hospital Civil de Basurto on the left and under the motorway. Continue along this road – the Avenida de la Autonomía – to the circular Plaza de Zabálburu. Take the fourth exit, the Calle de Hurtado de Amezaga, to the railway Estación de Abando where this route ends. Take a bus or taxi to the airport. The railway station is the focus for many local bus companies and car rental agencies. The railway station is the focus for many of the car rental agencies.

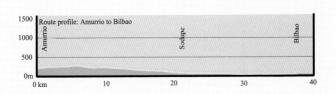

189

Staying on in Bilbao

The city's big draw is the titanium-clad Guggenheim Museum; more traditional is the Museo de Bellas Artes. The Casco Viejo (old quarter) is on the east side of the Ría de Bilbao, to the east of the Estación Abando. Here you will find the Gothic cathedral and streets worth exploring.

OPTION 1

Najerilla valley to Santo Domingo

Distance	59km (36.6 miles)
Type	Mountains and plain
Climb	756m (2480ft)
Cycling time	4hr 10min

An option for those who enjoy a challenging high-level route on mountain roads. The uphill climb is steep and the mountain road rough, but the shale ridge road is in good condition and almost level. The descent is on a good asphalt road. The ridge section provides excellent riding with great views.

Start at the road junction described in Stage 5 and head north uphill on the narrow asphalt road through scrubby pasture. Pass through beech, oak and birch woods. About 3.5km from the start the road bends sharply left, with a hardcore mountain road straight ahead. Take this mountain road and climb steeply through scrubby woodland. After a left bend the road levels through high pasture before climbing again steeply through beech woodland.

After 2.8km on the mountain road a right bend leaves the trees behind. Continue along a ridge. After a left bend the mountain road climbs the western side of Gatón (2037m). At an altitude of 1916m a T-junction is encountered; the views now include those over the valley of the Río Oja. The shale road has a lofty and exposed feel as it runs round the broad ridge. Steep slopes fall

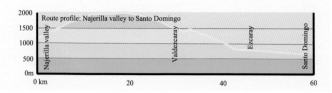

Route profile: Najerilla valley to Santo Domingo

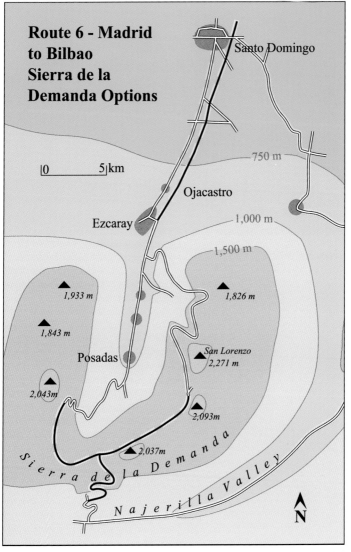

Sierra de la Demanda ridge

away in all directions and the summits are not that much higher than the track. Here beech trees grow to 1700m.

Turn right at the T-junction on a good-quality shale road. Pass north of Gatón then west of Salineros (2093m). In the shallow col between Salineros and San Lorenzo (2271m) the road surface changes to asphalt. Take the left fork and descend the west side of San Lorenzo on an extremely pitted road, which swings round huge spurs as it clings to the steep valley sides. Pass the Valdezcaray ski station where the road improves. Continue contouring round large spurs and valleys with a short climb before a steep hairpin bend descent to the valley road. Turn right at the T-junction on the valley road to **Ezcaray**. The Río Oja joins the road on the left. Where the road bends sharp left into Ezcaray, continue straight ahead to join the Vía Verde. The blue building is clearly the old railway station.

The Vía Verde is easy to follow; simply keep going straight ahead, gently downhill, on the well-made grit track for some 14km. This option ends on the eastern side of **Santo Domingo** directly opposite the start of the Vía Verde described in Stage 6. A visit into Santo Domingo is recommended.

OPTION 2
Sierra de la Demanda loop

Distance	94km (58.4 miles)
Type	Plain and mountains
Climb	1350m (4429ft)
Cycling time	6hr 25min

An excellent long day in the hills. Halfway round it joins the Najerilla valley to Santo Domingo option. Most of the route is on asphalt roads, with a well-made shale mountain road on the ridge.

Leave the centre of Santo Domingo, heading south towards Ezcaray on the LR111. The road climbs gently as it parallels the Río Oja, crossing it just before **Ojacastro**. The mountains gradually hem in the wide river plain. Pass through Ojacastro and into **Ezcaray**. In town turn left where the road bends right again, crossing the river and turning sharp right. It is at this bend that the Vía Verde used on the return begins. Continue up the very pretty valley overlooked by forest-flanked mountains.

Ignore the turns for Valdezcaray and Urdanta. Pass the villages of Zaldierna and Azarrulla, and go through Posadas with its substantial stone houses. After Posadas at the bridge across the river take the right fork. The road climbs much more steeply through a series of hairpin bends. The steep rocky hillsides are forested with blocks of beech and pine. The climb eases slightly as it climbs above the treeline, and at the ridge the asphalt road ends and the shale mountain road begins. (The climb just completed is often used in the Tour of Spain as the end of a stage.) The views now include the valley of the Río Oja

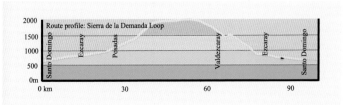

Route profile: Sierra de la Demanda Loop

and the surrounding mountains. Continue along the shale mountain road, keeping close to the ridgeline. The road heads south before bending left to head south-east. Where the road bends to the north-east there is a track on the right which is where the Najerilla valley option comes in. To complete the loop follow the directions given for Option 1.

ACCOMMODATION ON OR CLOSE TO ROUTE 6

Please note that this is not an exhaustive list. Hotel guide prices are in Euros, based on a double room with an en suite bathroom at high season. Rooms without en suite are typically 20% cheaper, as are single rooms. Please note that hotels are constantly opening, closing or being refurbished; it is always advisable to book ahead. Prices (where known) are indicated as follows: (1) up to 50 Euros; (2) 50–75 Euros; (3) 75–100 Euros; (4) over 100 Euros.

Alcobendas
(3) Frontón, Bulevar Salvador Allende, 16 (tel: 916 52 34 37)
(3) Grand Prix, Bulevar Salvador Allende, 10 (tel: 916 52 46 00)
(2) Arba, Huesca, 37 (tel: 916 54 34 12)
(1) Los Ángeles, Miño, 14 (tel: 916 51 50 06)
(1) Miraflores, Miraflores, 9 (tel: 916 63 97 17)

Fuente El Saz
(1) El Juncal, Palomares, 2 (tel: 916 22 33 49)
La Imprenta, Avenida Julián Sánchez, 5 (tel: 916 20 02 89)
Paqui, Calle Bodegas, 9 (tel: 918 41 52 73)

El Casar
(3) La Jara, Calle Falla, s/n, Urbanazación Monte Calderon (tel: 949 36 88 32)
(2) El Cruce, Polígono Los Charcones, 9 (tel: 949 33 52 67)

Cogolludo
(2) Ballestero, Comercio, 3 (tel: 949 85 50 34)
(2) Palacio, Palacio, 7 (tel: 949 85 54 11)

Arbancón
El Balcón de Arbancón, José Ingles, 2

Arroyo de las Fraguas
(1) Alto Rey, Cogolludo, 43 (tel: 949 82 36 03)

Galve de Sorbe
(1) Pensión Nuestra Señora del Pinar, Los Tallers, s/n (tel: 949 30 30 29)

Montejo de Tiermes
(2) Tiermes (tel: 975 35 20 55)

San Esteban de Gormaz
(3) Convento San Esteban, Calle del Convento (tel: 975 35 13 59)
(2) Moreno, Avda. de Valladolid, 10 (tel: 975 35 02 17)
(2) Rivera del Duro, Avda. Valladolid, 131 (tel: 975 35 00 59)
(1) El Alquerque, Plaza del General Mola (tel: 975 35 13 77)

Ucero
(1) Cañón del Río Lobos, Eruelas, 9 (tel: 975 36 35 45)
Camping Cañón del Río Lobos Ctra. Burgo de Osma-San Leonardo de Yagüe, km 17
(tel: 975 36 35 65)

San Leonardo de Yagüe
(1) La Posada El Chispo, Real, 15 (tel: 975 37 60 59)
(1) Torres, Magdalena, 4 (tel: 975 37 61 56)

Quintanar de la Sierra
(3) Posada Las Mayas, Calle Cerro, 5 (tel: 947 39 56 09)
(2) Casa Ramón III, Ctra. Neila km 2 (tel: 947 39 60 75)
(2) La Quinta de Nar, Ctra. Soria, s/n (tel: 947 39 53 50)
(1) Casa Ramón II, Ernesto Sanz y Sanz, 1 (tel: 947 39 50 07)
(1) Domingo, Calle del Conde Jordana, 28 (tel: 947 39 50 85)
San Cistobal, Conde Jordana, 21 (tel: 947 39 50 30)
Camping Arlanza, Ctra. Campamento, s/n (tel: 947 39 55 92)

Neila
(2) Villa de Neila, Campo de Santa María, s/n (tel: 947 39 51 87)

Viniegra de Abajo
(1) Goyo, Puente del Río Neila, 3 (tel: 941 37 80 07)

Anguiano
(2) Abadía de Valvanera, Monasterio de Valvanera (tel: 941 37 70 44)
(1) Valdevenados, Ctra. de Lerma, 12 (tel: 941 37 70 85)

San Millán de Cogolla
(3) La Calera, Prestiño, 3 (tel: 941 37 32 68)
Camping Berceo, A 200 m de Berceo y a 500 de San Millán de la Cogolla (tel: 941 37
32 27)

Santo Domingo de la Calzada
(3) El Corregidor, Mayor, 14–16 (tel: 941 34 21 28)
(2) Hospedería Cisterciense, Pinar, 2 (tel: 941 34 07 00)
(2) Rey Pedro 1, San Roque, 9 (tel: 941 34 11 60)
Miguel, Juan Carlos, 23-3° (tel: 941 34 32 52)
Albert, Beat Hermosilla, 26 (tel: 941 34 08 27)
Camping Bañares, Ctra. Logroño-Burgos, km 42.2, Bañares (tel: 941 34 01 31)

Cuzcurrita de Río Tirón

(2) El Botero, San Sebastián, s/n (tel: 941 30 15 00)

Miranda

(4) Tudanca, Ctra. N-1, Madrid-Irún, 318 (tel: 947 31 18 43)

(4) Achuri, Estación, 86 (tel: 947 34 72 72)

(3) Hospedería El Convento, San Francisco, 15 (tel: 947 332712)

(2) Ferroviaria, Ciudad Jardín, 1 (tel: 947 10 03 75)

Amurrio

(2) Aldama, Dionisio Aldama, 12 (tel: 945 06 66 46)

Ayala, Calle Aiala, 2 (tel: 945 890 452)

Artziniega

(3) Torre de Artziniega, Cuesta de Luciano, 3 (tel: 945 39 65 00)

Bilbao/Bilbo

The city has some 30 hotels and pensiónes. Contact the Turismo at Plaza del Ensanche 11 (tel: 944 79 57 60, www.bizkaia.net)

Options 1 and 2

Ezcaray

(4) Echarren, Padre José García, 19 (tel: 941 35 40 47)

(4) Palacio Azcárate, Calle del Padre José García, 17 (tel: 941 42 72 82)

(4) El Pago, Ctra. Santo Domingo, 29 (tel: 941 42 75 26)

(2) Iguareña, Lamberto Felipe Muñoz, 1 (tel: 941 35 41 44)

Hay meadow, Galve de Sorbe

ROUTE 7
LOS PIRENEOS

ROUTE SUMMARY

From	To	km	Type	Cycling time
San Sebastián	Leitza	49	Ascent up valley	4hr 10min
Leitza	Auritz	91	Valley and mountain passes	5hr 50min
Auritz	Ansó	85	Across valleys and passes	5hr 40min
Ansó	Jaca	67	Passes and valleys	4hr 55min
Jaca	Broto	55	Valley and mountain pass	3hr 50min
Broto	Campo	72	Valley descent and pass	4hr 45min
Campo	Pont de Suert	56	Valley and high passes	4hr 5min
Pont de Suert	Tremp	54	Mountain pass and valley	3hr 50min
Tremp	Coll de Nargó	61	Plain and mountain passes	4hr 20min
Coll de Nargó	Berga	84	High mountains	5hr 50min
Berga	Olot	73	Valleys with passes	4hr 45min
Olot	Girona airport	64	Hills and valley plain	4hr 30min
Option 1				
Hernani	Leitza	40	Ascent up valley	2hr 50min
Option 2				
Olot	Anglès	39	Hills and valley	2hr 10min

The route not only traverses topography but also different linguistic traditions, from the Basque language in Donastia, through Aragón with its own mountain dialects, and ending with Catalan in Girona. Many towns are named in the local language and Castilian (as with Donastia/San Sebastián) and there is a free interchange of the letters 'v' and 'b' (for example Arive/Aribe).

The route starts at the main railway station in San Sebastián, which connects with Biarritz in France and Bilbao to the west. Both have airports. The city has many car rental agencies for those using one-way hire. Cyclists travelling from the United Kingdom can use the Bike Express routes. The Atlantic route passes through Bayonne (just north of Biarritz) with its railway connections to San Sebastián. At the eastern end the Mediterranean route terminates on the coast some 40km east

ROUTE 7: CLIMATE DETAILS

	Jan	Feb	Mar	Apr	May	Jun	Jul	Aug	Sep	Oct	Nov	Dec
Pamplona/Iruñea												
av min temp °C	1	1	4	6	9	12	14	14	12	8	4	2
av max temp °C	8	10	14	16	20	24	27	27	24	19	12	9
rainfall mm	120	86	79	83	90	84	46	44	67	107	107	140
Lérida/Lleida												
av min temp °C	1	1	5	8	12	15	17	18	15	10	4	2
av max temp °C	10	13	18	21	25	29	32	31	27	21	15	9
rainfall mm	22	18	31	46	47	43	24	34	34	30	22	29
Barcelona												
sunrise	08:17	08:03	07:26	07:34	06:49	06:21	06:21	06:46	07:18	07:48	07:24	08:00
sunset	17:31	18:05	18:42	20:16	20:49	21:19	21:29	21:08	20:26	19:34	17:48	17:24
Best time	–	–	G	G	VG	VG	G	G	VG	G	–	–

(G= good time to go; VG = best time to go)

Public holidays

Throughout entire route Easter Monday
San Sebastián: 20 January and 31 March
Province of Huesca: 22 January and 10 August
Provinces of Lleida/Lérida, Barcelona and Girona: 11 September and 26 December

Province of Lleida/Lérida: 11 May and 29 September
Province of Barcelona: second Monday after Easter and 24 September
Province of Girona: 25 July and 29 October

of Girona airport. From San Sebastián the route uses Vías Verdes to start and finish with road options described. Otherwise the route is on asphalt roads.

The availability of accommodation has largely determined where the stages start and finish. However, most villages and hamlets have Fondas and Casas Rurales offering accommodation; the Pyrenees are a popular holiday destination throughout the year.

The route is covered by two Michelin Regional Maps: nos 573 Navarra and País Vasco/Euskadi (1:250 000) and 574 Cataluña/Catalunya (1:400 000) or three Zoom maps nos 144 Pireneos Atlánticos, 145 Pireneos Centrales and 146 Pireneos Orientales (all 1:150 000). For maps that show topographical information the Instituto Geográfico 1:200 000 provincial maps will be required. The Footprint Guides to Northern Spain and Catalunya cover the route.

The climate at the western end of the Pyrenees is largely driven by Atlantic weather systems resulting in mild wet winters and warm summers. The figures for Pamplona/Iruñea (466m) just south of Stage 2 reflect this. Moving east the climate becomes warmer and drier as reflected in the figures for Lérida/Lleida (203m), just south of Stage 8. Closer to the Mediterranean coast the temperatures moderate slightly and there is a small increase in rainfall. Most of the route is above 800m, rising to 1500m, so expect temperatures to be cooler than those given as height is gained. See 'Climate details' box (left) for temperature and rainfall information.

The Pyrenean mountains, stretching for 450km from the Atlantic Ocean to the Mediterranean Sea, form the mountainous border between Spain and the rest of Europe. This largely unspoilt wilderness provides excellent cycling over high passes and along wide valleys.

STAGE 1
San Sebastián to Leitza

Distance	49km (30.4 miles)
Type	Ascent up valley
Climb	710m (2330ft)
Cycling time	4hr 10min

This route provides an excellent way of getting away from the coastal plain and into the mountains. The alternative route follows the Río Urumea and is also worth doing.

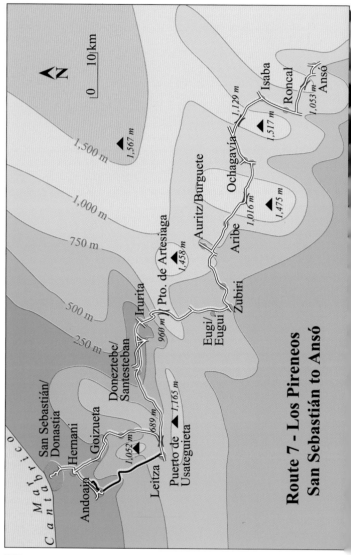

**Route 7 - Los Pireneos
San Sebastián to Ansó**

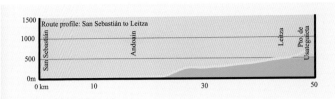

The stage is described from San Sebastián/Donastia to the Puerto de Usateguieta just beyond Leitza on the main route (where it meets the optional route). It uses the Andoain to Lekunberri Vía Verde. The disused railway trackbed has undergone a great deal of improvement and is perfectly rideable with a consolidated grit surface. There are several tunnels, up to 400m in length, only one of which is lit; the others are pitch black inside so some form of illumination is required. There are puddles and cow muck on the unimproved sections. The Vía Verde continues beyond Leitza, and features a 2.6km-long tunnel.

The route starts outside the main railway station in San Sebastián on the Paseo de Francia. Facing away from the station, turn left to join the one-way system. Turn first right and cross the river. Once across, turn first right to parallel the river then turn right again to recross the river. Having returned to the east bank take the first right fork (passing the road with the railway station) to join the dual carriageway that passes over the railway. Continue on this road as it bends sharp right into the Paseo Duque de Mandas. At the far end it bends left to become the Calle de Eguia, which in turn bends right and then left. One more right turn takes it across the river, followed by a left turn. Pass under the motorway, then turn left at the roundabout onto the Calle Sierra de Aralar. Pass under the railway. Continue to the T-junction and turn left.

Continue straight ahead on this road (Paseo Aintzieta then Martutene) and pass under the E80. At the first roundabout take the turn for Astigarraga and Hernani, at the second continue straight ahead, at the third turn right to **Hernan**i and at the fourth continue straight ahead and under the motorway. After the motorway continue

Vía Verde, Leizarán Valley, prior to improvements

straight ahead at all roundabouts. The third roundabout is where the road option to Leitza starts. Continue straight ahead taking the cycle-path to the left, cross the river and into Hernani. At the end of the cycle-path turn left, opposite the monastery, heading south-west. You may have to dismount. At the second plaza pass through the arch and continue straight ahead on Lizarraga Kalea to leave town. Pass over the motorway. Pass through Urnieta towards **Andoain** and at the second large roundabout turn left before bending right to parallel the railway to the right. After 1.5km on this road turn left before the large house with the balcony, turning right immediately behind it onto the red cycle-path. Follow this cycle-path into Andoain. There is a short road section before it restarts offset to the right at a T-junction. Continue to its end where it crosses the road to a red-brick path that climbs and becomes the Vía Verde.

Continue straight ahead, giving way to pedestrians. The route soon passes through the first of many tunnels and across the first of many bridges. In places the tunnels have collapsed and alternative tracks have been made. The Vía Verde follows the Río Leizarán which has cut a steep and now wooded valley, very pretty and quiet, with the river adding to the tranquillity. There are too many bridges and tunnels to keep count.

At some unmarked point the route leaves Guipúzcoa and enters Navarre. After 20km pass the electricity station and go onto the narrow asphalt road. Pass twice under the motorway. Where the asphalt track descends sharply take the narrow, level track on the left. Continue on the Vía Verde to the disused railway station. Turn right onto the road that becomes asphalt and leads downhill. Turn left at the T-junction and continue into the town centre.

From the centre of **Leitza** take the Doneztebe road for a bendy 5km climb to the **Puerto de Usateguieta** and the pensión Basa Kabi, where this stage finishes.

STAGE 2
Leitza to Auritz/Burguete

Distance	91km (56.5 miles)
Type	Valley and mountain passes
Climb	1223m (4013ft)
Cycling time	5hr 50min

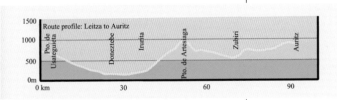

Head east from the Puerto de Usateguieta along the wooded ridge that overlooks the valley of the Río Urumea. The road soon starts a long and often twisty course down to the floor of a large and partly wooded valley that broadens as it descends through pasture and fields. Pass through the stone-built villages of Ezkurra, Lazorbian, Zubieta, Ituren and Elgorriaga before arriving at **Doneztebe/Santesteban** at the bottom. Pass through Doneztebe. Cross the river and turn right at the T-junction towards Pamplona/Iruña on the NA-1210 in a wide valley surrounded by wooded hills. In Oronoz-Mugairi continue straight ahead towards Elizondo. Turn left at the T-junction with the N121B again towards Elizondo.

On the N121B pass north of Arraioz and into **Irurita**. Turn right towards Berroeta and Eugi, and after a short distance turn left on the NA174 heading south. The road starts

Beech forest, Puerto de Artesiaga

in a flat-bottomed valley with steep sides, but soon starts its climb through a mixture of pasture and forest. As height is gained the big mountains ahead can be seen. There are extensive beechwoods. At the **Puerto de Artesiaga** (960m) expect to find grazing horses. The descent is initially steep through beech and conifer woods. At the T-junction turn right and pass the Embalse de Eugi on the right. Pass the villages of **Eugi/Eugui** and Urtasun. The descent ends in the village of **Zubiri**. Turn left at the T-junction.

The road climbs through conifers to a low pass (730m) before a gentle descent through Erro in a wide valley with lush pastures. Soon woods are again encountered before passing Bizkarreta-Guerendiain. The road continues its climb up through Aurizberri/Auzperri towards Auritz/Burguete. After Aurizberri-Espinal ignore the two significant right turns (the second of which is used on the next stage). Continue the climb to **Auritz/Burguete** (800m) where this stage ends; this height becomes the base altitude for the remainder of the route.

STAGE 3
Auritz/Burguete to Ansó

Distance	85km (52.8 miles)
Type	Across valleys and passes
Climb	1129m (3704ft)
Cycling time	5hr 40min

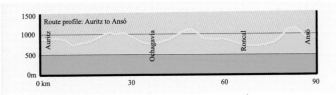

From Auritz/Burguete return down the valley and turn left at the first significant left turn towards Garralda on the

Aribe

NA140. The valley bottom is full of fields surrounded by steep wooded hillsides with limestone crags breaking out on the ridges. Pass Garralda. The valley narrows and the road drops to **Aribe** before climbing again. The vegetation becomes scrubbier as the road climbs along the foot of cliffs through the villages of Garaioa and Abaurrea Baja to peak at Abaurrea Alta. Looking north there are huge limestone cliffs in the distance. This is a country of high pasture. The road dips, then climbs again before descending through Jaurrieta to the Valle de Salazar with a twisty descent through pine forest into Ezcároz.

In the valley bottom turn left at the T-junction in Ezkaroze-Escároz. Head north in this narrow valley. The road bends right to pass through **Ochagavía-Otsagabia**, a very pretty riverside, stone-built mountain village. The road climbs through Izalzu and into the pine forest. About 5km from Izalzu bend right for the twisty ascent to the Puerto de Laza (1129m), with good views of mountains to the north and hills elsewhere. The most distinct peak is the layer-cake mountain of Oroel south of Jaca. The forest continues and the road descends through the village of Uztárroz-Uztarrotze to **Isaba**. Turn right at the T-junction in Isaba and descend through the wooded

Puerto de Laza

gorge of the Río Esca with sheer limestone cliffs and rock stacks. Pass through **Roncal-Erronkari** where the gorge widens temporarily; 1.5km beyond Roncal-Erronkari turn left into another gorge. It is as if the roads have had to squeeze between the blocks of mountains.

Pass through the village of Garde. From here the climb is long and challenging. The road climbs to the wooded ridge (1153m) where it enters the province of Huesca. Ignore the right turn to Fago. The steep descent is on a poor road into the **Valle de Ansó** and the village for which it is named.

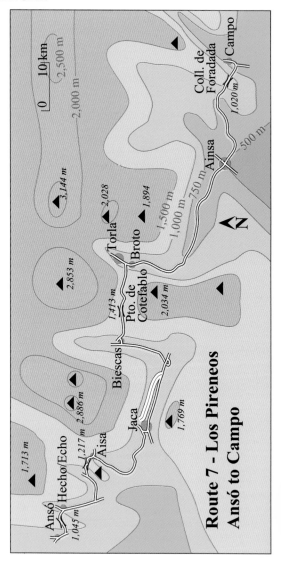

Route 7 - Los Pireneos
Ansó to Campo

STAGE 4
Ansó to Jaca

Distance	67km (41.6 miles)
Type	Passes and valleys
Climb	801m (2628ft)
Cycling time	4hr 55min

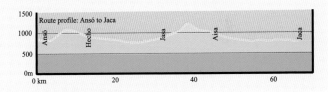

Leave Ansó heading south and down the valley, which narrows considerably. After 2km bend left into a steep-sided limestone valley and pass through two tunnels. Continue to climb through low pine-covered hills to a col (1045m) before descending into the **Valle de Hecho/Echo**. In the village of **Hecho/Echo** turn right at the T-junction. Proceed down the broad valley surrounded by wooded hills. Ignore the left turn to Urdués. The valley narrows to a gorge for a section. Take the left turn to Jasa. The road climbs the valley that narrows and then broadens as it follows the braided Río Osia. After 6km on this road turn right for a steep twisty climb through the pretty village of Jasa. Keep alert for the signs to **Aisa**. The road beyond the village is a badly maintained asphalt *pista forestal* that degrades to shale at times. The climb is steep and twisty in places, through scrubby pine forest, and reaches a pass at 1217m. The descent is again twisty but with views to the north of the snow-capped mountains around the ski resort of Candanchu.

Continue the descent, cross the river and pass through Aisa. Beyond the village turn right and continue down the broad valley, with lush pastures. As the road descends it crosses and recrosses the braided river, an indication of its juvenile nature. Continue into **Jaca**, ignoring the turn-off to Esposa, Sinués and Tieras, before passing by Novés. Enter Jaca across the Puente San Miguel and along the Paseo de la Constitución. The town centre is straight ahead.

Jaca is the first big town since leaving San Sebastián and has all the rest and recovery facilities needed after some hard riding. There are many hotels and restaurants, but most importantly there is a very good bike shop. The two big tourist attractions are the cathedral and the 16th-century fort, the Ciudadela.

Around Jaca

Cycling: the San Juan loop may be of interest. Head south out of town and follow the gaudy pink signs to the Monasterio de San Juan de la Peña. The road skirts Oroel (1769m) and visits the monastery built into the base of an impressively large cliff (hence the name) – it is a very pretty spot. Return via Santa Cruz de la Serós. On this ride expect to see black kites and lammergeiers.

STAGE 5
Jaca to Broto

Distance	55km (34.2 miles)
Type	Valley and mountain pass
Climb	599m (1965ft)
Cycling time	3hr 50min

From the centre of Jaca head south, taking any of the roads in that general direction. At the southern bypass on the edge of town turn left towards Sabiñánigo. The N330 is a relatively busy level road through large fertile fields on the terraces of the Río Gas. Keep to the N330 ignoring all options to join the A23 motorway. Ignore the turn off for

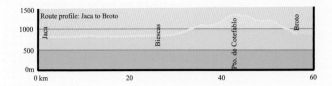

Baraguás, Espuéndolas, Borrés and then Sabiñánigo after the roads merge.

After a small rise turn right where the road is signposted to Biescas, doubling back under the main road. The road now heads north into the Valle de Tana, paralleling the Río Gállego, with big, pointy snow-covered mountains ahead. Around 11.5km along this road turn right into **Biescas**. Bear right in the town centre, cross the river and keep heading east to leave the town. At the T-junction on the outside of town turn right. Pass through Gavin. The road climbs along the valley side on a terrace with a gorge in the bottom, then enters pine forest. Pass through the tunnel and pass Yésero perched on a terrace on the far side of the gorge. The climb steepens before the **Puerto de Cotefablo** (1413m), located inside a tunnel. Descend without interruption to Broto and beyond. Pass

Linás de Broto

211

through Linás de Broto, where the road crosses a wide, flat valley floor with impressively terraced fields above. Shortly after, the floor of the Valle de Solana is visible well below. Ignore the turn-offs for Viu, Fragén and **Torla** before the hairpin descent into **Broto**.

STAGE 6
Broto to Campo

Distance	72km (44.7 miles)
Type	Valley descent and pass
Climb	451m (1478ft)
Cycling time	4hr 45min

Leave Broto on the through road, heading south along the Valle de Solana following the Río Ara. The valley is broad, with terraced slopes and wooded hills above; the pointy mountains bordering France are to the north.

Continue on this road ignoring the turns for Oto, Buesa, Sarvisé, Asín, Fiscal and Javierre. Beyond Javierre the river cuts a *garganta* (throat) through a ridge of hills, upended limestone beds interspersed with softer shale resulting in huge ribs of rock protruding from the hillside. The road is cut into the valley side and passes through two tunnels, after which the valley widens.

Pass through the southern edge of Boltaña where the valley broadens considerably. Continue on this road into **Ainsa**. At the crossroads continue straight ahead and cross the wide, braided Río Cinca that feeds into the

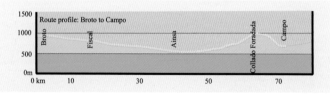

Garganta del Río Ara

Embalse de Mediano. As the road climbs slowly from the river terraces the landscape changes to that of dark shale with the odd band of limestone; the hills are badly eroded and the soils poor. Continue along the main road, ignoring the turns for El Puego, Usana, Gerbe, Arro, Fosado, Fuendecampo and Samper. As the **Collado Foradada** (1020m) is approached cliffs of upended limestone beds, often eroded to thin blades, rise out of the shale.

Descend from the Collado and pass through the village of Foradada. The road continues under the limestone ridge and through the shale badlands to end in the limestone gorge of the Río Esera. Keep on the main road as it bends left to Campo. Pass through the tunnel (800m) to Campo or consider going left on the remnants of the old road. Due to lack of maintenance the old road will become unusable.

STAGE 7
Campo to Pont de Suert

Distance	56km (34.7 miles)
Type	Valley and high passes
Climb	855m (2805ft)
Cycling time	4hr 5min

An alternative route from Campo is to take the road east through Aguascaldas, Egea and Villacarli. Then turn north through Beranuy and Bonansa. The Coll de Bonansa is 1380m. At the N-260 turn right to rejoin the main route. Recommended for its mountain scenery and canyons. There is a camp site at Bonansa.

Leave Campo on the through road, heading north, that gradually climbs along the bottom of the steep limestone valley by the river. Once again upended limestone beds form ribs that stand proud of the pine-covered hillsides. After passing a small *embalse* the road enters a narrow, deep, and sheer-sided limestone gorge cut by the Río Esera; a ledge has been carved for the road. The gorge gradually opens out into a wide basin containing the village of Seira, where there is an *embalse* and terraced fields sitting on eroded gravel beds. Pass through Seira, up the short, sharp climb and through the tunnel. Enter the impressive canyon of Congosto de Ventamillo. After a couple of kilometres the canyon opens to lush countryside

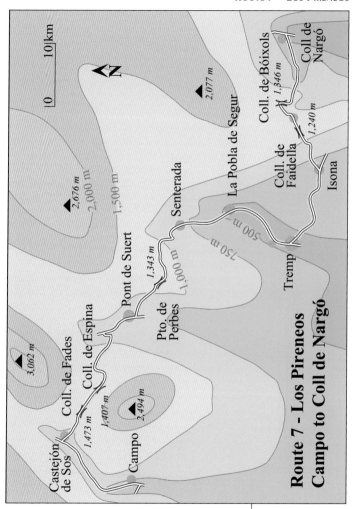

**Route 7 - Los Pireneos
Campo to Coll de Nargó**

surrounded by mountains. Pass through El Run, and after 1.2km turn right. Climb through the mountain resort of **Castejón de Sos**.

The shady subterranean route has now been left behind. Continue the climb through lush hillsides with excellent panoramas. Pass through Bisaurri, followed by hairpin climbs through fields and pinewoods. The views improve all the while. The road peaks at the **Coll de Fades** (1473m) and more or less maintains its lofty position, passing through coniferous and deciduous woods interspersed with pasture on hills of all sizes. Pass through the village of Laspaúles where the red shale makes the area appear messy. Climb to the **Coll de Espina** (1407m), after which the route is downhill, passing the fortified hamlet of Senin as the road switches back on itself. Continue the descent into the Vall del Noguera Ribagorçana and cross the river of the same name. Turn right at the T-junction. Pass through Les Bordes, heading south in a valley of varying width with limestone outcrops, and enter **Pont de Suert**.

STAGE 8
Pont de Suert to Tremp

This stage leaves the Pyrenees proper, but not its influence; the mountains return with an exhilarating vengeance in the following stage. This is one of the few stages on this route that connects with the railway system.

Distance	54km (33.5 miles)
Type	Mountain pass and valley
Climb	601m (1972ft)
Cycling time	3hr 50min

Leave Pont de Suert, heading south on the through road. After 1km turn left onto the N260 to pass around the top of the Pantà (*embalse*) d'Escale. The road remains level as far as the road tunnel. Pass through the tunnel and

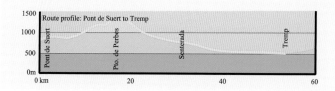

climb through Viu de Llevata (which erroneously claims to be at 1325m) before reaching the **Puerto de Perbes/ Perves** (1343m).

Descend, ignoring the turns for Perbes and Sarroca de Bellera. In the valley pass through the tunnel and cross the river several times. Continue down the valley into **Senterada**, ignoring the turn to La Pobleta de Bellveí. This is the wide valley of the Río El Flamisell, which narrows to a limestone gorge with tunnel. The valley widens again before **La Pobla de Segur** with its railway terminus. Ignore the turn to Claverol, and continue south down the western side of the Pantà de Sant Antoni. Continue south and downhill in a very wide valley; ignore the turns for Sant Joan and Salàs, then Talarn (perched on a cliff). Having left the *pantà* behind enter **Tremp**.

STAGE 9
Tremp to Coll de Nargó

Distance	61km (37.9 miles)
Type	Plain and mountain passes
Climb	1000m (3281ft)
Cycling time	4hr 20min

This stage continues outside the mountains at first, and visits 'the land of dinosaurs' before climbing back to high mountain valleys.

From the centre of Tremp take the C1412, heading east. The road drops to cross a canal before beginning a relentless climb back into the mountains over large plateaux and through eroded valleys. The subsoil is gravel, washed out from the mountains to produce

Coll de Bóixols

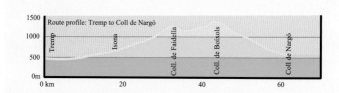

Route profile: Tremp to Coll de Nargó

fertile fields below infertile valley slopes. Pass through Vilamitjana, ignoring the turns for Gavet, Suterranya, Sant Salvador and Orcau. Turn left to pass through Figuerola D'Orcau then Conques before climbing to **Isona**, set among orchards and almond groves. In the village turn left.

Just 3km beyond Isona (opposite the turn for Abella) there is a right turn signed to the Ermita La Posa. ▶

Continue upwards on the main road from this junction, heading east. The road climbs above a gorge as the rugged mountains come in from the north. Ignore the turn for Siall, and continue up through pinewoods to the **Coll de Faidella** (1240m). From here there are spectacular views north to the limestone mountains. The road enters spectacular limestone country, descending along the north side of a very steep-sided, deep valley. Pass through the stone village of Bóixols, located in a col. Continue along the terraced valley beneath limestone cliffs before bending right to climb steeply through pinewoods to the **Coll de Bóixols** (1380m).

The road drops slightly before climbing to a saddle with a turn for Gavarra. Ignore this turn and descend through pine and deciduous woods along the northern edge of the sheer-sided *cañon* of the Riu Valldarques. Eventually the road descends the *cañon* side before it narrows to a tight gorge. Beyond this the country opens out to a rural scene of fields and pasture with a mountain vista straight ahead. Continue into the town of **Coll de Nargó** with its fine Romanesque church.

Turn right towards Ermita La Posa for 1.5km if you want to see the dinosaur footprints, visible on an exposed inclined limestone bedding plane located just below the *ermita*.

219

STAGE 10
Coll de Nargó to Berga

This stage is not the longest, but is the hilliest, making it probably the hardest day on the entire route. At the same time it is the most rewarding.

Distance	84km (52.2 miles)
Type	High mountains
Climb	1533m (5029ft)
Cycling time	5hr 50min

From the Romanesque church head east and south of Coll de Nargó. At the T-junction turn left, and beyond the end of the *embalse* turn right, onto the L-401 to Sant Llorenç. The road climbs in a steep wooded valley beside a braided river. Pass the turn to Perles where the landscape changes to bare limestone. Pass through the five tunnels. The road clings to an ledge cut out of the cliffs above a gorge, but before long terraced fields appear as the valley opens out. Pass through Alinyà (ignoring the turn for Llobera) and double back for the twisty climb up the valley side. Pass through the saddle that leads to good views to the west and south. Continue the climb and pass **Llinars** before descending into the head of a high valley that soon becomes a cañón. Pass through Cambrils. From here to the **Collado de Jeu/Jou** the road remains high, traversing under limestone cliffs to the north, while to the south there is a heavily eroded plateau of aggregate grits and gravels.

The town of Sant Llorenç has a superb position, in a deep bowl surrounded by hills with an *embalse* behind. The hills are wooded with mature pines, and the range to the south is a series of eroded upended limestone beds, reminiscent of the plates on a stegosaurus's back. Pray for good visibility.

Continue east on a relentless climb. The road is sometimes cut into the limestone cliffs, sometimes built on the grits. The cliffs are often enormous and at times recede north; the vegetation alternates between pines and pasture. The road occasionally diverts to cross rivers. The whole climb is spectacular and gentle except towards the end. At the Collado de Jeu (1466m) stop for a breather and take a good look down at the town of **Sant Llorenç.** Are there many places in such a setting? ◀

At the coll continue straight ahead at the bend right and then ignore the left turn for a hairpin descent into

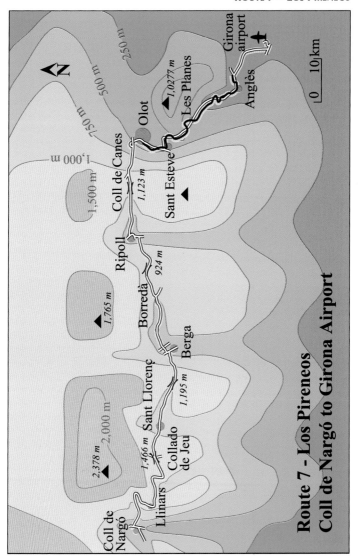

Route 7 - Los Pireneos
Coll de Nargó to Girona Airport

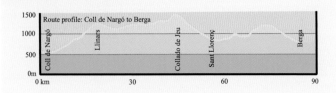

Sant Llorenç. In the centre of town turn right at the junction of main roads and continue the descent. Ignore the turn-off to Solsana and cross the Pantà de Llosa del Cavall. Pass the pulp factory. The road heads east for a gradual but undulating climb in the valley of the Aigua de Valls before passing through a gap in the hills to cross the Riu Aigua de Llinars. Wooded plate-shaped hills continue along the southern side of the valley. Pass the turn for Llinars, climb via hairpin bends and through the tunnel to the unmarked Pont de Llinars (1195m).

From here the road keeps to the hillside, but the valley to the south is more open. Some 7km beyond the tunnel the road descends a long north–south cliff line through evergreen oaks to the floor of what is either a huge valley or an incursion of plain into the mountains; the change in landscape is abrupt. The road continues downhill to **Berga**. Continue to the T-junction before turning right and downhill into town.

STAGE 11
Berga to Olot

Distance	73km (45.3 miles)
Type	Valleys with passes
Climb	569m (1867ft)
Cycling time	4hr 45min

Leave Berga by retracing the route back to the T-junction. At the junction continue straight on, heading north. After

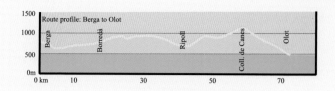

a short distance keep right and to Vilada and Ripoll. Pass under the E9/C16. Pass through wooded hills before crossing, then paralleling, the Pantà de la Baélls. From here the road climbs gently for the next 20km, mostly in a valley surrounded by wooded hills, made up of inclined rocks so that where bluffs combine with scarp and back slopes it appears that giant frogs surmount the hills. As there are no giant flies around here the appearance maybe more than fanciful...

Pass through Vilada and continue up the valley to **Borredà**. The chain of wooded hills continues to the south. Pass through Borredà and ignore the turn to Sant Jaume. About 2km after Borredà bend left after a climb through pine forest. The countryside is a mixture of pines and lush pasture with the hills continuing to the south. The road climbs to 918m before dropping, only to climb back to 924m. From this second rise continue the descent to the Riu El Ter valley.

At the T-junction turn left to **Ripoll**. At the second roundabout on the approach to Ripoll turn right. The road bends left and passes under the railway. Turn right onto the Carretera D'Olot. Climb along the northern side of the valley, heading east. The valley is wide with lush green pasture on the lower slopes and mixed woods higher up, very pleasing to the eye. The road peaks at the **Coll de Canes** (1123m) before the descent to Olot. Pass through the Coll de Coubet (1010m) and ignore the turn to Sant Joan. The descent is through enormous deciduous forests of beech, oak and evergreen oak on ridges that connect the plain with the mountains proper. Approaching **Olot** on the plain turn left to double back under the northern bypass, and enter the town.

223

Olot is the first large town since Jaca. It has a pleasant town centre, and plenty of accommodation that tends to get booked up at weekends. The Hostal Restaurante Sant Bernat is particularly recommended for good-value local cooking and accommodation. It has a secure garage for bicycles and its literature displays the international sign for such a facility.

Around Olot

The reason for the town's popularity is the nearby Parc Natural de la Zona Volcànica de la Garrotxa (*garrotxa* = twisted earth). The Parc contains the only evidence of volcanic activity in mainland Spain. There are a large number of cones made of volcanic ash, many of which are wooded and have well-signed walking itineraries. Leaflets are widely available.

STAGE 12
Olot to Girona airport

The Vía Verde makes use of a disused railway line that is generally easy to follow, but has been disrupted in places as towns have expanded. The track surface is generally very good.

Distance	64km (39.7 miles)
Type	Hills and valley plain
Climb	223m (732ft)
Cycling time	4hr 30min

This final stage follows the well-used Vía Verde between Olot and Gerona/Girona to just beyond Anglés/Anglès before seeking quiet roads to the airport. The opportunity may be taken to visit Girona or continue to the coast, but these options are not described. Option 2 uses the asphalt roads.

Return to the road into Olot from the bypass (at the end of the previous stage) and head south along it towards the town centre. Keep to the road as it bends left to head east. Turn right signed to Vic on the C152 heading south. Cross the appropriately named Río el Fluvia. Immediately across the river turn right down a back street beside it, signposted as the start of the Vía Verde.

Pass below a large pink building that was the railway station. At the road go straight ahead with a slight stagger to the left. The Vía Verde passes along a cutting through basalt. Pass the all-weather running track and then the renovated railway station. Cross the road. Approaching Les Preses continue straight ahead when the track becomes a road. Turn first left, and at the end cross the main road to rejoin the track. Bend right and continue straight ahead at the road. Turn left at the T-junction along the road that bends right before ending. The track restarts.

Cross the two roads, then pass under the main road to approach **Sant Esteve**. Cross the road and onto the end of the track. Continue straight ahead on the road, and at the T-junction turn left, then right, followed by a left bend. Where the road bends left a second time, take the track to the right followed by a left bend. Cross the stream and bend left, followed by a right. At the *fuente* turn right. The track bends gently left to the main road. Cross the main road. The track loops right back to the road before looping away again. When the track loops

Vía Verde, Olot

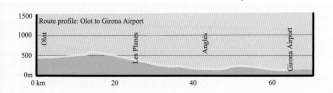

back to the road a second time, take the lay-by that used to be the main road.

The old road climbs over the new road on a ridge at 575m. The new road makes use of the old trackbed and tunnel underneath the pass. When the old road nears the new take the track that climbs briefly. Cross the next two roads and approach Sant Feliu. The track becomes a road for a short distance. Continue straight ahead at the crossroads behind the buildings and under the bridge. The road ends and the track takes over. The track crosses two bridges and exits Sant Feliu. Once again the track crosses under the main road. Cross the next road, pass over the river on the old railway bridge, cross the next road and join the road that stops in front of the Bar La Caseta in **Les Planes**.

Continue along the track to the left of the bar; it continues for some 8km before again becoming a road. After 300m turn right. When it loops back to the road turn right onto the lay-by/old road for a short distance before turning sharp right onto a track. Follow the track through the woods and across the road. Descend the steep concrete track and turn right at the bottom. The Vía Verde bends left and descends to the main road. Cross the main road. The track loops back under the road. At the end turn left onto the road, cross the river and repass under the main road. Just before the main road is rejoined turn left onto the straight track that passes the former station of El Pasteral. The track passes through Cellera de Ter, crossing two roads as it does so.

Approaching **Anglès** the track turns to concrete as it approaches a large roundabout. The Vía Verde skirts the town on the town side of the bypass before crossing to the north side of the road. Pass the two small roundabouts and 2.9km from the large Anglès roundabout turn right to Estanyol heading south. The road climbs as it bends through the woods. Pass through Estanyol, and at the T-junction turn left then right soon after towards Salitja. Bypass Salitja. At the T-junction turn left and follow this road for 700m before turning left. At the roundabout turn left and enter the airport to finish the route.

OPTION 1
Hernani to Leitza

Distance	40km (24.8 miles)
Type	Ascent up valley
Climb	721m (2366ft)
Cycling time	2hr 50min

This option can be used instead of the Vía Verde described in Stage 1; like the first stage, it ends at the Puerto de Usateguieta. It is worth cycling in its own right.

The option starts at the roundabout east of Hernani as described in Stage 1. Turn left heading south, continue straight ahead at the next roundabout and pass under the motorway. At the next roundabout take the second exit to Goizueta on the GI-3410. Keep to this road which becomes the NA-4150. The route is easy to follow, as there are no turns until the Puerto de Usateguieta. The road follows the Río Urumea up a peaceful and beautiful wooded valley, and passes through the villages of Ereñou, Pagoaga and **Goizueta/ Gozuolo**. Apart from a little industry near Hernani the valley is unspoilt, with the river adding sparkle and focus to the scene. The climb is initially very gentle, but steepens up considerably beyond Goizueta. The village is worth a visit with its mix of stone and half-timbered buildings. The hotel Bata Kabi sits at the **Puerto de Usateguieta** adjacent to the road junction, with the main route coming in from the right.

Route profile: Hernani to Puerto de Usateguieta

OPTION 2
Olot to Anglès

This option uses the road to avoid the Vía Verde but is nowhere near as enjoyable as the off-road option.

Distance	39km (24.2 miles)
Type	Hills and valley plain
Climb	114m (374ft)
Cycling time	2hr 10min

Return to the road into Olot from the bypass (at the end of Stage 11) and head south along it towards the town centre. Keep to the road as it bends left to head east. Turn right (signed to Vic) on the C152, heading south. Cross the Río el Fluvia. Continue heading south and straight ahead at the roundabout on the town's southern bypass. Pass through Les Preses, and at the next roundabout (approaching Sant Esteve d'En Bas) turn left towards Sant Feliu. Pass through Sant Feliu, Les Planes, Amer, El Pasteral and Cellera de Ter. At the large roundabout on the approach to **Anglès** turn left.

Continue straight ahead at the two small roundabouts and 2.9km from the large Anglès roundabout turn right to Estanyol heading south. The road climbs as it bends through the woods. Pass through Estanyol, and at the T-junction turn left then right soon after towards Salitja. Bypass Salitja. At the T-junction turn left and follow this road for 700m before turning left. At the roundabout turn left and enter the **airport** to finish the route.

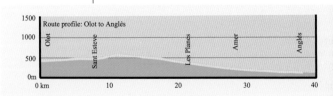

ACCOMMODATION ON OR CLOSE TO ROUTE 7

Please note that this is not an exhaustive list. Hotel guide prices are in Euros, based on a double room with an en suite bathroom at high season. Rooms without en suite are typically 20% cheaper, as are single rooms. Please note that hotels are constantly opening, closing or being refurbished; it is always advisable to book ahead. Prices (where known) are indicated as follows: (1) up to 50 Euros; (2) 50–75 Euros; (3) 75–100 Euros; (4) over 100 Euros.

San Sebastián/Donastia

There are some 45 hotels and pensiónes here; contact the Turismo at Boulevard, 8 (tel: 943 48 11 66, www.sansebastianturismo.com).

Hernani

(3) Pensión Zinkoenea, Mayor, 57 – 1o (tel: 670 39 08 97)

(2) Txintxua, Zikuñaga, 76 (tel: 943 33 36 80)

Urnieta

(2) Oianume, Calle de Ergoien Industrialdea, 18 (tel: 943 55 66 83)

(2) Pensión Guria, Calle de Idiazábal, 46 (tel: 943 00 56 50)

Leitza

(2) Jai-Alai, Polg. Ind. Landa, 23 (tel: 948 51 07 35)

(2) Basa Kabi, Ctra. Lecumberri – Hernani, km 17 (tel: 948 51 01 25)

(1) Musunzar, Elbarren, 14 (tel: 948 51 06 07)

Ezkurra

(1) Ezkurra, Asunción, 4 (tel: 948 61 50 80)

Zubieta

Herriko Ostatua, Mayor, 23 (tel: 948 45 17 71)

Ituren

(2) Plazaenea, Plaza de la Villa, 8 (tel: 948 45 00 18)

Doneztebe/Santesteban

(1) Ameztia, Ameztia, 31 – 1o (tel: 948 45 00 28)

(1) Santamaría, Mayor, 28 (tel: 948 45 00 43)

(1) Posada de Oitz, Calle Mayor, 1 (tel: 948 45 19 51)

Oronoz-Mugairi

(1) Urgain, Avda. Martín Urrutia s/n (tel: 948 59 20 63)

(1) Urgain II, Carretera de Pamplona, 0 (tel: 948 59 21 98)

Eugui-Eugi

(3) Mesón Quinto Real, Ctra. Pamplona-Francia, km 27 (tel: 948 30 40 44)

(2) Etxeberri, San Gil, 30 (tel: 948 30 44 54)

Zubiri

(4) Hostería de Zubiri, Avenida Roncesvalles, 6 (tel: 948 30 43 29)

(2) Gau Txori, Roncesvalles Etorbidea (tel: 948 30 40 76)

Erro

(2) Erro, Tr. Erro, 17 (tel: 948 76 81 20)

Auritzberri-Espinal

Hostal Haizea, Ctr. Pamplona – Valcarlos, km 41 (tel: 948 76 03 79)

Camping Urrobi, Ctra.N-135 Pamplona-Valcarlos, km 42 (tel: 948 76 02 00)

Auritz-Burguete

(3) Loizu, San Nicolás, 13 (tel: 948 76 00 08)

(2) Burguete, San Nicolás, 71 (tel: 948 76 00 05)

(1) Juandeaburre, San Nicolás, 28 (tel: 948 76 00 78)

(1) Don Jauregui, Calle de San Nicolás, 32 (tel: 948 76 00 31)

Aribe

(2) Aribe, Calle de Santa María, 33 (tel: 948 76 44 66)

Garaioa

(1) Pensión Lorea, Chiquirrín, s/n (tel: 948 76 40 48)

Abaurrea Baja

(2) Posada Sarigarri, Calle de San Martín, 1 (tel: 948 76 90 61)

Ochagavía-Otsagabia

(3) Auñamendi Plaza Gurpide, 1 (tel: 948 89 01 89)

Orialde, Urrutia, 6 (tel: 948 89 00 27)

Camping Osate, Ctra. Salazar (tel: 948 89 01 84)

Izalzu

(1) Hotel Rural Besaro, Calle Irigoien, 5 (tel: 948 89 03 50)

Isaba-Izaba

(2) Txiki, Mendigatxa, 17 (tel: 948 89 31 18)

(2) Ezkaurre, Garagardoia, 14 (tel: 948 89 33 03)

(2) Lola, Mendigatxa, 17 (tel: 948 89 30 12)

(2) Onki Xin, Izagentea, 25 (tel: 618 31 78 37)

(1) Casa Txarrantxulo, Burguíberria, 2 (tel: 948 89 32 81)

Camping Asolaze, Carretera Francia, km 39 (tel: 948 89 30 34)

Roncal-Erronkari

(2) Zaltua, Castillo, 23 (tel: 948 47 50 08)

Ansó

(2) Kimboa, Ctra. Zuriza (tel: 974 37 01 84)

(2) Posada Magoria, Calle Milagro, 32A (tel: 974 37 00 49)

(1) Aisa, Plaza Domingo Miral (tel: 974 37 00 09)

Camping Valle de Ansó, Extramuros, s/n (tel: 974 37 02 55)

Siresa

(2) Castillo D'Archer, Plaza Mayor, s/n (tel: 974 37 53 13)

Hecho-Echo

(2) Casa Blasquico, Pl. Palacio, 1 (tel: 974 37 50 07)
(2) Usón, Ctra. Selva de Oza, km 7 (tel: 974 37 53 58)
(2) De La Val, Cruz Alta, 1 (tel: 974 37 50 28)
(2) Lo Foratón 2, Urb. Cruz Alta, s/n (tel: 974 37 52 47)
Camping Borda Bisaltico, Ctra. Gabardito, km 2 (tel: 974 37 53 88)
Camping Valle de Hecho, Ctra. Puente de la Reina-Hecho (tel: 974 37 53 61)

Jaca

(3) Mur, Santa Orosia, 1 (tel: 974 36 01 00)
(3) La Paz, Mayor 41 (tel: 974 36 07 00)
(3) Charlé, Ctra. de Francia s/n, (tel: 974 36 00 44)
(3) Jaques, Unión Jaquesa, 4 (tel: 974 35 64 24)
(3) Somport, Echegaray, 11 (tel: 974 36 34 10)
(2) Pradas, Obispo, 12 (tel: 974 36 11 50)
(2) Ramiro I, Carmen, 23 (tel: 974 36 13 67)
(2) Ciudad de Jaca, Sancho Ramirez, 15 (tel: 974 36 43 11)
(2) A Nieu, Avenida Zaragoza, 22 (tel:974 36 16 79)
(2) Skipass, Mayor, 57 (tel: 974 36 43 19)
(1) París, Plaza San Pedro, 5 (tel: 974 36 10 20)
Camping Victoria, Avda. Victoria, 44 (tel: 974 35 70 08)
Camping Ain-Jaca, General, 5, Canfranc (tel: 656 47 77 12)

Senegüé

(2) Casbas, Unica (tel: 974 48 01 49)
Camping Valle de Tena, Calle del Acceso (tel: 974 48 09 77)

Biescas

(4) Los Jardines, Avda. Ramón y Cajal, 16 (tel: 974 49 55 55)
(2) Casa Ruba, Esperanza, 20 (tel: 974 48 50 01)
(2) La Rambla, Rambla de San Pedro, 7 (tel: 974 48 51 77)

Gavin

(3) Lausan, Avda. Ordesa, s/n (tel: 974 48 54 11)
Camping Gavin, Ctra. N-260, km 503 (tel: 974 48 50 90)

Linas de Broto

(2) Las Nieves, Avenida de Ordesa, s/n (tel: 974 48 61 09)
(1) Cazcarro, Ctra. Biescas, s/n (tel: 974 48 61 09)

Viu

Camping Viu, Carretera Nacional 260, (tel: 974 48 63 01)

Torla

(4) Villa Russell, Francia, s/n (tel: 974 48 67 70)
(4) Ordesa, Ctra. de Ordesa, s/n (tel: 974 48 61 25)
(2) Abetos, Ctra. Ordesa (tel: 974 48 64 48)
(2) Edelweiss, Ctra. Ordesa, s/n (tel: 974 48 61 73)
(2) Bujaruelo, Avenida de Ordesa, 5 (tel: 974 48 61 74)
(2) Villa de Torla, Plaza Nueva, 1 (tel: 974 48 61 56)
(2) Las Nieves, Avda. de Ordesa, s/n (tel: 974 48 61 09)
(1) Alto Aragón, Capuvita, s/n (tel: 974 48 61 72)
(1) Ballarín, Capuvita, 11 (tel: 974 48 61 55)
Camping Río Ara, Junto al Río Ara (tel: 974 48 62 48)
Camping San Anton, Ctra. Ordesa (tel: 974 48 60 63)
Camping Ordesa, Ctra. Ordesa, km 3 (tel: 974 48 61 46)
Camping San Nicolás de Bujaruelo, Bujaruelo (tel: 974 48 64 12)

Broto

(4) Pradas Ordesa, Avenida Ordesa, 7 (tel: 974 48 60 04)
(2) La Posada, Los Arcos, s/n (tel: 974 48 63 36)
(2) Sorrosal, Avenida Ordesa, 10 (tel: 974 48 60 10)
(1) Gabare, Avenida Ordesa, 6 (tel: 974 48 60 52)
El Mirador, Ctra. de Oto, km 0,7 (tel: 974 48 61 77)

Oto

Camping Oto, Ctra. N-260 Valle de Broto (tel: 974 48 60 75)

Fiscal

(2) Río Ara, Carretera, s/n (tel: 974 50 30 20)
(2) Casa Cardena, Alta, s/n (tel: 974 50 30 77)
Camping El Jabali Blanco, Ctra. N-260, km 463 (tel: 974 50 30 74)
Camping Ribera del Ara, Ctra. de Bergua, s/n (tel: 974 50 30 35)

Boltaña

Camping La Gorga, Av de Ordesa, (tel: 974 50 23 57)
Camping Boltaña, Ctra. N-260, km 442 (tel: 974 50 23 47)

Ainsa

(3)Dos Riós II, Avenida Central, 4 (tel: 974 50 09 61)
(3) Villa Románica, Santa Cruz, 21–23 (tel: 974 50 07 50)
(2) Apolo, Pineta, 4 (tel: 974 50 08 88)
(2) Dos Riós, Avenida Central, 2 (tel: 974 50 01 06)
(2) Mesón de L'Ainsa, Avenida Sobrarbe, 12 (tel: 974 50 00 28)
(2) Pireneos, Avenida Sobrarbe, 7 (tel: 974 50 00 08)
(2) Sánchez, Avenida Sobrarbe, 10 (tel: 974 50 00 14)

Campo

(3) Cotiella, Carretera Benasque s/n (tel: 974 55 03 03)

(2) Los Nogales, Nugueret, 30 (tel: 974 55 00 36)
(2) El Rebos de Campo, Ctra Benasque s/n (tel: 974 55 00 72)

Castejón de Sos

(2) Plaza, Plaza del Pilar, 2 (tel: 974 55 30 50)
(2) Pirineos, El Real, s/n (tel: 974 55 32 41)
(1) Casa Juan, Condes de Barcelona (tel: 974 55 35 42)
Camping Alto Esera, Afueras, s/n (tel: 974 55 34 56)

Laspaúles

Camping Laspaúles, Ctra. N-260, km 369 (tel: 974 55 33 20)

Bonansa

Camping Baliera, N-260, Km 355.5 (tel: 974 55 40 16)

Pont de Suert

(2) Can Mestre, Pl. Major, 8 (tel: 973 69 03 06)
(2) Hotel Flor De Neu, Calle Salencar, s/n (tel: 973 69 05 86)
(1) Canigó, Avenida Victoriá Muñoz, 16 (tel: 973 69 03 50)
(1) El Pedris, Canaleta, 9 (tel: 973 69 02 57)
(1) Fonda Isard, Carrer de Sant Aventí, 29A (tel: 973 69 01 39)
Camping Baliera, Carretera Nacional 260, Montanuy (tel: 974 55 40 16)

Senterada

(2) Casa Leonardo, Call La Bedoga, 2 (tel: 973 66 17 87)
Camping Senterada, Ctra. L-503, km 0.5 (tel: 973 66 18 18)

La Pobla de Segur

(3) Solé, Avinguda de l'Estació, 44 (tel: 973 68 04 52)
Fonda Can Fasersia, Major, 4 (tel: 695 169 181)

Talarn

(2) Casa Lola, Carrer Soldevila, 2 (tel: 973 65 08 14)
Camping Gasset, Ctra. C-147, km 57 (tel: 973 65 07 37)

Tremp

(2) Segle XX, Plaça de la Creu, 8 (tel: 973 65 00 00)
(1) Alegret, Plaça de la Creu, 30 (tel: 973 65 01 00)

Vilamitjana

(2) Nerets, Avinguda de Catalunya, 20 (tel: 973 65 17 22)

Coll de Nargó

Pensión Del Llac, Ctra. de la Seu, s/n (tel: 973 38 30 22)
Betriu, Carretera C-14 KM 156.4 (tel: 973 38 30 20)

Organyà

(2) Dom, Ctra. de Lleida, 56 (tel: 973 38 35 13)
Camping Organyà, Calle Piscina, s/n (tel: 973 38 20 39)

Fígols i Alinyà
(2) Cal Celso, Carrer Sol, s/n (tel: 973 37 00 92)

Cambrils
Camping La Comella, Camí de Cambrils a Solsona, (tel: 973 48 90 27)

Sant Llorenç de Morunys
(3) El Monegal, Monegal, s/n (tel: 973 49 23 69)
(2) Casa Joan, Ctra. de la Coma, 12 (tel: 973 49 20 55)
(2) Piteus, Ctra. Berga, 11 (tel: 973 49 23 40)
(1) La Catalana, Plaça Doctor Ferran, 1 (tel: 973 49 22 72)
Camping Morunys, Ctra. Coma, km 1.5 (tel: 973 49 22 13)

Berga
(3) Cal Nen, Drecera de Queralt, s/n (tel: 938 21 00 27)
(3) Arumì, Ctra. Arbúcies, 1–5 (tel: 938 89 53 32)
(2) Berga Park, Ctra. de Solsona, 1-A (tel: 938 21 66 66)
(2) Estel, Ctra. Sant Fruitós, 36 (tel: 938 21 34 63)
Queralt, Plaça de la Creu, 4 (tel: 938 21 06 11)
Camping Berga Resort, C-16, km 96.3 (tel: 938 21 12 50)

Borredà
Cal Bardolet, Plaça Major, 7 (tel: 629 65 56 74)

Ripoll
(3) Pensión La Trobada, Pg. Honorat Vilamayor, 5 (tel: 972 70 23 53)
(3) Hostal Del Ripollès, Plaça Nova, 11 (tel: 972 70 02 15)
Camping Solana de Ter, Ctra. N-152 Barcelona – Puigcerdá, km 104 (tel: 972 70 10 62)

Olot
(3) Borrell, Nònit Escubós, 8 (tel: 972 27 61 61)
(2) La Perla, Ctra. La Deu, 9 (tel: 972 26 23 26)
(2) Olot, Sant Pere Màrtir, 29 (tel: 972 26 12 12)
(2) Sant Bernat, Ctra. De Les Feixes, 29–31 (tel: 972 26 19 19)
(1) Amolls, Avet, 33 (tel: 972 26 75 21)
Camping Les Tries, Avinguda de Pere Badosa (tel: 972 26 24 05)
Camping La Fageda, Ctra. Olot-Santa Pau, km 3.5 (tel: 972 27 12 39)

Sant Feliu de Pallerols
Fonda Finet, Sant Antoni, 3 (tel: 972 44 40 24)
Camping Vall D'Hosteles, Playa de Bastons (tel: 972 44 41 04)

Anglès
(1) Fonda Tarres, Plaza de Catalunya, 5 (tel: 972 42 13 14)
(1) Massot, Industria, 62 (tel: 972 42 00 07)

ROUTE 8
PICOS DE EUROPA

ROUTE SUMMARY

From	To	km	Type	Cycling time
Llanes	Cangas de Onis	45	Hills then valley	3hr 10min
Cangas de Onis	Posada de Valdeón	62	Valley and mountain pass	4hr 15min
Posada de Valdeón	Potes	58	High passes/descent	3hr 45min
Potes	Llanes	88	Valley then hills	5hr 50min
Option 1 Pto de Pandetrave	Potes	36	Short climb, long descent	2hr 05min
Option 2 Puertos de Aliva loop		74	Big mountains then valley	6hr 20min
Option 3 Covadonga		40	One climb, then reverse	2hr 55min

The Picos de Europa are a group of spectacular limestone mountains extending north from the midpoint of the Cordillera Cantábrica. Starting 10km from the sea and measuring a compact 40km west to east and 25km north to south, the range is an exhilarating collection of well-defined peaks, deep gorges and lush high pastures. The Picos comprise three massifs (from west to east): El Cornión; Los Urrieles, containing Torre Cerredo (2648m); and Andara. Bounding the massifs are deep gorges. The Parque Nacional Los Picos de Europa encompasses most of the area.

As well as hosting the usual mountain activities the Picos are also a magnet for naturalists. The hay meadows are rich in flowers and a botanical wonder in late May and early June. The nutrient-poor soil provides perfect conditions for a multitude of meadow plants, and dozens of species of orchids have been recorded. There is a huge number and variety of butterflies. Birds include

ROUTE 8: CLIMATE DETAILS

	Jan	Feb	Mar	Apr	May	Jun	Jul	Aug	Sep	Oct	Nov	Dec
León												
av min temp °C	-1	-1	2	4	6	10	12	12	10	6	2	0
av max temp °C	7	9	13	16	19	24	28	27	23	18	12	7
rainfall mm	57	41	61	43	53	39	17	16	39	48	55	65
Santander												
av min temp °C	7	7	8	10	11	14	16	16	15	12	10	8
av max temp °C	12	12	14	15	17	20	22	22	21	18	15	12
rainfall mm	119	88	78	83	89	63	54	84	114	133	125	129
Bilbao												
sunrise	08:46	08:27	07:48	07:53	07:05	06:35	06:35	07:01	07:36	08:09	07:47	08:25
sunset	17:45	18:21	19:00	20:37	21:13	21:45	21:55	21:33	20:48	19:53	18:05	17:39
Best time	–	–	G	G	VG	VG	G	G	VG	G	G	–

(G = good time to go; VG = best time to go)

Public holidays
Cantabria: 15 September
Asturias: 8 September
León: 23 April, 2 May, 29 June and 5 October

griffon vultures, golden and booted eagles, house and crag martins, buzzards and harriers; there are wolves, bears, boars and chamois.

The route starts and finishes in Llanes on the coast. There are no really convenient airports for the Picos, but Llanes has a railway station and a couple of car hire agencies making connections with Bilbao possible. One-way car hire is probably the best way of getting to the Picos, and Llanes is the only town in the area with such agencies. The route circumscribes the Picos in an anticlockwise direction where road cycling is possible. Access to the heart of the mountains requires 'there and back' excursions, off-road cycling or walking options. The main route is cyclable on virtually any type of bicycle, as is the Covadonga option. However, the Puerto de Pandetrave and Puertos de Aliva options require at least a very robust road bike or hybrid.

There are several relevant maps, of which the best is the 1:80 000 Picos de Europa published by Adrados Ediciones. It is available outside Spain and sold widely within the Picos. Other maps include the Instituto Geográfico Nacional 1:200 000 Mapa Guía Cordillera Cantábrica. The Michelin 1:250 000 Regional Map 572 Asturias Cantabria is adequate for the road options only. The best guidebooks are available locally and are often written in Spanish.

Located close to Spain's northern coast, the Picos experience strong Atlantic influences with relatively mild winters, cool summers and high rainfall. Low pressures sweep in during autumn and winter. Winter snows can last on the higher peaks and sheltered crevices well into early summer. Snow can also block the higher road passes in winter and spring. The route keeps to a relatively small area located midway between Santander and León, so expect to encounter mixed weather. The table 'Climate details' table (left) will help you to work out the best time to go.

In the Picos, Covadonga (see Option 3) is something of a spiritual home for the Spanish: it was here that King Pelayo turned back the advance of the Moors in AD718. This action started the Christian Reconquests that largely created the Spain we know today.

STAGE 1
Llanes to Cangas de Onis

Distance	45km (27.9 miles)
Type	Hills then valley
Climb	699m (2293ft)
Cycling time	3hr 10min

The route starts outside Llanes railway station (FFCE). The road is a dead end blocked by the Albergue de Estación. From this point head east along the road, ignoring the immediate left turn. Take the first right turn signed to Pancar and Parres, heading south out of town on the LLN-7. Pass through the avenue of plane trees before going through Pancar. Cross the railway. Cross the dual carriageway, ignore the left turn and pass through the spread-out village of **Parres**. There is a gentle climb all the way. Ignore the left turn in Parres. Continue to climb on this relatively narrow road through pasture and plantations of eucalyptus and pine. Gradually the road becomes steeper and twistier with less shade. The hills to the north often host eagles.

Descend from the unmarked col at 470m. The descent is at first twisty along the north side of a steep lush valley before reaching the valley floor. Pass through the villages of El Mazuco, Cortines and Debodes. At the T-junction turn left, followed immediately by a second left to join a larger road heading south. Pass through **Meré** and continue up the steep and often rocky valley of Río de las Cabras.

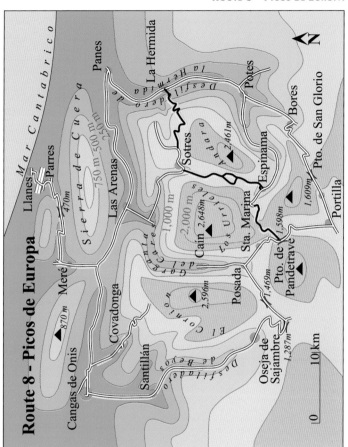

At the top of the climb turn right for a descent to **Cangas de Onis**. The Picos fill the view to the south. Pass by Robellada then through Avín, Benia, Villar Mestas de Con, La Estrada and Corao. The descent is along the valley of the Río Güeña. The valley is wide, green, lush and fertile. At Soto de Cangas continue straight ahead at the roundabout rather than left for Covadonga. It is from this roundabout that Option 3 Covadonga starts. Cangas de Onis with its hotels, restaurants and Roman bridge is 4km further on.

STAGE 2
Cangas de Onis to Posada de Valdeón

This stage goes to the heart of the Picos, and becomes more impressive the further it goes. Initially it follows the Río Sella, then via valley and gorge climbs between the massifs of El Cornión and the Cordillera Cantábrica before finishing in Posada de Valdeón.

The Río Sella has cut a 10km-long sheer-sided gorge through the limestone mountains, so deep and narrow that only the occasional glimpse of the surrounding peaks is possible.

Distance	62km (38.5 miles)
Type	Valley and mountain pass
Climb	1415m (4643ft)
Cycling time	4hr 15min

Take the road due south out of Cangas de Onis. The junction is a short distance east of the Roman bridge. The road climbs gently as it parallels the Río Sella in a broad, lush valley surrounded by hills. Pass through Caño, Tornín and Corigos. Pass through **Santillán** and Precendi and ignore the turn-offs in both villages. The valley narrows and the hills become bigger. The **Desfiladero de Beyos** defines the western limit of the Picos and starts beyond Ceneya. The road, high above the river and mostly in shadow, is an example of 1930s engineering bravado. Ignore all turn-offs.

Pass through the gorge. ◀ At the southern end the valley widens considerably to give excellent views of the mountains. Continue the climb. Ignore the left turn to Soto de Sajambre. Pass through **Oseja de Sajambre** and ignore the turn to Pío. Continue the ascent and pass through the tunnel. Beyond it the hillsides are covered

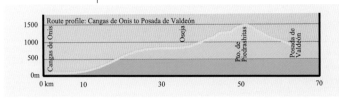

Route profile: Cangas de Onis to Posada de Valdeón

240

Posada de Valdeón during haymaking

in trees, mostly beech. The climb continues via a series of large open hairpin bends to the Puerto El Pontón (1287m). Descend for 0.5km and then turn left. Climb to the Puerto de Panderruedas (1469m) on a relatively steep but well-shaded road.

From the pass the descent is initially very twisty, through beech forest with wild strawberries growing on the shaded verges. Beyond are the hay meadows, a riot of wild flowers that flourish on the poor soil. Haymaking takes place in mid-June when the meadows are just past their best. **Posada** sits in the bottom of a valley surrounded by large, steep-sided, barren mountains.

Posada is a very popular village with walkers and sightseers and can be very busy during the day. Accommodation can be difficult at weekends.

Posada is also at one end of the mountain walk – one of Spain's classics – along the Cares gorge that separates the massifs of El Cornión and Los Urrieles. When a hydroelectric station was built at Poncebos, it took its headwater from the Río Cares at Caín via a canal built into the side of the gorge. A path was constructed alongside to service the canal, and this is open to the public – and a mighty fine path it is. It really starts at Caín some 9km north of and 480m lower than Posada. During summer (between the equinoxes) a bus service links both ends of the walk; at other times it is a 'there and back' affair. One option is to cycle to Caín and walk down for a couple of hours before returning.

There are interesting plants and a host of birds: griffon vultures circle high above on thermals, and rock hoppers skip about looking for insects. However, it is the agile house and crag martins that steal the aerial show. They have an ability to turn, flip and rotate in mid-air in pursuit of their prey that defies comprehension.

Caín is worth a visit for its setting alone, but do not even consider taking your bike down the gorge path: it is most unsuitable.

Garganta del Cares, one of Spain's classic walks

STAGE 3
Posada de Valdeón to Potes

Distance	58km (36 miles)
Type	High passes then descent
Climb	1084m (3557ft)
Cycling time	3hr 45min

Option 1 is shorter, with much less climb than the main route, but the off-road section can be rough and should only be undertaken on a bike with some off-road capability.

Leave Posada heading south-east, climbing through hay meadows on a very narrow road. Pass through the village of **Santa Marina de Valdeón**. Continue the climb through meadows then beechwoods via a couple of hairpin bends to the **Puerto de Pandetrave** (1598m). At the pass there is a Land Rover track on the left signed the 'Senda Collado de Remoña'; this is the start of Option 1 which can be used instead of the remainder of this stage.

The pass is one of the links between the Cordillera Cantábrica and the Picos. Continue on the road heading south down the valley of the Río Puerna to **Portilla de la Reina**. The rocks in the valley are shale rather than limestone, and those around Portilla are coarse conglomerates. Pass through Portilla and turn left at the T-junction to repass through the remainder of the village. The road climbs steeply through a desolate gorge. Pass through Llánaves de la Reina. The valley widens considerably as it climbs to the Puerto de San Glorio (1609m); there are extensive views over the Valle de Cereceda. There is a track heading north-east from the pass to Cosgaya via the Collado de Llesba. Do not be tempted by it as

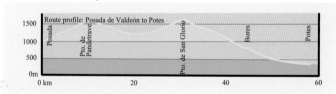

Route profile: Posada de Valdeón to Potes

Santa Marina de Valdéon and the massif of El Cornión

Picos de Europa from Frama

the track is in an appalling condition and is only for the most hardened of mountain bikers.

Instead, there's an uninterrupted 27km of descent ahead. Continue on the main road over the pass. The road is at first fairly straight, but beyond the Mirador del Corzo negotiates a series of hairpin bends before descending the hillside with only a couple of hairpins to contend with. Ignore the turns for Dobáganes, Dobares and Enterrías. Pass through **Bores**, and at the next main junction bend left down the valley, a delightful mix of pine forest and hay meadow. Pass straight through La Vega de Liébana then Norova before entering **Potes**.

Potes is a lovely mountain resort with lots of accommodation that fills up at weekends. It also has plenty of bars and restaurants. It is a popular centre for canoeing, horse riding, bungee jumping, canyoning and so on.

STAGE 4
Potes to Llanes

Distance	88km (54.6 miles)
Type	Valley then hills
Climb	725m (2379ft)
Cycling time	5hr 50min

A long but not too hilly stage. One option would be to split it and take time out for exploring.

From the centre of Potes head north-east on the main through road. In Ojedo turn left at the roundabout. Pass through the village and ignore all turns. Pass through Tama, following the river north. Ignore the turn-off to Castro; almost immediately the **Desfiladero de la Hermida** begins. ▶

The gorge widens at Lebeña where the Romanesque church of Santa María has a pre-Christian Celtic carved altar stone. Outside the church a yew and an olive tree, planted at the time of its building, may imply some form of insurance against future changes in religion. The gorge narrows again before widening slightly for **La Hermida**, where there is a Madonna carved in a cave above the village. The next section of gorge is the most impressive, being more wooded and deeper. Pass through the hamlets of Urdón, Rumenes and Estragueña to leave the gorge and the mountains behind. Continue into **Panes**.

This superb gorge, cut into limestone by the Río Deva, defines the eastern limit of the Picos. It is more open than the others, giving better views, and has a number of villages. The road can get very busy with coaches taking day trippers into the Picos.

Turn left in the centre of Panes, signed to Cangas de Onis. Cross the Río Deva and continue straight ahead, ignoring the right turn. Ignore the turn for Abándames. The river is the Río Cares, a tributary of the Río Deva. The

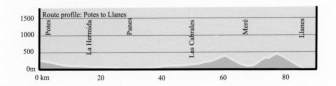

Route profile: Potes to Llanes

247

La Hermida

Cares has cut this deep east–west valley that varies in width along its length; it is very pretty. Ignore the turn for Cerébanes and Llonín. Approaching Niserias the valley narrows considerably. Pass through the village and keep to the main road. Pass through Trescares and then **Las Arenas**, set in a wide bowl of a valley. ▶

Beyond Arenas the road steepens and now parallels the Río Casaño. Pass through Carreña and Ortiguero. As the road climbs the views south improve, with the gorge of the Casaño next to the road before it bends south to cut into the mountains. About 2km from Ortiguero the road reaches its highest point at a roundabout. Turn left at this roundabout right towards **Posada** and **Llanes**, and retrace the first half of Stage 1 back to **Llanes** to finish the route.

This part of northern Spain is renowned for its cider (*sidra*) as evidenced by the number of bars dedicated to its sale.

OPTION 1
Puerto de Pandetrave to Potes

Distance	36km (22.4 miles)
Type	Short climb, long descent
Climb	193m (633ft)
Cycling time	2hr 5min

This option cuts short Stage 3. It is from the Puerto de Pandetrave to Potes via Fuente Dé and the valley of the Río Deva.

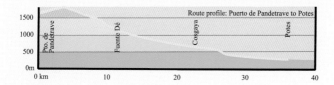

The first 12km of this option are on unmetalled mountain roads that can be very rough and steep. An all-terrain bike is recommended, otherwise there will be sections of pushing before Fuente Dé. The descent into Fuente Dé through the mountains and hay meadows is stunning.

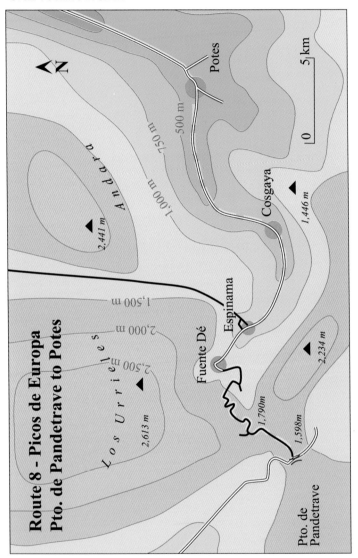

**Route 8 - Picos de Europa
Pto. de Pandetrave to Potes**

Los Urrielles

2,613 m

2,234 m

2,441 m

Andara

Fuente Dé

Espinama

Cosgaya

1,446 m

Potes

1,790m

1,598m

Pto. de Pandetrave

N

1,500 m
2,000 m
2,500 m
1,000 m
750 m
500 m

0   5 km

The village is worth visiting for its location alone, trapped by 800m-high cliffs in a tuck in the mountains. The Río Deva has in turn carved out one of the prettiest valleys in Spain.

Start from the Puerto de Pandetrave (1598m) described in Stage 3. Take the vehicle track heading east signed 'Senda Collado de Remoña'. The climb is steep and the mountain road rough in places. Gradually the view of Santa Marina and Posada to the northwest is revealed. After 4km and 192m of climb there is a side road to the left; ignore this. Continue on the main road, head-

Puerto de Pandetrave to Fuente Dé track

ing north-east, and climb over the ridge. The descent is through heather-covered hillsides. After a double hairpin the road straightens before another hairpin. Descend into a valley, cross the stream and contour round to the second stream. In each case the road passes through beechwoods before the stream. From the second stream (1524m) the road descends along the valley side through more beechwoods, through three sharp bends and a fourth in the open. At this fourth bend ignore the track to the right. Continue descending through hay meadow and woodland onto an asphalt road at Fuente Dé.

Continue on the main road and pass under the cable car. The route to Potes is simple. Continue straight ahead, stopping at as many of the roadside bars and cafés as required! Pass through **Espinama**, Cosgaya and Los Llanos before arriving in **Potes**, shaken *and* stirred.

OPTION 2
Puertos de Aliva loop

This option should only be approached on a robust all-terrain bike. There are mountain bike hire shops in Potes. Takes lots of food, water, suntan lotion and film, and hope for good weather.

Distance	74km (46 miles)
Type	Big mountains then valley
Climb	1736m (5696ft)
Cycling time	6hr 20min

This loop provides one of the best days of mountain cycling possible. It uses the eastern of the two central north–south incisions that cut the Picos into three massifs. Unlike the Cares gorge, this incision is a high valley. However, quality doesn't come cheap in terms of effort: it's tough, and some sections can be very rough.

Leave from the centre of Potes on the main through road, heading west. The road is along the bottom of the valley of the Río Deva. The first 20km are on asphalt roads with various gradients, climbing all the way. Pass through Los Llanos and Cosgaya to get to **Espinama**. There are two tracks leading north out of Espinama which come together after a short distance. Turn right beside the Bodegas Peña Vieja and pass under the arch. The concrete road starts level, but beyond the village becomes a steep rough mountain road. Fortunately there is plenty of tree cover for shade as the road climbs in a northerly direction up the valley of the Río Nevandi. About 2.5km from and 336m above Espinama the trees finish and the climb continues through rich hay meadow. Pass through Invernales (hay barns) de Igüedri. Expect to come across some local cows and lots of walkers. ◀

There are two types of Spanish sheepdog. One is small and cute with short curly hair and is used to direct sheep. The other is a huge hound with skinhead appearance and aggressive attitude, used to protect sheep from wolves. The latter will be with flocks of sheep and will announce their presence with a fairly lazy bark. They should be no trouble, but it's wise to keep clear.

Continue the climb through the Portillas del Boquerón, after which the road levels slightly. This is a land of limestone and high pasture. Ignore the road that comes in from the right. Continue north to the fork in the road at 1448m, one of the Puertos de Aliva. The left fork leads to the Refugio de Aliva where food and accommodation is available. Take the right fork, and descend

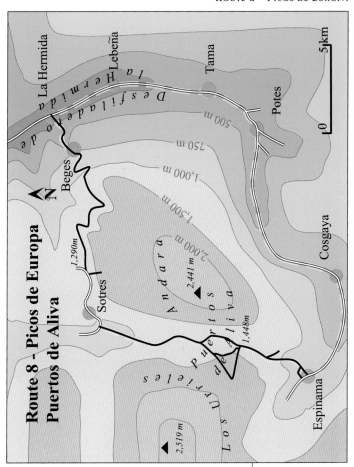

to the Ermita Nuestra Señora de las Nieves – an excellent picnic spot. Pass the *ermita* onto an area of level pasture, a very popular place for grazing sheep and cows. The road disappears, but continue north to the west side of the concrete barn ahead where it reappears. The road is disjointed as it climbs the small ridge to the west. On the

253

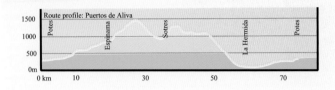

ridge turn right to join the road heading north along it. Descend through a gated fence into the Valle del Duje; the descent can be steep and very rough. The road levels. Pass through the barns of Vega de Sotres. At Invernales de Texu keep high and pass above; from here the climb to **Sotres** (1025m) begins. Turn right at the T-junction for a steep climb on a metalled road to the village. Pass straight through.

Continue the steep climb on the road through hay meadows to a height of 1290m where the route leaves the asphalt road for a rough mountain road, 3.8km from the centre of Sotres. Ignore the adjacent track that heads south up the side of a ridge. Turn right onto the vehicle track, heading east into a small valley. The track is rough and very twisty in places. Descend through trees and between huge limestone boulders. Cross the stream and enter the beechwoods after a descent of 170m. The track levels, and from here is wide with a good surface. It contours around the hill, and is exposed where it has been carved into the rocks.

Continue on this track round the end on the Sierra de la Corta to the high pasture above Majada La Cerezal. The track remains level to re-enter beechwoods as it crosses the Riega del Torno. Ignore the left turn 1km into the woods. The track contours around the Monte de la Llama to emerge again in the open before crossing the Riega de los Lobos. Contour in the open high above the Cañón del Urdón some 750m below. Pass the walled enclosures and ignore the road on the right heading uphill. The descent to the village of Bejes is on a very rough concrete track with hairpin bends built onto a cliff face.

Invernales de Texu, Valle del Duje

Pass through Bejes and join the improved concrete road. Ignore the right turn to La Quintana, and descend into the gorge of the Río Corvera. The road drops into the Desfiladero de la Hermida at **La Hermida**. Turn right at the T-junction for a 16km-long ride with 180m of climb back to Potes. Keep to the main road and follow the signs. On most afternoons a strong breeze blows through the gorge from the north, and makes the last stretch that bit easier.

OPTION 3
Covadonga

Covadonga is used as a mountain stage finish on the Tour of Spain: it's a tough, unremitting climb that ends in a spectacular setting.

The option starts from the roundabout at Soto de Cangas (towards the end of Stage 1) and continues past the village of Covadonga to the Lago de la Ercina.

Distance	40km (24.8 miles)
Type	One climb, then reverse
Climb	1044m (3425ft)
Cycling time	2hr 55min

Take the southern exit from the roundabout in Soto de Cangas, signed to **Covadonga**. The road follows the bottom of the valley of the Río Covadonga. Initially the climb is gentle, through small villages with tourist facilities. After 6.5km at the roundabout near to the Ermitaño de Covadonga turn left. The road steepens and climbs to the end. Above 600m the trees thin out to reveal rough, lumpy limestone country. There is a cruel dip in the road before the steep climb to the Lago de Enol. The road continues and ascends a small ridge to reach the Largo de la Ercina, where there is a large car park and a small bar.

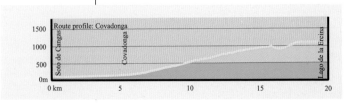

Route profile: Covadonga

256

This is a popular scenic spot. The limestone mountains of El Cornión rise in jagged lumps to the south. To return simply retrace the route.

Covadonga

ACCOMMODATION ON OR CLOSE TO ROUTE 8

Please note that this is not an exhaustive list. Hotel guide prices are in Euros, based on a double room with an en suite bathroom at high season. Rooms without en suite are typically 20% cheaper, as are single rooms. Please note that hotels are constantly opening, closing or being refurbished; it is always advisable to book ahead. Prices (where known) are indicated as follows: (1) up to 50 Euros; (2) 50–75 Euros; (3) 75–100 Euros; (4) over 100 Euros.

Llanes

(2) La Paz, Avenida La Paz, 5 (tel: 985 40 05 86)
(1) Albergue La Estación (tel: 985 40 14 58)
La Encina, Calle Celorio, 54 (tel: 985 40 04 66)
La Posada del Rey, Calle Mayor, 11 (tel: 985 40 13 32)
Camping Entre Playas, Av de Toro (tel: 985 40 08 88)
Camping Las Bárcenas (tel: 985 40 15 70)

Avín

(2) Alda, (tel: 985 94 02 12)
Camping Picos de Europa, Ctra. AS-114, km16 (tel: 985 84 40 70)

Soto de Cangas

(4) Bricial, La Venta (tel: 985 94 02 33)
(3) La Balsa (tel: 985 94 00 56)
(3) La Ablaneda, Ctra. de Covadonga, km 1 – Soto de Cangas (tel: 985 94 02 45)
Camping Covadonga, Cangas de Onís a Panes, km 3 (tel: 985 94 00 97)

Cangas de Onís

(4) Los Acebos Cangas, Avda. Covadonga, 53 (tel: 985 84 37 00)
(3) Eladia, Avenida Covadonga, 14 (tel: 985 84 80 00)
(3) Monteverde, Sargento Provisional, 5 (tel: 98584 80 79)
(2) Casa Fermin, Contranquil, 3 (tel: 985 94 75 62)
(2) Plaza, Roberto Frassinelli, 3 (tel: 985 84 83 08)
(2) Los Robles, San Pelayo, 8 (tel: 985 94 70 52)
(2) Pensión Susierra, Susierra (tel: 985 84 37 00)
(1) La Posada del Monasterio. La Vega-Villanueva (tel: 985 84 85 53)

Amieva

(2) Puente Vidosa, Vidosa s/n

Oseja de Sajambre

Hostal les Vedules, Carretera General, s/n (tel: 987 74 03 48)

Soto de Valdeón

Camping Valdeón, Ctra. Pontón – Posada de Valdeón km 13 (tel: 987 74 26 05)

Posada de Valdeón

(2) Abascal, El Salvador, s/n (tel: 987 74 05 07)

(2) Begoña, Llanos, 2 (tel: 987 74 05 16)
(1) Corona, Rabanal, 4 (tel: 987 74 05 78)
Cumbres Valdeón, Travesía Soto, 6 (tel: 987 74 27 10)
Hostal Campo, Camino Llanos (tel: 987 74 05 02)
Rojo, Santiago, 8 (tel: 987 74 05 23)

Caín
(2) La Posada del Montañero, Trv. del Cares, 3 (tel: 987 74 27 11)
(2) La Ruta, Trv. del Cares, 15 (tel: 987 74 27 02)

Santa Marina de Valdeón
(2) Posada Asturiano, Travesia de los Llanos, 1 (tel: 987 74 27 61)
La Ardilla Real, Pza. de la Esquina, 1 (tel: 987 74 26 77)
Camping El Cares, El Cardo (tel: 987 74 26 76)

Llánaves de la Reina
(2) San Glorio (tel: 987 74 04 18)

Enterrias
(2) Mirador de Enterrias, Lugar Barrio, s/n (tel: 942 73 62 24)

La Vega de Liébana
Pensión Violeta, Carretera General, 7 (tel: 942 73 60 23)
Camping El Molino, Ctra. San Glorio – La Vega de Liébana (tel: 942 73 60 09)

Potes
(3) Hostería Picos de Europa, San Roque, 6 (tel: 942 73 00 52)
(2) La Cabaña, La Molina, s/n (tel: 942 73 00 50)
(2) Picos de Valdecoro, Roscobado, s/n (tel: 942 73 00 25)
(2) Casa Cayo, Cantabra, 6 (tel: 942 73 01 50)
(1) El Fogón de Cus, Capitán Palacios, 2 (tel: 942 73 00 60)
La Antigua, Cántabra, 9 (tel: 942 73 00 37)
Camping Isla Picos de Europa, Ctra. Gral. Potes-Fuente – Turieno (tel: 942 73 08 96)
Camping La Viorna, Ctra. Santo Toribio (tel: 942 73 20 21)
Camping El Redondo Picos de Europa, Fuente de Camaleño (tel: 942 73 66 99)

Ojedo
(2) Infantado (tel: 942 73 09 39)
(2) Hosteria Peña Sagra, Calle Ojedo, s/n (tel: 942 73 07 92)

La Hermida
(3) Hotel Balneario La Hermida, Barrio las Caldas (tel: 942 73 36 25)
Posada La Cuadrona, C/ La Vea, 11 (tel: 942 73 35 65)
Posada Campo, Lugar Barrio la Vega, 25 – Bajo (tel: 942 73 35 10)

Panes
(3) El Tilo, Mayor, s/n (tel: 985 41 41 67)
(2) Covadonga, Plaza de la Iglesia (tel: 985 41 42 30)
(2) La Molinuca, Carretera de Cangas de Onís a Panes (tel: 985 41 40 30)

259

Arenas de Cabrales

(2) Picos De Europa, Calle Mayor s/n (tel: 985 84 64 91)

(2) El Ardinal Barrio de Río, s/n (tel: 985 84 04 34)

(2) El Naranjo de Bulnes, Carretera Arenas de Cabrales (tel: 985 84 65 19)

(2) Torrecerredo, Vega de Barrio, s/n (tel: 985 84 66 40)

Camping Naranjo de Bulnes, Ctra. Arenas – Panes km 32 (tel: 985 84 46 78)

Carreña

(2) Casa Ramón, Lg. Carreña, s/n (tel: 985 84 50 39)

Option 1

Fuente Dé

(3) Rebeco, Ctra. de Fuente Dé, s/n (tel: 942 73 66 01)

Espinama

(1) Nevandi, Ctra. Fuente Dé (tel: 942 73 66 08)

(1) Puente Deva, Ctra. Espinama – Camaleño (tel: 942 73 66 58)

(1) Ramoña (tel: 942 73 66 05)

(1) Sebrango, (tel: 942 73 66 15)

Cosgaya

(4) Cosgaya, Bo Areños. Ctra. Potes-Fuente Dé, s/n (tel: 942 73 32 30)

(3) Del Oso, Ctra. Potes Fuente De (tel: 942 73 30 18)

Option 2

Cosgaya

(4) Cosgaya, Bo Areños. Ctra. Potes-Fuente Dé, s/n (tel: 942 73 32 30)

(3) Del Oso Pardo, Ctra. Potes Fuente De (tel: 942 73 30 18)

Espinama

(1) Nevandi, Ctra. Fuente Dé (tel: 942 73 66 08)

(1) Puente Deva, Ctra. Espinama – Camaleño (tel: 942 73 66 58)

(1) Ramoña (tel: 942 73 66 05)

(1) Sebrango, (tel: 942 73 66 15)

Sotres

(2) Pensión La Perdíz (tel: 985 94 50 11)

(2) Peña Castil (tel: 985 94 50 49)

Option 3

Covadonga

(2) Auseva, El Repelao (tel: 985 84 60 23)

FURTHER READING

MAPS

The Instituto Geográfico Nacional produces two series of maps at 1:200 000. The scale and level of detail is just right for cycling: they show all roads including most forest and other major tracks, rivers, contours at 100m and most geographical features. There are two caveats: changes to the road networks are not updated very quickly, and town details can be very poor. The two series show the same level of detail but are presented differently. The series of Mapa Provincial covers the whole of Spain on a province-by-province basis. Within each province boundary the map has all the detail listed above, but outside only the road system is continued and sometimes the contours, but not vegetation detail. The series of Mapa Guía covers only the more popular areas, but does not suffer a drop-off in detail at provincial borders. Stanfords of Long Acre in London (020-7836 1321 or www.stanfords.co.uk) is a good stockist.

The other maps worth considering are Michelin Regional 1:250 00 to 1:400 000 and the more detailed Zoom series, which show all the public roads along with some limited topographic detail. They are revised annually so try and get an up-to-date one, otherwise new roads may be missing. These maps are widely available in bookshops.

CYCLING GUIDEBOOKS

There are three books that open up off-road cycling.

Guía de Vías Verdes Volumen 1, 2 & 3 – published in Spanish. See www.viasverdes. com. Available from www.elcorteingles.es/tienda/libros. Each contains 30 or so routes along disused railways and canals spread throughout Spain. The maps, route notes and supporting information is excellent. The nature of the dislocated routes means that they cannot be used to compile an extended tour in their own right, but may be incorporated into rides to add variety and access parts of the country that are not serviced by roads. They are highly recommended.

GENERAL GUIDEBOOKS

There are many guidebooks published on Spain, its regions and cities. Carrying even one would be onerous and a waste of effort, particularly as nearly all towns have tourist offices that provide the same town maps and information free of charge and fresh off the press (but do make sure you take a good dictionary and phrase book with you; these need not be heavy). The sites of interest often have free multilingual brochures detailing the history of the site and points of interest. For background reading and route planning try the *Rough Guide to Spain* or the more specific *Rough Guide to Andalucía* or *The Pyrenees*. These lively books have proved to be reliable. For more information on the wilder parts of Spain try the following.

Wild Spain, A Traveller's Guide – Frederick V. Grunwald (Sheldrake Press)
The geography, fauna and flora of each wild area are described in detail.

OTHER READING
Visiting Spain and writing is a popular pastime, particularly so in the 1920s and
1930s. Much is worth searching out and can be interesting background reading.

Homage to Catalonia – George Orwell
Orwell fought on the Republican side in the trenches of Huesca, then witnessed the
infighting shenanigans in Barcelona before being badly wounded. Worth reading for
the description of trench fighting and an explanation of the destructive power strug-
gles within the Republican side.

South from Grenada – Gerald Brenan
After the Great War Brenan moved to Yegen in the Alpujarras. An excellent description
of the country and customs of the time. Of particular interest is the description of the
flat-roofed houses, the same as those of the Berbers of the Atlas Mountains.

Driving Over Lemons – Chris Stewart
Drummer and sheep shearer Stewart buys a valley farm in the Alpujarras, settles in with
his family and raises sheep. An up-to-date account of living in the area.

Voices of the Old Sea – Norman Lewis
After World War II Lewis settled in a fishing village on the Costa Brava, and here describes
the village and its inhabitants. Slowly tourism develops and changes the village forever.

Don Quixote – Miguel de Cervantes Saavedra
Certainly a fictitious story that can be funny and touching at the same time. Does not
give any insight into modern Spain. The locations of many of the stories that are still to
be found include the famous windmills.

Our Lady of the Sewers – Paul Richardson
Richardson searches out the Spanish customs that are on the verge of extinction or are
being revived, or are such fun that they will last forever. They include communal pig
butchering, pilgrimages, sheep drives and plough lifting.

Roads to Santiago – Cees Nooteboom
Nooteboom travels throughout Spain, describing its art and history, before eventually
arriving in Santiago. The detours can be deep and challenging but give a deeper insight
into Spain than found in most books.

The author, Cubillas de Arbas, Léon

APPENDIX 1: Temperatures and Rainfall

	Jan	Feb	Mar	Apr	May	Jun	Jul	Aug	Sep	Oct	Nov	Dec
Madrid												
min	-10	-9	-4	-1	1	6	8	7	4	0	-3	-8
av min	2	2	5	7	10	14	17	17	14	9	5	2
av max	9	11	15	18	21	27	31	30	25	19	12	9
max	18	22	16	29	33	37	39	38	36	28	22	16
rainfall	39	34	43	48	47	27	11	15	32	53	47	48
Sevilla												
min	-3	-3	1	2	3	5	11	12	9	4	0	-3
av min	6	7	9	11	13	17	20	20	18	14	10	7
av max	15	17	20	24	27	32	36	36	32	26	20	16
max	24	27	32	36	42	44	46	49	41	39	32	24
rainfall	66	61	90	57	41	8	1	5	19	70	67	79
Almería												
min	2	0	3	5	8	13	15	16	10	8	5	3
av min	8	9	11	13	15	18	21	22	20	16	12	9
av max	16	16	18	20	22	26	29	29	27	23	19	17
max	23	26	27	30	35	36	38	37	36	32	27	25
rainfall	31	21	21	28	18	4	0	6	16	25	27	36

	Jan	Feb	Mar	Apr	May	Jun	Jul	Aug	Sep	Oct	Nov	Dec
Barcelona												
min	-2	-7	1	4	5	11	14	13	10	5	3	-3
av min	6	7	9	11	14	18	21	21	19	15	11	8
av max	13	14	16	18	21	25	28	28	25	21	16	13
max	23	21	24	28	32	35	35	36	32	28	25	21
rainfall	31	39	48	43	54	37	27	49	76	86	52	45
Finisterre												
min	-2	-1	3	2	5	8	9	9	4	3	1	2
av min	8	7	9	10	11	13	15	15	15	13	11	9
av max	12	13	15	16	18	20	22	22	21	19	15	13
max	21	24	29	29	31	33	35	37	32	29	25	20
rainfall	96	67	92	51	55	38	19	41	57	76	127	124
Santander												
min	-2	-4	-4	2	4	8	11	12	3	5	2	0
av min	7	7	8	10	11	14	16	16	15	12	10	8
av max	12	12	14	15	17	20	22	22	21	18	15	13
max	21	26	30	33	31	34	35	40	34	30	24	21
rainfall	119	88	78	83	89	63	54	84	114	133	125	159

Min and max show the extreme temperature recorded over an extended period; av min is the average daily minimum temperature, av max the average daily maximum temperature. All are in degrees Celsius. Rainfall is the monthly average in mm.

APPENDIX 2: Sunrise and Sunset Based on First Day of Each Month

	Jan	Feb	Mar	Apr	May	Jun	Jul	Aug	Sep	Oct	Nov	Dec
Madrid												
sunrise	08:37	08:24	07:48	07:58	07:14	06:47	06:48	07:11	07:42	08:11	07:45	08:20
sunset	17:57	18:30	19:06	20:38	21:10	21:39	21:48	21:29	20:48	19:57	18:13	17:50
Málaga												
sunrise	08:28	08:18	07:47	08:02	07:23	07:00	07:01	07:22	07:48	08:12	07:41	08:12
sunset	18:10	18:40	19:11	20:38	21:05	21:38	21:39	21:22	20:46	20:00	18:21	18:02
Barcelona												
sunrise	08:17	08:03	07:26	07:34	06:49	06:21	06:21	06:46	07:18	07:48	07:24	08:00
sunset	17:31	18:05	18:42	20:16	20:49	21:19	21:29	21:08	20:26	19:34	17:48	17:24
Bilbao												
sunrise	08:43	08:27	07:48	07:53	07:05	06:35	06:35	07:01	07:36	08:09	07:47	08:25
sunset	17:45	18:21	19:00	20:37	21:13	21:45	21:55	21:33	20:48	19:53	18:05	17:39
Alicante												
sunrise	08:18	08:07	07:34	07:46	07:05	06:40	06:41	07:03	07:32	07:57	07:29	08:01
sunset	17:50	18:21	18:54	20:24	20:53	21:20	21:29	21:11	20:32	19:45	18:03	17:43
Cadiz												
sunrise	08:36	08:26	07:55	08:10	07:31	07:08	07:10	07:38	07:56	08:19	07:49	08:19
sunset	18:18	18:46	19:19	20:46	21:13	21:38	21:46	21:30	20:54	20:09	18:29	18:11

APPENDIX 3
Language Notes

The Spanish language as we know it takes second place in the language league table behind English. It is well ahead of French. Apart from Spain it is used in Argentina, Chile, Uruguay, Paraguay, Bolivia, Peru, Ecuador, Columbia, Venezuela, Panama, Costa Rica, Nicaragua, El Salvador, Honduras, Guatemala, Mexico, Cuba, Dominican Republic, Puerto Rico, Equatorial Guinea and the Philippines. In the USA some 22 million people speak Spanish.

Spanish is not the only language in Spain. It is joined by *gallego* in Galicia, *catalán* in Cataluña (Catalonia), *vasco* or *euskera* in the Basque Country, *mallorquín* in Mallorca and *valenciano* in Valencia. The Spanish we know should really be referred to as Castilian Spanish, which is accepted almost everywhere. English speaking is increasingly widespread, but do not depend on it; there are still villages where only the schoolchildren speak some English.

Although it is relatively easy to get by without knowing any Spanish by judicious use of a phrase book and pointing, learning at least some of the most useful words and phrases is a good idea. Contact your local college; most put on a range of courses, from beginners to detailed academic study. During the summer term you will find that many also run conversation-based courses aimed at holidaymakers. Should going back to school not appeal, or time commitments be a problem, there are a number of teach-yourself programmes commercially available and widely advertised.

Pronunciation

Spanish is, like French, a derivative of Latin, but unlike French the whole word is pronounced. Normally emphasis in a word is given to:

- the penultimate syllable if the word ends in a vowel or 'n' or 's': eg zap**a**to
- the last syllable if the word ends in a consonant that is not 'n' or 's': eg Mad**ri**d
- elsewhere if marked with a written accent: eg Ávila.

Greetings and pleasantries

The Spanish use the equivalents of 'please' and 'thank you' infrequently and when really meant, and not as a linguistic lubricant. This is not rudeness, but arises because they frequently use the conditional tense, making excess pleasantries unnecessary.

Letters are pronounced as follows:

a	as in back	casa
b	as in bag	baño
c	before a, o, u as in car	casa
c	before e and I like th in thee	cien
d	as in dentist at start of words	dentista
	less harsh in the middle	adiós
	like th in thee at the end	Madrid
e	as in end	escoba
f	as in few	fácil
g	before a, o, u as in gas	gasolina
	before e, i like ch in loch	gente
gu	before e, i like g in gas	guitara
	before a like gw	agua
h	always silent	hola
i	like ee in reed	litro
j	like ch in loch	Jerez
k	as in kink	kilo
l	as in large	libro
ll	like lli in million	llave
m	as in Michael	mantequilla

n	as in never	nunco
ñ	like ny in canyon	niño
o	as in cot	oficina
p	as in Peter	pan
qu	like k in keel	q u e
r	at start of word rolled	r o s a
	elsewhere as in rule	pero
rr	rolled as in curry	perro
s	as in soon	sopa
t	as in tent	tanto
u	like oo in boot	usted
v	mix of English v & b	vivo
w	like v in view	water
x	like s at the beginning	Xaviar
	like s before consonant	excusa
	like ks between vowels	taxi
y	as in yes	mayor
	the word y like ee	y
z	like th in thee	zapatos

hola	hello
buenos días	good day
buenas tardes	good afternoon/ evening
buenas noches	good night
adiós	goodbye
hasta luego	until later
hasta mañana	until tomorrow
por favor	please
gracias	thank you
de nada	it's nothing
si	yes
no	no
disculpame	excuse me
perdone	excuse me

lo siento	I am sorry
no comprendo	I do not understand
¿habla Inglés?	do you speak English?
no hablo Español	I do not speak Spanish

Numbers and Quantities

uno	1
dos	2
tres	3
cuatro	4
cinco	5
seis	6
siete	7
ocho	8
nueve	9

diez	10
once	11
doce	12
trece	13
catorce	14
quince	15
dieciseis	16
diecisiete	17
dieciocho	18
diecinueve	19
veinte	20
veintiuno	21
veintidós	22
veintitrés etc	23
treinta	30
treinto y uno	31
cuarenta	40
cincuenta	50
sesenta	60
setenta	70
ochenta	80
noventa	90
cien	100
qinientos	500
mil	1000

primero/a	first
segundo/a	second
tercero/a	third

alguno/a	some
bastar	enough
más o menos	approximately
muy	very
un poco de	a little of
ninguno/a	none
unos/unas	some
varios/a	various

The calendar

lunes	Monday
martes	Tuesday
miércoles	Wednesday
jueves	Thursday
viernes	Friday
sabádo	Saturday
domingo	Sunday
enero	January
febrero	February
marzo	March
abril	April
mayo	May
junio	June
julio	July
agosto	August
septiembre	September
octobre	October
noviembre	November
diciembre	December
invierno	winter
verano	summer
primavera	spring
otoño	autumn
ahora	now
ayer	yesterday
el fin de semana	weekend
hoy	today
mañana	tomorrow
medianoche	midnight
mediodia	midday

Accommodation

¿tiene una habitación…	Do you have a room…
…para este noche?	…for tonight?

269

...para dos/tres noches?	...for two/three nights?
¿cuanto es?	How much is it?
doble double	
individual/solo	single
con baño/sin baño	with/without bath

Eating and Restaurants

bebeda	drink
café	coffee
café con leche	with hot milk
café solo	without milk
cerveza	beer
glarra	shandy
dulce	sweet
limonada	lemonade
mazanilla	camomile tea
nata	cream
seco	dry
sidra	cider
té	tea
el vino	wine
vino blanco	white wine
vino tinto	red wine
zumo	juice
carne	meat
cerdo	pork
conejo	rabbit
cordero	lamb
huesos	bones
jamón de york	processed ham
jamón serrano	air-dried ham
pollo	chicken
ternera	veal
huevos	eggs
comestibles	groceries
el aceite	oil

almendras	almonds
azúcar	sugar
confitura	jam
fideos	noodles
empanada	pie/pasty
empanado	in breadcrumbs
las galletas	biscuits
garbanzos	chick peas
judías	beans
lenteja	lentil
mahonesa	mayonnaise
mantequilla	butter
mermelada	jam
nuez	nut
pan	bread
el queso	cheese
sal	salt
fruto	fruit
aguacate	avocado
albaricoque	apricot
ananás	pineapple
fresa	strawberry
lima	lime
limón	lemon
manzana	apple
melocotón	peach
naranja	orange
pera	pear
piña	pineapple
plátano	banana
pomelo	grapefruit
sandía	watermelon
uvas	grapes
pan y pasteles	bread and cakes
madalena	sponge cakes
pan	bread
pan integral	wholemeal bread
pastel	cake

pescado	fish	comida	lunch
atún	tuna	el desayuno	breakfast
boqueron	whitebait	copa	wine glass
calamares	squid	cubiertos	cutlery
cangrejo	crab	cuchara	spoon
la langosta	lobster	cucharadita	teaspooon
mejillones	mussels	cuchillo	knife
merluza	hake	merienda	afternoon tea
pulpo	squid	tenedor	fork
el salmón	salmon	vaso	tumbler
las sardinas	sardines		
trucha	trout		

Weather

calor	hot
chubascos	showers
despejado	clear
granizo	hail
lluvia	rain
nieve	snow
niebla	fog
nublado	cloudy
relampago	lightning
sol	sun
solneado	sunny
temperatura	temperature
tormenta	storm
trueno	thunder
viento	wind

verduras	vegetables
aceituna	olive
ajo	garlic
alcachofa	artichoke
arroz	rice
berenjana	aubergine
berza	cabbage
calabacín	courgette
cebolla	onion
cebollín	spring onion
col	cabbage
coliflor	cauliflower
espárrago	asparagus
guisantes	peas
lechuga	lettuce
nabo	turnip
patatas	potatoes
pepino	cucumber
pimiento rojo/verde	pepper red/green
puerro	leek
seta	mushroom
tomates	tomatoes
zanahoria	carrot

Countryside and Geography

alto	high
el campo	the country
barranco	ravine
caliza	limestone
canaleta	irrigation channel
casa de nieve	snow pit
collado	col
cordillera	mountain range
cresta	crest
cueva	cave

Miscellaneous

almuerzo	lunch
cena	evening meal

cumbre	summit/top
embalse	reservoir
fuente	spring
largo	lake
montaña	mountain
morro	clifftop
palustre	marshy
peña	cliff
peñones	walls of rock
pico	mountain
piedra	rock/stone
pizzaro	slate
planicie	plain
río	river
sierra	mountain range
tajo	cleft
torrente	stream
albergue	shelter
atalaya	watchtower
camino	road/pathway
chubasquero	cagoule
cuesta abajo	downhill
cuesta arriba	uphill
ermita	hermitage
finca	farm
horno de cal	lime oven
llano	flat
mapa	map
paseo	walk/walkway
pozo	well
refugio	mountain hut
sendero	path/trail
subida	ascent/climb
arbusto	shrub
flor	flower
orquídeas	orchids

Directions and Locations

¿hay una farmacia por aquí?
 Is there a pharmacist around here?

sí, hay un en la calle San Pedro
 Yes, there is one in San Pedro street

¿dónde est?	Where is?
¿cómo voy a?	How do I go to…?
a	to/at
al lado de	beside the
aquí	here
cerca de	around or near
de	of/from
delante de	in front of
detrás de	behind
en	in or on
enfrente de	opposite(facing)
lejos de	far from
lugar	place
sobre	on or above
a la izquierda	to the left
a la derecha	to the right
este	east
norte	north
oeste	west
sur/sud	south
después	then
hasta	until
luego	until
todo recto	straight on

APPENDIX 4
Travelling to Spain

FROM THE UNITED KINGDOM AND EIRE

Although for the majority air travel will be the most economic and convenient option, there are also sea and road routes.

Sea

Brittany Ferries run two services a week each between Portsmouth and Santander and Bilbao. They run a weekly service between Plymouth and Santander. Tel: 0871 244 0744 or www.brittanyferries.com.

Land

It is certainly possible to use France as a land bridge and travel by car or by train. Try Rail Europe (tel: 08448 484 064) or www.raileurope.com. European Bike Express operates four routes, two of which could be of interest. The coaches start in Middlesbrough and head south via Dover with pick-up points on route. The coach can set down anywhere on route and pick up anywhere on a return service. Cycles are carried in trailers and the only preparation required is to turn handlebars through 90º. The Mediterranean route terminates in Empuriabrava on the Costa Brava some 100km up the coast from Barcelona. The Atlantic route loops round Bayonne and Lourdes in France. Cycling between these routes would allow a good exploration of the Pyrenees. Tel: 01430 422111, fax: 01430 422877, email: info@bike-express.co.uk or www.bike-express.co.uk

Scheduled Flights

The main operators such as Aer Lingus, British Airways, British Midland and Iberia have been joined by the budget airlines such as EasyJet and Ryanair. As many flights are operated daily, visits can be any length, and single tickets allow airport-to-airport options even if a different carrier is required.

AIRLINE DETAILS

The following UK and Eire departure airport abbreviations have been used:
A Aberdeen, Bt Belfast, B Birmingham, Bk Blackpool, Bh Bournemouth, Bl Bristol, Cd Cardiff, C Cork, Cv Coventry, De Derry, Do Doncaster, D Dublin, Dtv Durham Tees Valley, E Edinburgh, Ex Exeter, Em Nottingham East Midlands, H Humberside, I Inverness, IOM Isle of Man, G Glasgow, Ke Kerry, Kn Knock,

L Liverpool, Lb Leeds, Lg London Gatwick, Lh London Heathrow, Ll London Luton, Le London Southend, Ls London Stanstead, M Manchester, N Newcastle Nh Norwich, S Shannon, So Southampton.
In addition to direct flights many also offer feeder flights.

Aer Lingus: tel: 0818 365044 (Eire), tel: +44 (0) 871 718 2020 (UK and NI) www.aerlingus.com.

Direct flights from Eire to Alicante (D, C, Bt), Barcelona (D, C, Bt), Bilbao (D), Madrid (D), Málaga (D, C, Bt), Palma (D, C), Santiago de Compostela (D).

British Airways: tel: 0844 493 0787 (UK), www.britishairways.com or travel agents. At the time of revising British Airways are in the process of merging with Iberia. This will open up a vast range of routes both direct and indirect between the UK and Spain. See the BA and Iberia websites for the full range of departure and arrival airports.

Iberia: tel: 0870 609 0500 (UK), tel: 0818 462000 (Eire), www.iberia.com or travel agents. As a national carrier, now tied in with British Airways, Iberia goes everywhere in Spain and its islands but not always directly. It is worth checking that any connecting flights will also take your bicycle.

Direct flights from London Heathrow to Madrid but also code sharing with British Airways.

Airports in Spain include Almería, Alicante, Badajoz, Bilbao, Gerona, Granada, Jerez de la Frontera, La Coruña, León, Madrid, Málaga, Santiago de Compostela, Seville, València, Valladolid, Vigo, Vitoria and Zaragoza.

Iberia Express: tel: 902 100 424 (Spain), 0034 954 983 070 (Rest of Europe) or www.iberiaexpress.com. Expensive to take bikes. Operate into Madrid with connections to other Spanish cities or into the Iberia network.

Direct flights to Madrid (D, E).

EasyJet: tel: 0846 104 5000 (UK) or www.easyjet.com. EasyJet allows online booking of bicycles and has clear guidance on how to prepare it for carriage.

Direct flights to Alicante (Bt, Bl, E, G, L, Lg, Ll, Le, Ls, M, N), Almería (Lg), Asturias (Ls), Barcelona (Bl, Bt, L, Lg, Ll, Le, Ls, N), Bilbao (Ls, M), Madrid (Bl, E, L, Lg, Ll, M), Málaga (Bt, Bl, G, L, Le, Lg, Ll, Ls, M, N), Murcia (Bl, Lg), Palma (Bt, Bl, E, G, L, Lg, Le, Ll, Ls, M, N) Sevilla (LG) and València (Lg).

Monarch Airlines: tel: 08719 405040 or www.flymonarch.com.

Direct flights to Alicante (B, Em, Lg, Ll, M), Almería (B), Barcelona (B, Lb, Lg, M), Málaga (B, Em, Lg, Ll, M) and Palma (B, Em, Lb, Ll, M).

Thomson: tel: 0871 231 4787 or www.thomsonfly.com.

Direct flights to Alicante (B, Bl, Cd, Do, Dtv, Em, G, Lg, M),Almería (M), Gerona (B, Lg, M), Jerez (Lg), Málaga (B, Bl, Bt, Cd, Do, Em, G, Lg, Ll, M, N), Palma (A,

B, Bh, Bl, Bt, Cd, De, Do, E, Em, Ex, G, Lg, Ll, M, N, Nh, So) and Reus (B, Bl, Bt, Cd, De, Do, G, Lg, Ll, N).

Thomas Cook: www.flythomascook.com.

Direct flights to Alicante (Bt, B, Cd, Em, G, Lg, M, N), Almería (B, Lg, M), Málaga (B, G, Lg, M), Palma (A, B, Bl, Bt, Cd, Do, E, Em, Ex, G, H, IOM, Lb, Le, Lg, Ll, Ls, M, N, Nh) and Reus (A, B, Bl, Bt, Cd, E, G, IOM, Lg, M, N).

Jet2: tel: 0871 226 1737 (UK) or 00 44 203 8336 (Rest of World) or www.jet2.com.

Direct flights to Alicante (Bk, Bt, E, Em, G, Lb, M, N), Barcelona (G, Lb, M), Málaga (Bk, E, Em, G, Lb, M, N), Murcia (Bt, Bk, E, Em, Lb, M, N), Palma (Bt, Bk, E, Em, Lb, M, N) and Reus (Bt, M, N).

Ryanair: tel: 0871 246 0000 (UK), 1520 444 004 (Eire) or www.ryanair.com.

Direct flights to Alicante (B, Bh, D, E, Em, G, Ke, Kn, L, Lb, Ls, M), Almería (Em, Ls), Barcelona (B, D, E, Em, G, L, Lb, Ls), Gerona (B, Bh, Bl, C, D, Do, Ll, Ls, M, N), Jerez (Ls), Madrid (D, Ls, M), Málaga (B, Bh, Bl, C, D, E, Em, G, L, Lb, Ls, M, S), Murcia (B, Bh, D, Em, G, L, Lb, Ll, Ls, M), Palma (B, Bh, Bl, D, Em, G, L, Lb, Ls, M), Reus (B, Bl, Em, D, G, L, Ll, Ls, M), Santander (D, Ls), Santiago de Compostela (Ls), Sevilla (D, Lg, Ls), València (Bl, D, Em, Ls, M), Valladolid (Ls) and Zaragoza (Ls).

FROM THE LOW COUNTRIES AND GERMANY

Travel to Spain is relatively easy by land or air.

Land

A good network of motorways makes Spain easily accessible by car, but journeys can be very long and tiring. Secure parking will often be available at the airports where most of the routes in this book start and finish.

Rail journeys can be very time consuming and not all services will simultaneously carry bikes. There are direct rail services from Paris to Madrid calling at Vitoria-Gasteiz, Burgos and Valladolid, wand to Barcelona calling at Figueres and Girona. There are also direct services from Milan and Zurich to Barcelona calling at Figueres and Girona. For details contact RENFE (tel: 0034 90 22 40 20 2 or www.renfe.com). For services from Germany further information can be obtained from Die Bahn (tel: 0180 5 996633 or www.bahn.de) and for the Netherlands from Nederlandse Spoorwegen (tel: 0900 9296 or www.ns.nl).

Air

Travel by air is generally quick and is often the least expensive route.

AIRLINE DETAILS

The following departure airport abbreviations have been used:

Am Amsterdam, Bm Basel-Mulhouse, Be Berlin, Bb Berlin Brandenburg, Bs Berlin Schoenenfeld, Bn Bremen, Br Brussels, Bc Brussels/Charleroi, Cb Cologne – Bonn, Dd Dortmund, Df Düsseldorf, Dw Düsseldorf Weeze, Eh Eindhoven, Fr Frankfurt, Fh Frankfurt/Hahn, Gg Groningen, Ha Hamburg, Hl Hamburg Lubeck, Hr Hannover, Kb Karlsruhe Baden, Ko Köln – Bonn, Lz Leipzig Halle, Ma Maastricht, Mc Magdeburg Cochstedt, Mn Memmingen, Mu Munich, Nu Nuremburg, Ro Rotterdam, St Stuttgart.

In addition to direct flights many also offer feeder flights.

EasyJet: tel. 01805 666 000 (DE), 0900 040 1048 (NL) or www.easyjet.com.
  Direct flights to Barcelona (Am, Bb, Bs, Dd), Madrid (Am, Bb, Bs), Málaga (Bb, Bs) and Palma (Bb, Bs, Dd).
Ryanair: tel: 0900 116 0500 (DE), 0902 33 660 (B French), 0902 33 600 (B Dutch), 0900 04 00 860 (NL English) or www.ryanair.com.
  Direct flights to Alicante (Bc, BN, Dw, Eh, Fh, Kb, Ma, Mn), Almería (Bc, Dw), Barcelona (Bc, Hl), Bilbao (Dw), Gerona (Bc, Bn, Cb, Eh, Dw, Fh, Kb, Ma), Jerez (Dw, Fh), Madrid (Bc, Dw, Fh), Málaga (Bc, Bn, Dw, Eh, Fh, Kb, Lz, Ma, Mn), Palma (Bc, Bn, Cb, Dw, Eh, Fh, Gg, Hl, Kb, Ma, Mc, Mn), Reus (Bc, Dw, Eh, Fh), Santander (Bc, Fh), Santiago de Compostela (Fh), Sevilla (Bc, Dw, Eh), València (Bc, Dw, Fh, Mm), Valladolid (Bc) and Zaragoza (Bc).
TUIfly: tel 0900 1000 2000 (DE), 0900 249 9 990 (NL) or www.tuifly.com.
  TUIfly provides a comprehensive service from throughout Germany to Spain.
Vueling: tel: 0902 33429 (B), tel: 0900 777 0005 (NL), 0900 1100 520 (DE) or www.vueling.com. Operate throughout Spain from their Barcelona hub.
  Direct flights to A Coruña (Am), Alicante (Am), Bilbao (Am, Be), Barcelona (Am, Be, Br, Gg, Ha, Mu, Nu), Malaga (Am), Palma (Am), Sevilla (Am) and València (Am, Br).
Transavia: tel 0900 0737 (NL), 00 32 (0) 70 66 0305 (B) or www.transavia.com.
  Direct flights to Alicante (Am, Dw, Eh, Ro), Almería (Am), Barcelona (Am, Eh, Ro), Girona (Am, Ro), Madrid (Ro), Málaga (Am, Dw, Eh, Gg, Ma, Ro), Palma (Am, Br, Dw, Eh, Gg, Ro), Sevilla (Am) and València (Am, Eh).
Air Berlin: tel: 030 3434 3434 (DE), 0871 5000 737 (UK) or www.airberlin.com.
  Air Berlin has a comprehensive range of direct flights from Germany to Spain.
Germanwings: tel: 0900-19 19 100 (DE) or www.germanwings.com.
  Germanwings has a comprehensive range of direct flights from Germany to Spain including Barcelona, Bilbao, Jerez, Málaga, and Palma.

Iberia: tel: 0707 00050 (B), 0034 954589786 (LUX), 069 50073874 (DE), 0900 777 7717 (NL) or www.iberia.com.

Iberia has an unrivalled network of internal connections listed under the UK and Eire section.

Direct flights to Madrid (Be, Br, Df, Fr, Mu).

Iberia Express: tel: 902 100 424 (Spain), 0034 954 983 070 (Rest of Europe) or www.iberiaexpress.com. Expensive to take bikes. Operate into Madrid with connections to other Spanish cities or into the Iberia network.

Direct flights to Madrid (Am, Be, Df, Fr)

KLM: tel: 0900 040 0252 (NL), www.klm.com or travel agents.

Direct flights to Barcelona (Am) and Madrid (Am).

Lufthansa: www.lufthansa.com or travel agents.

Lufthansa provides a comprehensive service from throughout Germany to Spain although a number of flights are not direct.

FROM THE USA AND CANADA

Air travel is the most convenient option for cyclists. Iberia offers the most comprehensive network if internal connections are included.

Air Canada: Air Canada: tel: 1-888-247-2262 (Canada and USA) or www.aircanada.ca.

Direct flights to Barcelona from Montreal and Toronto. Connecting flights via Frankfurt and Munich to Madrid. Other connecting flights in alliance with other carriers.

Air Europa: tel: 1-800 238 7672 (USA) or www.air-europa.com.

Direct flights to Madrid from New York JFK.

American Airlines: tel: 1-800 433 7300 (USA) or www.aa.com. Operates with Iberia offering a good network in Spain.

Direct flights to Madrid from Dallas/Fort Worth, Miami and New York JFK.

United Airlines: tel: 1-800-864-8331 or www.united.com.

Direct flights to Barcelona and Madrid from Newark New York. Connecting flights throughout the USA and Canada.

Delta: tel: 1-800 241 4141 or www.delta.com.

Direct flights to Madrid from Atlanta, New York Newark and San Diego, Barcelona from Atlanta, Detroit and New York Newark and Málaga from New York Newark. Connecting flights throughout the USA and Canada.

Iberia: tel: 1-800 772 4642 (USA) or www.iberia.com or travel agents. Iberia operates with American Airlines and has an unrivalled network of internal connections listed under the UK and Eire section.

Direct flights to Madrid from Boston, Chicago, New York JFK, Los Angeles and Miami. Feeder flights from throughout North America.

APPENDIX 5
Spanish Airports: Routes and Maps

AEROPUERTO DE MADRID–BARAJAS

Like many other major airports Barajas is surrounded by roads from which cyclists are either banned or are highly unpleasant for cycling. However, there are routes that can be used and some are described below.

From T1: Arrivals at T1 find themselves at ground level. Ascend to the Departure area using the stairs, escalator or lifts and leave the building. Once outside turn right and keep to the right hand side of the road heading north. Bear right at the first fork at the end of the terminal building and right again at the second heading towards T2 departures (Salidas). The road bends to the right and is joined by a road from the right, from T2 T3, and then one from the left. This one has priority and it will need crossing to get in the correct lane. Follow this road round the large car park on the left. Pass the terminals on the right and at the next fork keep right and descend to the roundabout at the bottom of the hill. It is marked on the map with pink infill.

From here those heading north and east should go to Route 6 Stage 1 for a description of the route to Alcobendas. Those heading south, west or into Madrid should take the exit marked 'Bolsas de taxi' heading south, pass under the flyover then over the M13 autovía and straight ahead at the two roundabouts. Turn left at the T-junction. After a few metres you will now arrive at the Avenida de Logroño, which is numbered the M110 on most maps.

From T2 and T3: Turn left out of terminal and cycle on the right hand side of the road. Shortly the road splits into three. Take the right hand fork heading towards T2 departures (Salidas). The road bends to the right and is joined by a road on the left from T1. From here follow the route description given from T1.

From T4: Those starting at T4 should head for the multi-storey car parks opposite; make their way to the ground floor and exit turning right and north. After the pay booths continue straight ahead. Take the right fork immediately before the flyovers and again fork right after them. At the roundabout next to the Repsol service station at the dual carriageway turn right for Alcobendas (north and east) and left for Madrid (and west). Follow the map to the Avenida de Logroño and at the roundabout with the chapel join Route 5 Stage 1.

To return to the airport: simply follow the routes in reverse. Departures (Salidas) are well signed. Those using T4 will need to approach from the roundabout southwest of the terminal and hope that cyclists are accepted as authorised vehicles otherwise it will be a detour through the car parks.

AEROPUERTO DE MÁLAGA

Málaga airport provides one of Spain's better arrival points, and is located some 8km south-west of Málaga next to the former N430 Carretera Nacional. At one time this dual carriageway was infamous for the horrendous number of accidents as drivers sped through coastal villages and towns with little regard for anybody's safety. Fortunately the section we use has now been bypassed, but care is still needed, so take it easy and be alert.

Towards Málaga
From Terminals 1, 2 and **3**: arrivals will find themselves at ground level. On leaving the building turn right and join the flow of traffic. Join the road coming in from

the right just before the roundabout. At the roundabout turn right, and when safe to do so move into the outside, or left hand, lane and go up and over the bridge that crosses the dual carriageway (MA-21). The road curves to the right and joins the MA-21 immediately before passing under the bridge just crossed.

Towards Torremolinos
From Terminals 1, 2 and 3: arrivals will find themselves at ground level. On leaving the building turn right and join the flow of traffic. Join the road coming in from the right just before the roundabout. At the roundabout turn right, staying in the near-side, or right-hand, lane and join the dual carriageway via the slip road.

Returning to the airport
Follow the signs from the MA-21 to the airport link road and go straight ahead at the roundabout. All the terminals are well signed.

AEROPUERTO DE ALMERÍA

This is a small airport and getting in and out is easy. On leaving the terminal turn right and follow the road as it bends to the left and then straight ahead. Ignore the fork left that goes behind the car parks. At the junction with the main road turn right for routes east and north or left for Almería. The return is just as easy: simply follow the signs.

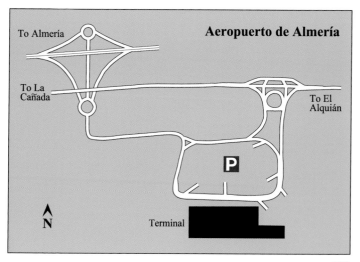

AEROPUERTO DE GIRONA

Girona airport is so cycle-friendly and easy to find your way around that a description would be superfluous. A map is included for completeness.

AEROPUERTO/AIREPORTA DE BILBAO/BILBO

Bilbao airport terminal is an architectural delight, and inside functionality is as good as it gets. However, Bilbao airport is all but impossible to reach from the city by bike. A taxi is the recommended method of linkage.

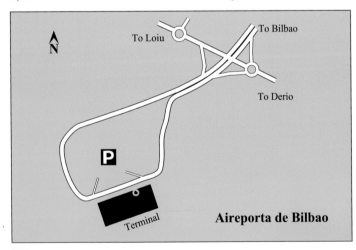

APPENDIX 6
Car Hire Companies

Autos Abroad: Arrange car hire with regional, national and international providers and often offer better value than booking direct.
UK Tel: 0844 826 6536 or www.autosabroad.com

Avis
USA Tel: 1-800-331-1212 or www.avis.com
Canada Tel: 1-800-879-2847 or www.avis.com
Eire Tel: 021 4281111 or www.avis.ie
UK Tel: 08445 81 81 81 or www.avis.co.uk
Germany Tel: 018 05 / 55 77 55 or www.avis.de
Netherlands Tel: 088-2847 000 or www.avis.nl

Budget
USA Tel: 800-527-0700 or www.budget.com
Canada Tel: 800-268-8900 or www.budget.com
Eire Tel: 09066 27711 or www.budget.ie
UK Tel: 08445 443455 or www.budget.co.uk
Germany Tel: 01805 / 21 77 11 or www.budget.de
Netherlands Tel: 088 - 2847 500 or www.budget.nl

Europcar (www.europcar.com)
USA and Canada Tel: 1 877 940 6900 or www.europcar.com/americas
Eire Tel: 00353 61 206025 or www.europcar.ie
UK Tel: 0845 758 5375 or www.europcar.co.uk
Germany Tel: 018/5 8000 or www.europcar.de
Netherlands Tel: 0900 0540 or www.europcar.nl

Hertz
USA and Canada Tel: 800 654 3131 or www.hertz.com
Eire Tel: 01 676 7476 or www.hertz.ie
UK Tel: 0843 309 3099 or www.hertz.co.uk
Germany Tel: 01 805 333 535 or www.hertz.de
Netherlands Tel: 020 201 3512 or www.hertz.nl

Holiday Autos (www.holidayautos.com)
Eire Tel: 0818 270 978 or www.holidayautos.ie
UK Tel: 0800 093 3111 or www.holidayautos.co.uk
Germany Tel: 089 1792 3002 or www.holidayautos.de
Netherlands Tel: 0900 202 26 34 or www.holidayautos.nl

APPENDIX 7
Organised Cycle Holiday Companies

There is a great variety of what is offered on an organised cycle holiday and not just location. Things to consider include:

Support provided:
This could be as little as airport transfers, hotel bookings, luggage transfer and route maps and notes. Something like this guide with the logistics sorted giving the freedom to divert, explore and set your own pace. At the other extreme are fully guided rides. What happens if something goes wrong or you are not up to finishing that day's ride? Will there be someone there at the end of the day to show you the best bars and restaurants?

Daily rides:
With some give and take are they the right distance and climb? Do they allow you to see and do what you came for?

Booking policy:
When you book is your holiday 'go' or is it subject to minimum numbers (with the possibility of your tour of the Picos turning into hill walking in Holland)?

The bike:
Who provides what is important and is the bike offered of the type you would normally ride? Taking your own pedals, cycling shoes and saddle can help make friends with a different bike.

Group size:
Will there be just your party or will there be others and how many?

Escorted rides:
What is the nature of the escort? Will the group be topped & tailed by guides keeping the group together like some prison chain gang? It happens.

Those who offer cycling holidays in Spain include:
Iberocycle: Tel: +34 942 58 10 92 or www.iberocycle.com
CTC: Tel: 01628 473300 or www.cyclingholidays.org
Exodus: Tel: 0845 869 8216 or www.exodus.co.uk
Inntravel: Tel: 01653 617017 or www.inntravel.co.uk
Freedomtreks: Tel: 01273 224066 or www.freedomtreks.co.uk
Bikespain: Tel: +34 915 59 06 53 or www.bikespain.info

LISTING OF CICERONE GUIDES

For full information on all
our guides, and to order
books and eBooks,
visit our website:
www.cicerone.co.uk.

Walking – Trekking – Mountaineering – Climbing – Cycling

Over 40 years, Cicerone have built up an outstanding collection of 300 guides, inspiring all sorts of amazing adventures.

Every guide comes from extensive exploration and research by our expert authors, all with a passion for their subjects. They are frequently praised, endorsed and used by clubs, instructors and outdoor organisations.

All our titles can now be bought as **e-books** and many as iPad and Kindle files and we will continue to make all our guides available for these and many other devices.

Our website shows any **new information** we've received since a book was published. Please do let us know if you find anything has changed, so that we can pass on the latest details. On our **website** you'll also find some great ideas and lots of information, including sample chapters, contents lists, reviews, articles and a photo gallery.

It's easy to keep in touch with what's going on at Cicerone, by getting our monthly **free e-newsletter**, which is full of offers, competitions, up-to-date information and topical articles. You can subscribe on our home page and also follow us on **Facebook** and **Twitter**, as well as our **blog**.

Cicerone – the very best guides for exploring the world.

CICERONE

2 Police Square Milnthorpe Cumbria LA7 7PY
Tel: 015395 62069 info@cicerone.co.uk
www.cicerone.co.uk